DATE DUE

Neutrality and the Academic Ethic

ISSUES IN ACADEMIC ETHICS
General Editor: Steven M. Cahn

NEUTRALITY
AND THE ACADEMIC ETHIC

Robert L. Simon

ROWMAN & LITTLEFIELD PUBLISHERS, INC.

ROWMAN & LITTLEFIELD PUBLISHERS, INC.

Published in the United States of America
by Rowman & Littlefield Publishers, Inc.
4720 Boston Way, Lanham, Maryland 20706

3 Henrietta Street, London WC2E 8LU, England

British Cataloging in Publication Information Available

Library of Congress Cataloging-in-Publication Data

Simon, Robert L., 1941–
Neutrality and the academic ethic / by Robert L. Simon.
p.   cm. — (Issues in academic ethics)
Includes bibliographical references and index.
1. Education, Higher—Moral and ethical aspects.   2. Education,
Higher—Social aspects.   I. Title.   II. Series.
LB2324.S55   1994   378'.001—dc20   94–764 CIP

ISBN 0–8476–7954–3 (cloth : alk. paper)
ISBN 0–8476–7955–1 (pbk. : alk. paper)

Printed in the United States of America

 ™ The paper used in this publication meets the minimum requirements of
American National Standard for Information Sciences—Permanence of
Paper for Printed Library Materials, ANSI Z39.48–1984.

Issues in Academic Ethics

Academic life generates a variety of moral issues. These may be faced by students, staff, administrators, or trustees but most often revolve around the rights and responsibilities of the faculty. In my 1986 book *Saints and Scamps: Ethics in Academia* (Rowman & Littlefield), I set out to enumerate, explain, and emphasize the most fundamental of these professorial obligations. To do justice to the complexities of academic ethics, however, requires the work of many scholars focused on numerous areas of investigation. The results of such an effort are embodied in this series.

Each volume concentrates on one set of connected issues and combines a single-authored monograph with reprinted sources chosen by the author to exemplify or amplify materials in the text. This format is intended to guide readers while encouraging them to develop and defend their own beliefs.

In recent years philosophers have examined the appropriate standards of conduct for physicians, nurses, lawyers, journalists, business managers, and government policymakers but have not given equal attention to formulating guidelines for their own profession. The time has come to observe the Delphic motto "Know thyself." Granted, the issues in need of critical examination are not exotic, but as the history of philosophy demonstrates, self-knowledge is often the most important to seek and the most difficult to attain.

Steven M. Cahn

To my sons Bruce and Marc, who both attended
Hamilton College where I teach, who
consequently found it difficult to be "saved from
their parents" (see the Introduction) since their
father not only was a professor but also was
their golf coach, and managed to thrive
at college anyway.

Contents

Preface

Most of my academic career has been spent as a faculty member at a small liberal arts college, a life I have enjoyed immensely. I have had the pleasure of teaching enthusiastic and interested students, have participated actively in the life of the institution, and have had the opportunity to coach a highly ranked college golf team. Although there have been moments when such pervasive involvement with a college has seemed more a cost than a blessing, on the whole it has been extremely rewarding, not only personally but intellectually as well.

To many of my colleagues at larger institutions that emphasize research, heavy involvement in the life of the institution might at best seem to be a sometimes pleasant distraction from their scholarly efforts. I would argue, however, that on the contrary, not only are there benefits such as the pleasure of working closely with undergraduates but also the more mixed intellectual blessing of proximity to the various educational and political controversies that arise on campus. Of course, there is the personal satisfaction of having at least some influence on the life of an institution and its members. But there are scholarly benefits as well. One faces a variety of views, is forced to defend one's own, and is often forced to formulate positions on topics that might not otherwise have seemed interesting or provocative.

During more than twenty years of teaching at Hamilton College in upstate New York, the issue of institutional neutrality has been much more than an abstraction. The issue of whether a college or university can be and should be politically neutral has arisen on my campus, as on many others, in the 1960s in connection with protests over the Vietnam War, during the 1980s in the controversy over divestment and South Africa, and in the 1990s in disputes over the politicization of the curriculum and alleged pressures for political correctness. In each case, debate over the proper role of the institution was lively, provocative, and engaged. In fact, two of the pieces in this volume began either as contributions to the debate on my campus (Richard Werner on divestment) or reflections upon it (David Paris on "political correctness").

Institutional neutrality is an issue, moreover, not only at times when the academy is torn by sometimes highly publicized controversies but also in everyday matters of educational and administrative policy. Values seem at stake in the issuing of invitations to speakers, in regulation (or lack of regulation) of student social life, and in revision of degree requirements or curriculum. But if such decisions are inevitably value laden, how can neutrality be possible?

My own interest in the question of neutrality within the academy arises, then, not only from its philosophical complexity but because of its importance for higher education. In fact, one of the claims of my contribution to this volume is that neutrality, properly understood, is a prerequisite for the kind of free inquiry and reasoned debate that should be fostered in colleges and universities.

In coming to this conclusion, I have profited enormously from discussion with colleagues, particularly in the Philosophy and Government departments at Hamilton, especially Russell Blackwood and Richard Werner, and with students and friends. The students in my seminars on Theories of Justice and Ethical Theory have presented excellent criticisms of early drafts of my work, and while I cannot acknowledge them all individually here, their refusal simply to accept my point of view (in fact most were quite critical of it) and their reasoned defenses of their own position were not only especially stimulating to me, but also illustrated the intellectual benefits of the close student-teacher relations fostered by small liberal arts colleges.

I also want to thank Virginia Held who, in spite of disagreement with my views, first encouraged me to write on neutrality at an early stage in my career, and Steven M. Cahn who encouraged me to further develop my ideas some years later. I am also grateful to Hamilton College for its support for my research and particularly for provision of a leave during the spring of 1993 that enabled me to complete this book.

In discussing neutrality, the first reaction I get from audiences often is somewhat blunt and inflexible. "Neutrality—that's impossible!" is a typical response, particularly in recent years when notions such as "neutrality," "objectivity," and "impartiality" are either under attack or being interpreted in new and controversial ways in many disciplines. I hope the discussion in this volume illustrates that neutrality is a complex topic. While those who argue that it is impossible to be neutral (a thesis I reject) may ultimately prove correct, it is hardly self-evident that they are correct. In my view, it would be a great loss to our educational institutions if they had no alternative but to be partisans in the major political disputes of the day. Above all, I hope to show that examination of the issue of institutional neutrality of colleges and universities can improve how we carry out one of our most important missions as a society: the induction of each generation into the domain of reasoned discourse and critical inquiry.

Robert L. Simon
Clinton, N.Y.
June 1993

Acknowledgments

I gratefully acknowledge permission to reprint material from the following sources:

Steven M. Cahn, "A Puzzle Concerning Divestiture," *Analysis,* Vol. 47, No. 3 (1987), © Steven M. Cahn, reprinted by permission of the author.

Steven M. Cahn, "A Note on Divestiture," *Analysis,* Vol. 49, No. 3 (1989), © Steven M. Cahn, reprinted by permission of the author.

Steven M. Cahn, "Principled Divestiture and Moral Integrity," *Analysis,* Vol. 51, No. 2 (1991), © Steven M. Cahn, reprinted by permission of the author.

Daniel H. Cohen, "A Reply to Cahn," *Analysis,* Vol. 48, No. 2 (1988), © Daniel H. Cohen, reprinted by permission of the author.

David Gordon and James Sadowsky, "Morally Principled Divestiture?" *Analysis,* Vol. 49, No. 3 (1989), © David Gordon and James Sadowsky, reprinted by permission of the authors.

Robert Holmes, "University Neutrality and ROTC," from *Ethics,* Vol. 83, No. 3 (1973), © University of Chicago Press, reprinted by permission of the publisher.

Sidney Hook, "From the Platitudinous to the Absurd: A Reply to Henry David Aiken," from Sidney Hook, *Convictions* (Buffalo: Prometheus Books, 1990), © Ann Hook, reprinted with the permission of Ann Hook.

John Searle, "The Storm Over the University," from *The New York Review of Books,* December 6, 1990, reprinted with the permission of *The New York Review of Books,* © 1990 Nyrev, Inc.

Roger A. Shiner, "The Divestiture Puzzle Dissolved," *Analysis,* Vol. 50, No. 3 (1990), © Roger A. Shiner, reprinted by permission of the author.

Temple University Press for permission to reprint material from Robert L. Simon, "A Defense of the Neutral University," in Steven M. Cahn, ed., *Morality, Responsibility, and the University* (Philadelphia: Temple University Press, 1990), © Temple University Press.

PART I

Academic Ethics and the Neutral University

Robert L. Simon

CHAPTER 1

Introduction

Some years ago, I remember being struck by an article on the ethics of teaching in which a philosophy professor declared that his goal as a teacher was to "save students from their parents."[1] At the time, I agreed strongly with the statement, but as my children grew I began to have increasing doubts, and by the time they had entered college, I had rejected it entirely.

Part of what troubles me about the statement is its suggestion (perhaps not the one intended by the author) that professors should function primarily as saviors whose principal aim is undermining the presumably more traditional and therefore presumably incorrect values students have inherited from their families. As I interpreted the statement, it reflected less a Socratic concern for continual examination of different views, including those of the instructor, than a certainty as to where the correct views were to be found.

Can't it be argued, however, that teachers should try to impart some values to their students? After all, even professors who are as critical of their own views as those of their colleagues, their students, or even the parents of their students, seem to be illustrating the *value* of critical examination and inquiry.

If individual instructors often express, illustrate, promote, or stand for certain values, shouldn't the institutions at which they teach do the same? Can't it be argued with some plausibility that colleges and universities should try to promote some values in their students and even in society at large? Values such as concern for truth, willingness to consider evidence in scholarly inquiry, and the appeal to reason rather than force in debate come immediately to mind. But if those values can be promtoed, what about others, such as the rejection of sexism, racism, and antisemitism? But why stop there? If the university community is convinced, for example, that a particular war is

3

unjust, or that investment in particular companies is wrong, or that research that might support a war effort is unjustified, or that a certain political stance toward capitalism or toward Western culture is politically correct, why shouldn't those values be supported by colleges and universities as well? After all, once a normative or value-laden stance is adopted with respect to some values, it seems arbitrary to draw a line in the dust and deny that other value issues are out of bounds. The only alternative, some would argue, is the totally value-neutral university; one that is so normatively sterile that it cannot even stand for the pursuit of truth rather than distortion, indoctrination, and propaganda.

Such questions seem to suggest that colleges and universities cannot (and perhaps should not) be politically neutral. On the other hand, if neutrality is a snare and delusion, whose political values should colleges and universities promote? Should they be partisans in behalf of particular causes, and, if so, which ones? What are the implications of such partisanship for academic freedom? Would education become simply indoctrination of students? Reflection suggests that the idea of the politically partisan university, designed to "save" students and perhaps even society at large from suspect political ideologies, has troublesome implications of its own.

More broadly, ideals such as impartiality, concern for truth, honest evaluation of evidence, and objectivity have long been thought to be among the major values that should govern scholarship. In fact, they seem to be the core values of what might be called the academic ethic: a normative code that ought to govern not only scholarship but rational discussion of issues in broader social and political contexts as well. Yet each of these values has come under increasing attack. Impartiality and objectivity too often are dismissed as at best unattainable and at worst ideological weapons that disguise the partisan interests of powerful social groups.

In the face of such skepticism about basic scholarly values, one might wonder what function colleges and universities should play in our society. Should their principal role be simply to train workers to fit into an increasingly complex and technical socioeconomic system? Should it be to instill radical doubts about the justice and fairness of that system? On the other hand, is there something still to be said for the more traditional idea of the university as a center of objective scholarship, the pursuit of truth, and transmission of great ideas? If so, does that traditional mission require that colleges and universities as institutions refrain from becoming partisan advocates of social causes so they can protect critical inquiry undertaken from a variety of perspectives? What of the claim that political neutrality, like the other ideas of the traditional academic ethic, is unattainable, or even worse, an ideological disguise used by traditionalists to protect their own interests and those of dominant groups from criticism and change?

Current debate within universities over such issues as "political correctness," limitations on "hate speech," and multiculturalism often reflect deeper disputes over the role and function of academic institutions themselves. Apparently abstract philosophical questions about such ideas as neutrality, objectivity, and the ethics of scholarship have significant practical implications for the education provided in colleges and universities. For example, some leading advocates of a reformed multicultural curriculum view adherence to the values of the traditional academic ethic as inherently conservative and hostile to the interests of racial minorities and other groups that have been left out of the American mainstream. Even temperate advocates of moderate forms of curricular revision often raise doubts about traditional academic values such as political neutrality and scholarly objectivity. Thus, according to one writer,

> many who are prepared . . . to do battle against the new Afrocentric and multicultural curricular ideas and to raise the flag of objectivity and factuality are doing the same as those who are attempting to assert the integrity of African civilization. . . . Which is to say that on both sides the advocates are partisans in an intellectual struggle . . . pious pretense to the contrary. The curriculum that we have today in American society is a by-product of power. The effort to change the current curriculum is an effort to destroy the political orthodoxy which has established itself through power.[2]

These comments suggest that the curriculum itself, which is the very heart of the academic enterprise, is inherently political. How then can colleges and universities claim to be neutral, or claim that neutrality is even possible as an ideal when the educational enterprise itself is permeated with political values?

Should colleges and universities be properly viewed as political organizations that can be used to instill an ideology in the next generation, as institutions that can and should be used overtly or covertly as a weapon in the moral and ideological struggles of the day? On the other hand, can and should institutions of higher education be politically neutral centers of critical inquiry and scholarship? Why are these issues important and what hangs on their resolution?

Colleges and universities are among the most influential institutions in our society. Although it may once have been true that the heat generated in argument in faculty meetings was so great precisely because the issues being discussed were so trivial, decisions made today in institutions of higher education often have important ramifications for the rest of society. At stake is not only the kind of education millions of our citizens will receive within institutions of higher education, but also the kind of research that will be conducted, and, perhaps most significant, the kinds of values that will be examined and considered by influential and articulate segments of society.

At a time when higher education is virtually a prerequisite for many of the most desired careers, and when research conducted at large universities may affect almost everyone, it is unsurprising that ethical issues that arise inside the academic community should receive increasing attention. Although academics, and ethicists in particular, have been among the leaders in raising ethical questions in such areas of social and professional concern as medicine, law, business, and even sports, they have paid relatively less attention to the ethical requirements that should apply within their own domain and to their own behavior.

However, as universities have become enmeshed through their research, investments, and curriculum in broader social issues, it is to be expected that the mission of institutions of higher education in our society be debated. In addition, as faculties and student bodies become more culturally and ethnically diverse, there is a tendency on the part of some groups to view traditionally academic values in at least some of their guises as at best irrelevant to their needs and at worst as disguised political weapons designed to insure the hegemony of the values of the more established and powerful social groups. Moreover, as a result of a number of intellectual movements in the humanities, there is increasing suspicion among academics themselves about such traditional intellectual values as truth, objectivity, and impartiality. What has been called the academic ethic, committed to the ideal of the university as a refuge for disinterested and objective scholarship as well as transmission of the major works of Western culture, has been called into deep question.

Are such critiques of traditional academic values justified? What should be the mission of the university in an increasingly pluralistic society? What code of ethics should govern the behavior of academics, as individuals and as members of institutions?

In what follows, such questions will be approached by examination of one central element of the traditional academic ethic: namely, the thesis that colleges and universities should be *politically neutral*. Why is the question of neutrality central? We can begin by considering the relationship of the thesis of neutrality to the ideal of the university as a refuge for objective scholarship and transmission and examination of the great intellectual achievements of the past.

Notes

1. The quotation is from Richard Mohr, "Teaching as Politics," Report from the Center for Philosophy and Public Policy, Vol. 6 (1986), pp. 247–48. Professor Mohr may not have intended the quoted remark in the sense I found troublesome.

2. Ronald Walters, "A Different View: 'Afrocentrism' Means Providing the Neglected Black Perspective," *American Educator,* Vol. 15, No. 3 (Winter 1991), p. 26.

CHAPTER 2

Neutrality, Skepticism, and the Academic Ethic

I. Neutrality and Academic Values

The thesis that colleges and universities ought to be politically neutral has been advanced for a variety of reasons, many connected with the traditional view of the university as a refuge for scholarship, objective critical inquiry, and transmission of knowledge of great achievements in the sciences, arts, and humanities. Historically, the doctrine was formally asserted by A. O. Lovejoy, John Dewey, and E. R. A. Seligman in their justly famous 1915 *General Report on Academic Freedom and Academic Tenure* to the newly formed Association of American University Professors (AAUP) as a protection for the academic freedom of professors against incursions against radical academic thinkers by trustees and politicians. The neutrality of colleges and universities themselves, it was hoped, would allow them to be both disassociated from and protective of a variety of partisan positions that might be adopted by the faculty. Thus, as Walter Metzger reminds us, "The norm of institutional neutrality was not just an ethicist's abstraction: it was a denial of the proprietary claims of trustees, donors, and their spokesmen."[1]

To understand the climate of the times, consider the remark of University of Pennsylvania Trustee George Wharton Pepper after the firing of economist Scott Nearing, probably because of his leftist political views, who remarked on the incident, "If I am dissatisfied with my secretary, I suppose I would be within my rights in terminating his employment."[2] This proprietary view of the university was asserted in an editorial in the *New York Times* as follows:

Men who through toil and ability have got together enough money to endow universities or professor's chairs do not generally have it in mind that their money should be spent for the dissemination of the dogmas of Socialism or in the teaching of ingenuous youth how to live without work. Yet when Trustees conscientiously endeavor to carry out the purposes of the founder by taking proper measures to prevent misuse of the endowment, we always hear a loud howl about academic freedom.[3]

The origins of the doctrine of institutional neutrality in the United States may suggest that its justification is primarily pragmatic. Neutrality, in this view, is *pragmatically necessary* to protect the university from outside interference, for if colleges and universities acted overtly as political agents they would then be vulnerable to political counterattack by more powerful interests. However, neutrality has also been justified by the important purposes of the university for which it is needed as protection. Thus, neutrality has been regarded as *educationally necessary,* since inquiry might be biased by institutional interests if not conducted within a neutral framework. Neutrality also has been regarded as *morally necessary,* since individual autonomy can best be developed and protected within institutions that are not committed to particular views that they might influence, require, or encourage their constituents to adopt.[4]

Is the doctrine of institutional neutrality sound? In times of major social controversy, should colleges and universities function as agents on behalf of particular social causes? Although this issue often is forgotten in times of political quiescence, it rises to the surface again during times of political conflict. In the 1960s, protesters against the Vietnam War often argued that universities as institutions should not only condemn the war but actively oppose it. In many cases, protesters felt justified in disrupting speeches by proponents of the policy of American government or what they felt was its support structure. More recently, in the 1980s, the divestment movement urged universities to rid themselves of investments in corporations doing business in South Africa, but some trustees refused on the grounds that to do so would violate the traditional neutrality of academic institutions. In the 1990s, debates over the multicultural curriculum and so-called "political correctness" raise issues of whether universities can and should be politically neutral, or whether they should stand for, support, and endorse a particular set of "progressive" values. For example, shouldn't universities fight racism and sexism? If the traditional neutrality of the university does not allow a moral response to such evils, isn't neutrality itself to be rejected?

Thus, political controversies over the justice of our policy in Vietnam and in other wars, over divestment, and over the universities' role in fighting social injustice have led to criticism of the doctrine that colleges and universities should be politically neutral. Can and should academic institutions remain silent and inactive in the face of genocide, the waging of unjust wars, systematic racial discrimination, political oppression, and world hunger? Is neutrality even possible? Do claims of neutrality function only ideologically as a covert disguise for a hidden agenda of promoting the conservative values of the dominant and powerful?

On the other hand, if a university or college becomes a partisan political agent, can it fulfill other functions, including the academic ones that presumably are its very reasons for being? Are there moral reasons, based on the academic function of colleges and universities, for them to refrain from partisan political action?

The issue of whether or not neutrality is desirable is practically significant only if it is *possible* to be neutral in the first place. If neutrality is impossible no matter how hard we try to attain it, it is pointless to consider whether we ought to be neutral. Many critics of the thesis that universities ought to be politically neutral deny that neutrality is possible in the first place. If they are right, the debate over whether institutional neutrality is good or bad, just or unjust, or right or wrong, never gets off the ground. Our first question, therefore, must be whether or not institutional neutrality is even possible.

II. Skepticism and the Concept of Neutrality

Many critics of the ideal of a politically neutral university point out that it makes sense to say colleges and universities *ought* to be neutral only if they *can* be neutral. Since, in the view of these critics, universities cannot be neutral, the whole issue of whether they ought to be neutral is derailed right from the start. Are these critics correct?

What the skeptics about the possibility of neutrality may fail to notice is that "neutrality" itself can be interpreted or understood in different ways. Thus, even if a skeptical argument shows that neutrality, *understood in one way,* is impossible, it does not follow that neutrality *understood in some other way* also is impossible. Perhaps, as philosopher John Searle has suggested, skeptics about the very possibility of neutrality are like certain sorts of epistemological skeptics who question whether knowledge is possible.[5] The kind of skeptic

Searle has in mind simply defines knowledge in such a way that it can never be attained. But, of course, just because knowledge as the skeptic defines it is unattainable, it does not follow that knowledge in other significant senses also is unattainable. Similarly, even if the skeptic is correct in claiming that certain kinds of institutional neutrality are unattainable, it does not follow that institutional neutrality of other kinds also must be beyond our grasp. An important goal of analysis, then, is to distinguish different conceptions of neutrality in order to discern which ones are and which ones are not attainable for particular agents.

For example, one popular argument is that no university can be neutral because the principle that the university ought to be neutral itself expresses a value judgment. A second, closely related argument points out that a university by its very nature (or at least as conceived of by proponents of the traditional academic ethic) is committed to such values as knowledge, truth, and rational discourse. Therefore, the university cannot be neutral because it is committed to certain values rather than others.

Such arguments may well be successful in showing that no university can be totally value free. Indeed, these kinds of arguments bring out the salutary point that the commitment to be neutral, like other value commitments, requires a rational defense. However, they undermine the thesis that universities ought to be politically neutral only if such neutrality is conceived of as total value freedom. But, as we will see, that is hardly the only relevant conception of neutrality that needs to be considered. Indeed, it is doubtful if proponents of the traditional academic ethic conceive of neutrality in terms of total value freedom. Hence, even if it is impossible for the university to be value free, that is irrelevant to the claim that the university ought to be neutral in some sense of neutrality different from that of value freedom.

Other skeptics point out that the university's action or inaction has political consequences. Therefore, they conclude that neutrality is impossible, for in their view even the failure to take any stand on controversial issues has significant causal implications. Therefore, no matter what the university does or does not do, there are political implications. At the very least, the status quo is left unchanged. In effect, failure to oppose the existing order is to support it. As Robert Paul Wolff argues in *The Ideal of the University,*

> Omissions are frequently even more significant politically than commissions in American politics, for those in positions of decision usually rule

by default rather than by consent. Hence, acquiescence in governmental acts, under the guise of impartiality, actually strengthens the established forces and makes successful opposition all the harder.[6]

Like other skeptical arguments, Wolff's approach also rests on a particular conception of neutrality. Of course, this is not a defect in the argument, since any discussion of neutrality will involve some specific conception or account of the general concept under discussion. It does mean, however, that a critique of neutrality as conceived of in one particular way need not apply to neutrality as conceived of in other ways.

Two elements in particular characterize Wolff's conception of neutrality. First of all, he thinks of it in consequentialist terms. In this view, an agent is neutral with respect to conflicting parties if the agent's actions (or inactions) do not have the consequence of improving the position of one particular side or party in a dispute. Let us call this the *consequentialist* conception of neutrality.

Second, and more controversially, Wolff assumes that failure to oppose one side has the consequence of benefiting the other side. Thus, his comment that failure to support critics of the government constitutes "acquiescence in governmental acts," and in fact actually stengthens the government, suggests that Wolff considers failure to oppose the government as tantamount to supporting it.[7]

Both of Wolff's assumptions need to be recognized as elements of a particular conception of neutrality; one that not all supporters of institutional neutrality need accept. In fact, consequentialist neutrality is far from the only significant form of neutrality worth considering. For example, an advocate of neutrality might require not that the consequences for all parties be equivalent but rather than one's *reasons* for making a particular decision be neutral. Thus, a referee who makes a crucial call in a basketball game may be neutral if his reason for making the decision was his belief that it was required by the rules, even if the decision benefits one team at the expense of the other. It would be absurd to criticize a referee as biased simply because his calls had unequal consequences for the competing teams; one team may simply have committed more infractions than its opponent.

What about the suggestion, which Wolff appears to endorse, that to fail to oppose government policy is in effect to support it? Taken more generally, this amounts to the view that "you must be either with us or against us." Clearly, granted that assumption, neutrality is impossible since if you do not take one side, you must be supporting the opponent.

However, the logic of "you must be either with us or against us" is called into question by examples such as the American constitutional requirement of the separation of church and state. Whatever else this doctrine implies, at a minimum it requires that the government not support one particular religion over others. It is minimally satisfied if the government does not favor one religion over any other. The skeptic might reply, using the logic of "you are either with us or against us," that by not favoring a particular religion, the state actually is favoring some other religion. But the point seems absurd since proponents of *all* religions could make the same claim. The logic of "you are either with us or against us" is faulty precisely because all parties to a dispute can make the same claim.

Let us consider this point more fully. The skeptical argument seems to go as follows:

1. Failure to support me has the consequence of making my opponent's position better off than it would have been if you had supported me.

2. Hence, your failure to support me makes my opponent better off.

3. Therefore, you actually have supported my opponent.

4. Therefore, your claim to neutrality is a sham for you too are my opponent.

The problem with this argument, however, is that premise 1 above is no more plausible than premise 1a below.

1a. Your failure to support my opponents makes my position better off than if you had supported them.

The rest of the argument then follows as before.

2a. Hence, your failure to support them makes me better off.

3a. Therefore, you actually have supported me.

4a. Therefore, your claim to neutrality is a sham for you are my ally.

In other words, by substituting (1a) for (1) and then making the same inferences in both cases, one can with equal plausibility conclude that you have chosen my side rather than that of my opponents. Of course it is true, as the skeptic claims, that failure to take a stand deprives the position one might have supported of an ally. But that is equally true for the other side. That is exactly why it is neutral, not necessarily in the sense of being consequence free, but in the sense of being nonpartisan. The fallacy involved in the assertion that you either are with us or against us is that it can be said by either side. The consequences of this are logically devastating. Both sides can regard a third party as an opponent (since it is not with us, it is against us) or with equal plausibility as an ally (since it is not against our opponents, it is with us). Surely any formula that implies such blatant contradictions is incoherent and should be rejected as such.

We can illustrate the points we have made about neutrality by reference to the example of the neutrality of the state toward particular religions. To claim that the university is actually supporting the status quo simply because it fails actively to support radical critics of the existing order is no more plausible than the parallel claim that the state, since it does not actively favor Christianity over Judaism, is actually supporting Judaism. The fallacy in both cases is the same. By applying the principle that "you either are with us or against us," one could just as well argue that by not supporting the status quo, the university is actually aiding the radicals, and by not actively supporting Judaism, the state in reality is aiding Christianity. More specifically, the inference that "if you are not with us you are against us" is fallacious since, as we have seen, by applying it consistently, one derives the contradictory conclusion that A is both supporting and opposing both sides in the dispute.

However, if, in spite of this critique, the skeptic still wants to maintain that failure to support one side is tantamount to supporting the other, then it does follow trivially that any decision including the decision not to make a decision about a dispute has political consequences and is not neutral. Let us call the kind of neutrality the skeptic is undermining *broad consequential neutrality* and admit it is unattainable by colleges and universities.[8]

However, this concession should bring little joy to the skeptic since even if the incoherence pointed out above is ignored, the failure of universities to be broadly consequentially neutral does not show they fail to be neutral in some other significant sense. Similarly, even if the government fails to be broadly consequentially neutral, it still can be neutral in other senses. For example, it can refrain from making any decisions on the *grounds* that they favor one religion over another. Moreover, it may be quite important that it refrain from making decisions on such a basis. Similarly, the university can refrain from making decisions simply because they favor one side or another in a political dispute, and it may be equally important that it too act with neutral intent.

Accordingly, it is doubtful if the skeptical arguments we have considered so far show that there is no important conception of political neutrality that colleges and universities (or the state, for that matter) can satisfy. Even if the skeptics do show that some conceptions of neutrality, such as neutrality as value freedom or neutrality as broadly consequentialist, are incoherent or impossible to attain, they leave open the question of whether other forms of neutrality are equally incoherent or attainable. Of course, this does not imply that any conception of neutrality is desirable, let alone that universities are morally required to be neutral. Whether an individual or institution ought to be neutral is an ethical issue that must be decided on appropriate normative grounds. Be that as it may, it is a genuine issue. For all we have seen, it remains possible that colleges and universities *can* be neutral. Whether they *ought* to be neutral is an issue of significance that cannot be avoided by appeal to the skeptical arguments we have examined so far.

What important kinds of neutrality are open to colleges and universities? Before dealing with the question of *institutional* neutrality, it will prove useful to examine first the question of neutrality at the *individual* level. What kind of neutrality, if any, should be adopted by the individual professor in the classroom? Sometimes, by focusing on issues that arise at the level of the individual, conclusions can be drawn that have some application for the institution as well.

Notes

1. Walter P. Metzger, "Academic Freedom in Delocalized Academic Institutions," in Metzger et al., *Dimensions of Academic Freedom* (Urbana: University of Illinois Press, 1969), p. 14.

2. Ibid., p. 13.

3. Quoted in Metzger, ibid., pp. 13–14.

4. This approach resembles the liberal view of the state that has been developed by such writers as Ronald Dworkin in his essay, "Liberalism," in Dworkin, *A Matter of Principle* (Cambridge, Mass.: Harvard University Press, 1985), and more extensively in John Rawls, *A Theory of Justice* (Cambridge, Mass.: Harvard University Press, 1971) and Bruce Ackerman, *Social Justice in the Liberal State* (New Haven: Yale University Press, 1980). According to

this view, the state should be neutral toward conceptions of the good and not impose ideals of the good life on its citizens. By referring to the "liberal" version of the doctrine of institutional neutrality, I do not mean to imply that it is liberal in any way other than that of resembling the liberal doctrine that the political institutions should provide a neutral framework within which individuals can pursue their own conceptions of the good life. For example, it need not be liberal in the sense of being connected with a liberal view of abortion or of provision of welfare by the state.

5. John Searle, *The Campus War: A Sympathetic Look at the University in Agony* (New York: World, 1971), pp. 199–200.

6. Robert Paul Wolff, *The Ideal of the University* (Boston: Beacon Press, 1969), p. 71.

7. Perhaps Wolff does not intend to make the conceptual point that failure to oppose one side is tantamount to supporting it. Perhaps he intends instead to make the factual claim that "under the guise of impartiality," colleges and universities actually or in fact provide covert positive support for the establishment.

8. Indeed, once broad neutrality is defined as existing only when an agent has no effect on the relative position of any party to a dispute, and failure to aid one side is counted as having a beneficial effect on the other side, neutrality has been defined as impossible to attain. But why accept the definition as picking out the only kind of neutrality with which we ought to be concerned (or even a kind of neutrality that is of significance)?

CHAPTER 3

Critical Neutrality: Individual and Institutional

I. Critical Neutrality in the Classroom

In this section, we will make a start by characterizing a kind of neutrality that may be appropriate for colleges and universities. We can begin by considering how neutrality might apply in the individual classroom. For example, should a professor in a course on ethics attempt to get students to question their own values? Should the professor go further and aim at having the students reject a specific set of values, such as the traditional values they may have learned at home? May a professor permissibly attempt to convince students to adopt that set of values he or she deems correct? If the professor thinks the values in question are sufficiently important, may any techniques, including rhetorical excess, emotive appeals, distortions, and failure to present other points of view fairly, be employed to promote them? On the other hand, is there any legitimate sense in which the individual instructor in the college classroom should be neutral with respect to ethical or political values?

Perhaps it will help to approach these questions by considering two, admittedly extreme, hypothetical responses to these questions. According to the first, which we can call the model of partisanship, professors should try, using whatever means of persuasion will prove most effective, to get students to adopt the values they think most important. According to the second model, which we can call the model of absolute neutrality, professors should be absolutely value neutral in the classroom. The instructor's role, in this view, is just to present information, not to evaluate it. Where there is controversy in a discipline, the professor should fairly present the different positions but refrain from taking a stand on which is most plausible. No special weight should ever be given to a position just because it is the one favored by the instructor. Thereby, professors show respect for the autonomy of their students, since no one attempts to impose a position upon the students, and instructors refrain from using their prestige or position to influence students by nonrational means.

The model of partisanship, at least in its more extreme forms, is likely to have few adherents. In effect, it presents the professor as an agent of a particular ideology whose role is to indoctrinate students. Since it is permissible according to the model to use any persuasive technique that works, students are not treated as rational persons in their own right but as things to be manipulated. In effect, the veneer of education is employed to cloak what really is going on: namely, indoctrination of the less powerful by the more powerful. Indeed, intentionally using one's status as a professor to impose one's values on students through nonrational means can be regarded as a form of harassment, one that resembles some forms of sexual harassment, in that persons use a position of power to bend others to their will in ways the victims might not rationally consent to being used.

It might be replied that unattractive as the model of partisanship may appear, there is no real alternative since no rules of rational inquiry have an objective justification. According to this retort, even to adopt ground rules of critical inquiry is a political act that has covert political implications. For example, even to be committed to scientific inquiry is not value neutral since there are different and contested forms of scientific investigation, and to be committed to science itself represents allegiance to a particular form of knowing that rules out alternate forms such as intuition and revelation.

In a trivial sense, this defense of partisanship is correct, since as we have seen, the commitment to rational inquiry itself is not value neutral. Commitment to rationality, to considering evidence, and to critical inquiry is itself the adoption of specific values. Moreover, the decision to adopt a certain set of rational procedures may have as a consequence that certain political positions receive more support from investigators than others, since those positions receive the greatest confirmation by investigators using the adopted procedures.

However, from the premise that teaching itself is not value free, or even that it is not consequentially neutral, it does not follow that it need be partisan in any other way. In particular, even if teachers and scholars must adopt some values, it does not follow that they must adopt the value of imposing their own ideologies on students by nonrational persuasive techniques. Indeed, one of their values might be the rejection of manipulation of students in the classroom. Moreover, adherents of the model of partisanship must themselves appeal to some rules of justification or inquiry in order to defend their own model of teaching. If no such rules had any more warrant or justification than any others, the whole institution of rational discourse and critical inquiry would be an illusion. The very process of justification would itself be a purely ideological exercise with no goal other than the conversion of others. In this extreme view, its advocates can give us no good reasons for accepting the model of partisanship, since "good reasons" are themselves a fiction to be used for ideological purposes. If the extreme forms of the model are correct, the university is nothing more than a Hobbesian state of nature in which proponents of different ideologies use the form but not the substance (since there is no such thing) of rational inquiry and critical discussion to convert those naive students who are deceived by the outward form of inquiry to their own point of view.[1] This surely is too high a price to be paid for the model of partisanship. Accordingly, the model, at least in its more extreme forms, must be rejected by all those committed to the university as a center of rational inquiry and critical discussion.

This point does not necessarily presuppose that totally uncontroversial principles of inquiry or justification can be employed. Rather, it does imply that the instructor is committed to employing some standards of justification and evaluation that are regarded as at least provisionally warranted, and not simply because their use supports the ideology or personal values of the user. Such warrant may be broadly pragmatic and value laden, but must constitute an independent test of the positions the user attempts to evaluate in discussion and investigation. Thus, even the Rawlsian method of reflective equilibrium, which requires us to test our considered moral judgments about particular cases against our principles so as to promote overall systematic coherence in our moral conceptual scheme, allows the possibility that some of our most cherished beliefs may be undermined by the weight of overall systematic considerations with which they might clash.[2]

Now consider the second model of absolute neutrality. According to this model, the professor must be absolutely value neutral in the classroom. While the respect for the individual autonomy of the student underlying this model is admirable, it is far from clear that the model is coherent. Surely, the instructor *must* make some value judgments *qua* instructor of a course. For example, the instructor must decide what material should be included in the course, determine what controversies are worth exploring and what positions are worth developing in depth, and select the methods for best evaluating the work of students. Moreover, the instructor's commitment to respecting the autonomy of students is itself a fundamental moral commitment. As was already suggested in Chapter 2, total value freedom cannot be applied within the educational process, even when practiced by the individual instructor.

Accordingly, neither the model of absolute neutrality nor the model of partisanship are fully acceptable, at least in their most uncompromising forms. Of course, the extreme forms of each model may be modified so as to avoid the sort of objections we have considered. For example, an advocate of absolute neutrality may attempt to distinguish between *professional* value judgments, such as judgments about what texts to use or what issues to cover, which are unavoidable, and *personal* moral and political judgments, which are avoidable in classroom instruction. On the other hand, an advocate of partisanship may acknowledge that there are rational constraints on the kind of advocacy that is permitted in class, but add that as long as nonrational persuasive techniques are avoided, it is permissible to defend moral and political judgments within the confines of critical inquiry.

Rather than examine such modifications in depth, the important point for understanding neutrality is that both sorts of modifications limit the partisanship of the instructor. Both require that the instructor be a scholar first and a partisan second. More precisely, even in the modified version of the model of partisanship, partisanship is governed and restricted by ground rules of rational discourse and critical inquiry. In both cases, students are to be persuaded by rational discourse or not persuaded at all. Manipulation by persuasive but nonrational techniques is prohibited.

There is a sense, then, in which proponents of the modified forms of both models concede that the professor can and should be neutral. Proponents of defensible forms of both models acknowledge that classroom discussion should be regulated by rules of critical inquiry and rational discussion. Adherence to these rules is neutral in the sense that regulation by the rules does not dictate the substantive position that emerges from discussion, and in that the rules normally are acceptable to different sides in debate.[3]

Let us call this kind of neutrality *critical neutrality* because it requires adherence to rules of critical inquiry. Such rules need not be value free, uncontroversial, or neutral in any sense other than constituting a court of appeal independent of the personal preferences of the investigators whose inquiries they govern. Thus, adherence to critical neutrality does not require commitment to neutrality in any sense that the skeptic has found incoherent. It requires neither value freedom nor consequential neutrality. On the contrary, adherence to canons of critical neutrality may have profound effects on students, instructors, and society at large. Neither does it require that the professor totally avoid advocacy of substantive positions in class. As long as advocacy is carried out in accord with rules and standards of critical inquiry and rational discourse, it not only is permissible but also may be educationally desirable, so long as students are sufficiently mature, informed, and skilled to form reasonable independent judgments of their own.

Before turning to issues concerning the content of such rules, we need to consider first if critical neutrality is any more possible than absolute neutrality or consequential neutrality. Moreover, even if it is possible, what makes it desirable? Whether critical neutrality is possible depends upon whether rules of critical inquiry exist for various disciplines which have warrant for rational investigators independent of the partisan stands such investigators take on substantive issues within the discipline. Here, we can distinguish *weak* from *strong* forms of critical neutrality. According to the strongest versions of critical neutrality, the rules must be totally independent of any substantive issue that arises within the discipline. Progressively weaker versions might loosen the requirement of total independence requiring instead that the justification of the rules be at least partially independent of substantive issues within the discipline, thus making room for models of justification that appeal to broad criteria of coherence among positions at different levels of inquiry. Weaker conceptions of critical inquiry, moreover, might not require partial independence from all substantive issues that arise within a discipline, but only independence from those at stake in a particular controversy. Alternately, independence might only be required from positions at stake in controversial political or moral controversies. Accordingly, critical neutrality itself is not a simple concept, but can be understood in a variety of ways along a variety of dimensions.

Are there any independent rules of critical inquiry, even in the weaker senses? It is doubtful if a full-fledged proof of their justification can be provided and, in any case, a full examination of this cannot be undertaken here. For our purposes, it is perhaps sufficient to point out that the skeptics (and other critics of neutrality) face severe problems if no such rules or standards exist. Indeed, if skeptics about neutrality claim that their own position is warranted or justified, they seem to themselves presuppose standards of argument and critical discussion that they can cite in support of their own view. Of course, skeptics can reply that they presuppose only minimal rules of logic, not the existence of broad standards of inquiry in all disciplines, but once the door has been opened, the burden of proof may shift to them to show why such standards cannot be found elsewhere.

Even more important, if such standards do not exist in certain areas of study or disciplines, critical inquiry and rational discussion is impossible there. Faculty and students arc at best engaged only in a kind of narrowly circular process in which each restates his or her favorite positions, using persuasive techniques rather than rational ones to promote conversion. In short, intellectual inquiry would be a sham, disguising a naked struggle for power. Moreover, if it were widely acknowledged that what passes for education could only be a nonrational struggle for power, it is doubtful if professors in those areas would be able to attract diverse kinds of students or receive public support for their activities, particularly if they represented partisan positions unpopular with the general public. Standards of critical inquiry, then, seem to be presupposed by the academic enterprise itself and play an important pragmatic role in explaining the value of the academic enterprise to society. We will return to this issue later, but for now, we can provisionally conclude that unless we are willing to accept a radical revision or even abandonment of the idea of education as involving critical development and rational examination of issues, and its replacement with a kind of indoctrination, some form of critical neutrality must be applicable to the classroom.

Assuming then, at least for the moment, that at least some of the weaker forms of critical neutrality are possible to implement, is there reason to believe that adherence to critical neutrality is desirable, or even morally required for faculty at colleges and universities? Three principal kinds of supporting arguments are particularly important.

The first is based on the rights or entitlements generated by the autonomy of students and colleagues.[4] As autonomous agents, such individuals are wronged if they are manipulated by the intentional presentation of misinformation or by the intentional persuasive use of nonrational emotive techniques designed to distort inquiry so as to promote acceptance of a particular point of view. In such a case, the offending instructor behaves in a manner relevantly similar in important respects to one who uses professorial authority to coerce students into engaging in sexual relations. Although the cases are dissimilar in important ways, in each case the power and prestige that arise from holding a position of authority and respect within an educational institution is wrongly used to manipulate others without their informed consent, thereby limiting the victims' opportunities for autonomous choice.

Second, violation of critical neutrality is a violation of the canons of inquiry that should govern the central activities and mission of the university. That is, respect for critical inquiry can be seen as valuable precisely because institutions where critical inquiry is carried out are perhaps the most important places where issues of the greatest importance can be examined and debated. Colleges and universities are engaged in the examination of different viewpoints so that those who engage in the examination can best distinguish truth from falsehood, or at least distinguish the more justified from the less justified position. To the extent this activity is intrinsically valuable and deserves protection, critical neutrality must be valued and enforced as well.

Finally, truth and justification may not only be intrinsically important, but as John Stuart Mill argued so eloquently in *On Liberty,* they may have social value as well. Without critical inquiry, our capacity to revise our views may be crippled, and so we may be doomed to act disastrously upon false assumptions precisely because alternatives are never given a fair hearing. Equally, because we have not adequately studied our own moral, intellectual, scientific, or artistic heritage, we may fail even to appreciate or understand those very factors that can enhance not only our enjoyment of life but our understanding of our problems and what to do about them.

In short, violation of critical neutrality endangers the rights of students and colleagues to exercise autonomous choice, undermines the endeavor to find the best-supported conclusions in an area of study, and incurs the social costs of substituting the teaching of one person's or group's pieties for the general development of critical faculties and skills. While none of these arguments is uncontroversial, their combined force may be sufficient to create at least a *presumptive* case for critical neutrality in the classroom.

A presumptive case is one that places the burden of proof on opponents. To say critical neutrality in the college or university classroom is presumptively justified is to say principles of critical neutrality should be applied unless trumped by some overriding moral arguments that apply in a particular context. Given the kind of arguments supporting critical neutrality, arguments for overriding the presumption in neutrality's favor would have to be especially weighty to carry the day.

Little has been said, however, about the *content* of principles of critical neutrality. This is partly because it is likely that many such principles are specific to context and to the subject matter of different disciplines. However, a core set of principles is likely to be presupposed by critical inquiry in virtually all contexts and so to be central to the academic ethic itself. For example, one such principle might require that conclusions be based on evidence and reason, not use of force. Another might require that students in a discipline be given a fair representation of opposing views on controversial issues that arise in a particular class. For example, if a professor's reading of a text is highly controversial within a field, students normally should be informed of that and told something of other interpretations and the reasons for holding them.[5] As noted earlier, this does not preclude instructors from defending their own viewpoints, although it requires them to do so in a way that presents different major positions fairly.

Although I myself believe that such principles are at the core of the academic enterprise, they are not always uncontroversial. Thus, I have heard faculty argue that they are not under an obligation to present positions other than their own on controversial topics to their classes since colleagues who hold dissenting views also are on the faculty and can more effectively present their own views in their own classes. While there are some contexts where such a view is plausible, there are others where it is quite controversial, and still others where it seems clearly mistaken.

For example, philosophers often disagree on which method or manner of doing philosophy is most appropriate. Philosophers who stress linguistic analysis, pragmatism, foundationalism, existentialism, phenomenology, and various so-called postmodern epistemologies may make radically different methodological assumptions. Now, in a philosophy concentration in which students will be exposed to several different approaches in different classes, it does not seem necessary for an instructor in a class devoted to, say, the movement of linguistic analysis to devote any large part of the course to a detailed examination of phenomenology since that will be covered elsewhere in the curriculum. However, it is quite another thing for a philosopher in a small department to present linguistic analysis as if it were the only way of doing philosophy, and as if there were no alternatives defended by theorists of repute.[6]

Where controversial political topics are at stake, the issue is even more complex. For one thing, course offerings are seldom if ever organized according to the ideology of the instructors. Thus, it is far from clear that students actually will have instructors who hold significantly different political views of the topic under discussion during their course of study. In fact, that topic may come up only in certain courses and not in others. In such cases, it does seem to be a positive duty not only to inform students that the instructor's views are controversial, but also to attempt fairly and forcefully to present the most plausible opposing positions along with supporting arguments. Of course, it is also permissible for instructors to indicate why they reject the alternatives and to present a reasoned case for their own view. What is impermissible is to load the dice so that controversial material is presented as if it were unchallenged wisdom. I remember inadvertently violating this rule in a course on philosophical issues in law during the first year of my first appointment as an instructor. In a lecture, I quickly dismissed the retributive theory of punishment as based only on primitive emotions of revenge, when (as my colleagues reminded me!) sophisticated Kantian defenses of retributivism based on ideals of justice and equity existed in the field and should have been given a fair hearing.

In any case, we can conclude that individual instructors should be committed to neither the model of extreme partisanship nor the model of absolute neutrality or total value freedom. Rather, they should be committed to a general policy of adherence to the ethics of critical inquiry. While interpretations of that ethic sometimes will be controversial, and a variety of approaches to teaching are compatible with it, it hardly is vacuous. Indeed, proponents of radical political positions as well as defenders of traditional values all implicitly appeal to such an ethic insofar as they maintain that their positions can be supported in free and rational dialogue within the university community.

II. Institutional Critical Neutrality

Although the university cannot be neutral in the sense of being value free or in the sense of being consequentially neutral, there may be other kinds of neutrality worth considering that are attainable by colleges and universities. In particular, our discussion suggests that just as individual instructors are obligated to respect the norms of critical inquiry in the classroom, so the college or university is morally required to maintain an institutional climate in which the academic ethic governs discourse and inquiry. If so, it can be argued that the university can and should be neutral to at least the extent the referee in a sports contest is neutral. That is, referees are prohibited from making decisions simply because the decision favors one side or the other and are obligated to apply the rules governing the contest impartially. Similarly, universities may be prohibited from making decisions simply because they favor one side or another in a partisan debate, and may be required to promulgate, enforce, and protect rules and norms central to rational discourse and critical inquiry. That is, the minimal kind of neutrality appropriate for colleges and universities may be *institutional critical neutrality;* namely, adherence to the values, rules, and principles of critical inquiry and discussion regardless of which substantive positions are thereby advanced.

In part, this kind of institutional critical neutrality can be called *internal* since it focuses on the neutral application of a set of rules within an institution or practice.[7] Critics may regard internal neutrality as trivial. After all, they may point out, to say the rules of critical neutrality are internally neutral is only to say they are applied impartially and consistently. But so may a rule that says, "Only voters who are registered Democrats will be allowed to vote in the next U.S. presidential election." That rule may be applied impartially and consistently in that only Democrats are allowed to vote. However, the content of the rule is hardly neutral between Republicans and Democrats.

The critics clearly are correct here. Accordingly, we need to consider whether institutional critical neutrality also is neutral in still a further sense, which we will call *external* neutrality. This second kind of neutrality is external in that it concerns the neutrality of the content of the rules rather than merely the neutrality of their application. To say the rules of basketball are externally neutral is to say not only that they are impartially and consistently applied but also that they are regarded as having a justification independent of the interests of any particular team or competitor. Thus, they may be mutually agreeable to all teams and competitors. Similarly, to say that the rules of critical inquiry are externally neutral is to say they too have a justification independent of the specific interests and partisan perspectives of parties within the university.

However, the rules of critical inquiry are externally neutral in a broader sense than the rules of basketball. After all, basketball itself is simply another practice, and skeptics will point out with some justice that mere consensus or agreement on the rules is one thing, but to claim they are justified or true is quite another. The rules of critical inquiry, while part of a social practice, are claimed to be not merely part of an intellectual consensus but also to have normative force for all investigators. That is, all investigators or participants in rational discourse ought to follow the rules.

Skeptics will deny that there are externally neutral rules of critical inquiry. They will point out there is much that is not only controversial but also unclear about the claim that there are externally neutral standards of critical inquiry, including the way such terms as "partisan perspective," "rational discourse," and "critical inquiry" are to be understood. Indeed, there can be different conceptions of critical inquiry and rational discourse, just as there can be different conceptions of justice, equality, and liberty. Thus, critical inquiry itself is arguably an essentially contested concept conceived of in different ways by proponents of different ideologies. The kinds of standards or rules of critical inquiry supported by a Marxist may differ from those of a pragmatist and still more from those supported by Kantians or libertarians. Therefore, according to the objection, there may be no set rules of critical neutrality that are externally neutral among all major ideological positions.

Moreover, even if there were an externally neutral set of rules, controversy among different ideological perspectives might arise over their interpretation. For example, disagreement over whether a protest is disruptive or whether it is a legitimate exercise of free speech might easily arise between protesters and their critics even though both sides accept the same abstract principle permitting free expression so long as it is not disruptive. Indeed, at my own institution, it was precisely such a controversy over what behavior counts as disruptive that led to the suspension of several students by the administration after a sit-in in a college building to protest the school's failure to divest.

However, once again, it is far from clear that these skeptical points are decisive. For one thing, even if the notion of critical inquiry is contested, it does not follow that institutions must take stands on which conception to support just because of the effect on one side or another in a partisan political dispute. That is, the *reasons* for the choice, the *justification,* can be independent of who gains and who loses. Similarly, a referee in a basketball game may have to decide between two conceptions of how to enforce the rules, one of which requires the referee to play a relatively passive role, calling only the most extreme fouls, and the other requiring stricter control of play. These conceptions may be embedded in two different views of the game and the permissible role of physical contact within it. The referee may have to choose between different conceptions, but the justification for the choice need not arise from a preference for one of the teams but rather can be supported by an overall philosophy of the game. Thus, both the referee and the university can be neutral at the level of justification, even when the proper understanding of the rules they are to enforce is contested.

Second, a commitment to institutional neutrality does not necessarily require colleges and universities to take stands on controversial epistemological issues, especially not the very same issues that are at stake in specific partisan disputes. Rather, the commitment is to an institution where such disputes can be pursued, where positions are defended by argument rather than force, and where debate is open to those qualified to participate in it. This commitment does not require the university to decide between radically different epistemologies that might be explored in advanced seminars in philosophy but only to ensure that scholarly debate about the merits of those epistemologies can be carried on.

Arguably, then, there is a common core of broad principles of inquiry that all constituents of the university community who are committed to supporting their views in a context of reasoned discourse must accept, including the commitment to consider evidence on its merits, even evidence against one's own position, and the rejection of coercion when used for the sole purpose of silencing opponents. Without allegiance to core elements such as these, no rational debate seems possible to begin with.

Moreover, even if we ignore the case for core elements of critical inquiry and rational discourse, it does not follow that institutional critical neutrality is undermined. Even if the nature of critical inquiry is itself inherently controversial, it doesn't follow that the values at stake in debate among various conceptions of critical inquiry are political values, let alone the same political values at stake in specific controversial issues. That is, the position one takes in epistemological debate need not determine or be determined by one's partisan political stance. For example, parties who disagree on divestment can still agree that different sides should be heard in debates on the issue. Similarly, proponents of divestment might hold vastly different epistemological views at the philosophical level.

Accordingly, proponents of institutional critical neutrality can make three sorts of replies to the criticism that critical inquiry itself does not admit of neutral interpretation. First, they can point out that institutional policies about controversial interpretations of critical inquiry can be neutral if their justification is independent of any particular moral or political controversy at issue. Second, they can maintain that there are at least some core values, that if not entirely uncontroversial, are initially plausible and seem to cut across epistemologies that conflict in more controversial philosophical areas.[8] Third, even if there are no core values acceptable to all sides to a political or moral controversy, their epistemological disagreements might not be relevant to their political and moral ones. That is, for every political or moral controversy, there may be some rules of critical inquiry, some epistemic values, that are common to the disputants in that particular case, even if there are no rules that are independent of all disputes or perspectives.

Finally, assume the worst possible case such that epistemological and moral-political controversies are inseparable in a particular context. Parties to the conflict deny that justifications for institutional policies are neutral, reject the case for core values, and are unable to find epistemic principles of inquiry they all regard as independent of the specific dispute at hand. Nevertheless, there may still be agreement on the need to preserve a common institutional framework within which the entire dispute, as well as others, can be examined and mediated. That is, all the parties may prefer the continued existence of an institution committed to the neutral enforcement of rules of critical inquiry, even if they acknowledge that critical neutrality cannot be attained *in this particular case.* Their preference may be merely political in that they fear a partisan institution may ultimately turn against them, or principled in that they believe in the policy of preserving a neutral framework for the protection of diverse viewpoints in the majority of cases, even if it is inapplicable in the particular one they currently face.

We will return to this point when we consider the *value* of institutional critical neutrality. Nevertheless, it seems clear that the mere possibility of dispute over the nature of critical inquiry itself is not sufficient to show that institutional critical neutrality is impossible. However, still more needs to be said about the implications of institutional critical neutrality.

Consider, for example, the claim that the university necessarily adopts a partisan conception of critical inquiry to begin with. Thus, aren't proponents of many eccentric epistemological positions excluded from the university? There is no department of astrology on campus, nor is creationism often defended, let alone given equal footing with evolutionary biology. And isn't there a bias against regarding individual testimony of private religious experiences as veridical and a bias in favor of the public kind of evidence and repeatable experimentation characteristic of scientific inquiry?

Clearly, not all epistemological positions, worldviews, or perspectives are represented equally (or even represented at all) within the university. But it does not follow that institutional critical neutrality is a fraud, or that the university has violated such neutrality by not allowing for the (equal) representation of all views. To see why, consider the constitutional requirement that prohibits government action to establish a religion in the United States. As interpreted by the courts, the antiestablishment clause requires that at a minimum there be no official religion in America and prohibits government support of one religion over another.

Now it would be absurd to argue that government neutrality toward religion has been violated simply because some religions have more adherents than others and because some have no adherents at all. After all, the point of neutrality in this context is not to ensure that every religion has some supporters, or that all religions have equal numbers of supporters, but to make sure that government policy does not officially sanction some religions and suppress others. However, if commitment to particular religions is based on the free decisions of the citizens themselves, government neutrality has not been violated.

A related point can be made about institutional critical neutrality within the university. Just as individual citizens have the right to make their own religious commitments, so scholars have the right (and obligation) to determine what views to explore and examine within their areas of professional competence. If such scholars, as the result of their inquiry, determine that some approaches are not worth examining within critical inquiry, then institutional critical neutrality is not violated. The point of institutional critical neutrality is to provide a neutral framework within which reasoned intellectual debate can be pursued, not to dictate the results of that debate. Thus, if the community of investigators agrees that astrology is a fraud, or that creationism is not a science, neutrality is not violated if the science department does not offer courses in creationism or astrology. On the other hand, neutrality would be violated if the university dictated in *advance of inquiry* and *independent of evidence* that, say, creationism must (or must not) be regarded as equal in intellectual worth to evolutionary biology.

It is helpful to keep in mind here the distinction between limitations in debate *within* a field and limitations on metadebate *about* the limitations within that discipline. Thus, no respectable scientific department would offer courses based on astrological methods, but debate on whether there is a significant epistemic difference between astrology and the natural sciences would be very appropriate in a course in the philosophy of science. Accordingly, limits on what perspectives and methodologies are represented in a university's curriculum may be compatible with institutional neutrality when (1) the limitations are supportable by appeal to the publicly accessible results of critical inquiry, (2) the limitations are proportional in force to the degree of support in their favor, and (3) the limitations are debatable in metainquiry about the discipline in question. These conditions allow inquirers to concentrate on areas of interest they deem significant, while also containing checks against dogmatism and intolerance. Moreover, they indicate that the point of institutional critical neutrality is not to provide equal access in the university for every point of view or perspective, but rather to ensure that the process that determines which problems, perspectives, and points of view get examined and studied is itself critical and rational.

III. Justifying the Neutral University

Perhaps enough has been said to show that the notion of institutional critical neutrality cannot be easily dismissed as inapplicable to colleges and universities. However, to say that it is possible for colleges and universities to be critically neutral is one thing, but to say that it is desirable for them to be neutral, or that they ought to be neutral, is quite another. What sorts of considerations, if any, justify the claim that colleges and universities ought to be critically neutral as institutions?

To begin with, it is doubtful if we will find one "knock-down" argument that all by itself should persuade all rational people of good will that a policy of institutional critical neutrality is justified. Moreover, different sorts of justification need to be kept distinct. In claiming that institutional critical neutrality is justified, is that claim merely that such neutrality is a good thing that the university may implement if it chooses but that it may decide not to implement without committing a wrong? Or is the claim that colleges and universities commit a wrong by not being critically neutral? That is, is commitment to critical neutrality by colleges and universities morally allowed or morally required? Finally, if institutional critical neutrality is required of colleges and universities, is the requirement absolute or *prima facie* (i.e., is it always morally overriding or can it be trumped by more weighty moral considerations)?

We can make a start toward answering these questions by considering the different sorts of arguments that can be advanced in favor of institutional critical neutrality, and then by considering types of cases where neutrality, even if possible, might seem open to moral objection. Then we will be in a better position to assess the nature and strength of the case for institutional critical neutrality. We need to keep in mind as we proceed that the case for institutional critical neutrality is multifaceted, in that a plurality of factors each lends some weight to the justification. The argument gains force as the weight of the different factors is aggregated.

To begin, there are practical consequences to a policy of partisanship rather than neutrality. In fact, as we have seen, the doctrine of institutional neutrality was originally intended by its American supporters to protect the university from interference by trustees and donors who wished to bend the university in the direction of the views they regarded as politically correct. In our own day, once the university is recognized as a partisan political agent, it can expect to be on the receiving as well as giving end of many political battles. The privileges and immunities extended to it because of its nonpartisan character are all too likely to come under fire and even be removed. Thus, why should opponents of the university's political stances allow it to keep its tax exemptions due to its educational status when an increasing amount of its energy and resources are devoted to advancing political views contrary to their own? Why not treat it like any other political opponent instead? Why not try to weaken it? As still more of the university's resources are devoted to fighting off such attacks, fewer resources will be available for support of critical inquiry and rational discourse within the university itself.

Consider further that when the university takes a partisan political stand as an institution in an area outside the sphere of values tied to critical inquiry, it lends its authority, prestige, and power to a particular side. The university then becomes open to conflicts of interest between its partisan commitments and the values of critical inquiry.

For example, if the university *qua* university takes the stand that it is wrongful discrimination for gays not to be allowed to serve in the military, what policy implications follow for issuing invitations to speakers who hold contrary views; appointing and retaining professors who strongly dissent from the university's stand; allowing military recruiters on campus; permitting and protecting opposing demonstrations; and the like? Although it may be possible for the university just to issue a statement of its views and take no further action, it is likely that the same arguments used to persuade the university to take a stand in the first place will be used to support more direct and forceful action as well. Moreover, even if the university only issues statements, its decisions in relevant areas often will appear to be politically motivated even when that is not the case, as might happen if the university also decided not to allow ROTC programs on its campus for entirely *neutral* reasons.[9]

However, even if the university can avoid conflicts of interest, and even the appearance of such conflict, the consequences for critical inquiry still are likely to be dire. For example, even if the university is willing to appoint and retain faculty and invite speakers who dissent from its official political stance, is it likely that such people will be attracted to an institution that has rejected their own views as immoral or unwise? Even those who have been attracted, or who remain at their posts, implicitly have been labeled as dissenters from an officially sanctioned position and must argue under an imposed handicap that arises not from the weaknesses of their arguments but from a political act by the institution that employs them. Loss of neutrality is all too likely to result in the partisan university that stands for a set of political and ideological principles and is far too intellectually homogeneous as a result. The intellectual diversity so essential for effective critical inquiry would be absent or, at best, in severe jeopardy.

Moreover, who is to decide for the university? Do only the trustees speak for the university? Many faculty think that they constitute the core of the university and speak for it, but why should faculty values dominate over those of students, alumni, administrators, and staff? Must the faculty be unanimous, or can a majority of the faculty, perhaps only a bare majority, speak for the whole institution? Universities have not been structured to act as corporate political agents. What in fact is all too likely to happen in the partisan university is that the most active and noisy groups will come to speak for the institution, although in fact they often will be expressing the viewpoint of their own group rather than that of the college or university itself.

Most important, in the partisan university, wouldn't the autonomy of each individual to pursue inquiry where it led and to adopt and advocate dissenting views be severely restricted? Not only would individuals be all too likely to feel pressure to conform to the views of the institution that employed them, but those views would also gain prestige from being the officially sanctioned perspective of the university itself. If so, individuals would be under pressure from a variety of sources to conform to the prevailing views. As a result, all of us would be intellectually impoverished in the same way we are impoverished whenever any view becomes orthodox, not because its merits are established in open inquiry but rather because it has been artificially protected from the challenges such inquiry generates.

But hasn't it been conceded already that at the individual level, the classroom instructor may argue for substantive positions under certain conditions without undermining the autonomy of students? Why doesn't a similar conclusion follow about the taking of substantive political stands by the university itself?

This objection would be decisive if the roles of the individual teacher and the college or university were logically parallel. However, consider whether the two sets of roles are relevantly different. Classroom instructors are individuals whose primary professional obligations are to engage in inquiry and disseminate the results. The scholar's findings are to reflect fair and judicious evaluation of the evidence and can be evaluated and criticized in appropriate professional forums, such as journals and presentations at professional meetings. Individual scholars, in other words, are charged with the responsibility of basing conclusions on evidence and on submitting their results, along with supporting arguments, to the judgment of their peers. The university, on the other hand, is likely to take overt stands not because of any evaluation of evidence but because of political pressures among its various constituencies and factions. Moreover, there is no forum in which the university is obligated to present its arguments for judgment by professional peers. That is, the university's taking of a political stance is not a contribution to inquiry in the same way as is the taking of a substantive position by a serious scholar.

More important, the individual does not play the same institutional role as guardian of critical inquiry as does the university. The latter but not the former is the guardian of the values necessary for critical inquiry. For the very institution designed to umpire the critical process also to be a participant within that process raises the very kinds of problems discussed above. Thus, it is at best doubtful if the analysis of the rights and obligations of scholars to take positions within critical inquiry can be applied in parallel fashion to the university itself. To assume that the two are parallel is as dangerous as assuming that because individuals may adopt particular religious perspectives, it follows that the state may do so as well.

Accordingly, an advocate of institutional critical neutrality can plausibly distinguish between the effects of a partisan professor and a partisan institution on the autonomy of students and faculty. The partisan professor, as long as his or her work is governed by intellectual standards of critical inquiry, is carrying out the activity the university is designed to promote: namely, critical inquiry subject to rational review. The university's role, however, is to nurture and protect such inquiry, not to be a participant in it. It is doubtful if it can carry out that role while being a partisan political agent as well.

To summarize, the partisan university faces inherent conflicts of interest among different kinds of goals. Thus, the prestige and influence of the university would be placed on one side of important political debates; yet the university also would have the obligation to encourage independent thinking and the formation of diverse perspectives on those very same issues, and to refrain from loading the dice on one side or another in advance of inquiry. The same institution charged with the responsibility of protecting the value of critical inquiry would become committed to a second set of values, which might on occasion call for limiting such inquiry or, at the very least, for diverting resources from it. It would be as if the state at one and the same time were to be trusted as the protector of religious tolerance and the advocate of a particular religion. Because the potential for conflict of interest is so great, and the threat to autonomy so large, we require state neutrality toward religion. Surely the case for university neutrality is no less defensible.

This does not mean that universities generally *are* neutral. Violations of neutrality may occur, but their existence does not refute the thesis that universities *ought* to be critically neutral. Violations of institutional critical neutrality are grounds for criticism in the name of neutrality, not reasons for rejecting neutrality itself.

Our discussion suggests, then, that an important case can be made for the claim that colleges and universities ought to be politically neutral in the relevant sense (i.e., be institutionally critically neutral). Just as state neutrality toward religion is a significant protection for the freedom of individuals to make their own religious choices, so too does institutional critical neutrality provide similar protection for individuals to make autonomous decisions within critical inquiry. By so doing, it protects the integrity and enhances the efficacy of critical inquiry and rational discourse. Indeed, not only do individuals need to be free to follow the argument where it leads within critical inquiry, but the framework provided by the rules, principles, and values of critical inquiry also provides the critical tests that help us distinguish justified from unjustified claims and separate truth from falsehood.

It is plausible to conclude, then, that critical neutrality is not simply desirable, but that it would normally be wrong for universities not to be institutionally critically neutral. By violating neutrality, they not only threaten the autonomy of their students and faculty, but also undermine the very framework that allows them to perform their most important function: the constant rational evaluation and transmission of our social, scientific, and cultural heritage.

However, while colleges and universities normally ought to be institutionally critically neutral, there may be instances where the case for neutrality is overridden by even weightier moral considerations. That is, adherence to neutrality may have its limits. Critics of neutrality point to hard cases in which it is far from clear that universities ought to be neutral in the face of the serious problems involved. In the next section, we will test the limits of the neutrality thesis by considering such cases and the difficulties they raise for advocates of neutrality.

Notes

1. Indeed, it is something of a mystery on this point of view why adherents of different ideologies would hold them so strongly since there are no better reasons on the extreme view for holding some positions rather than others. The result seems to be a kind of emotivism that leaves unclear why the passions are so strongly engaged in the first place.

2. John Rawls, *A Theory of Justice* (Cambridge, Mass.: Harvard University Press, 1971), particularly pp. 46–53. For appeal to "wide" reflective equilibrium in favor of greater equality in distribution of goods than Rawls appears to support, see Kai Nielson, *Equality and Liberty* (Totowa, N.J.: Rowman and Allenheld, 1985), pp. 13–44.

3. Similarly, the rules of a sport normally wil be mutually acceptable to the competitors. However, as we will see, this does not necessarily preclude important debate over the substance of the rules themselves, either in competitive sports or critical inquiry.

4. Those who would avoid the language of rights can put the point in terms of not wronging students and colleagues. That is, rather than saying students and colleagues have a right to autonomy, we can say instead, perhaps without substantial loss of meaning, that it wrongs them to deny their autonomy in educational contexts.

5. Of course, this does not preclude instructors from using their authority

to move the discussion along, for example by giving different students a chance to speak, or even of closing off debate at appropriate times so the syllabus for the course can be covered in the time allowed. It prohibits the instructor from using professorial authority arbitrarily or for purely partisan purposes, but not for using it for educationally valid goals.

6. It would be proper, however, for the instructor to defend such a view as the conclusion of an argument after a fair presentation of alternatives and criticisms.

7. The distinction between internal and external neutrality is essentially that drawn by David Paris in his article in Part II of this volume.

8. For example, a commitment to considering the evidence relevant to an issue, and to be open to consideration of objections.

9. For an argument that neutrality counts against allowing ROTC programs on campus, see the essay by Robert Holmes in Part II of this volume.

CHAPTER 4

Hard Cases for the Neutrality Thesis

I. Individual Behavior and University Values

One set of hard cases for the neutrality thesis concerns university regulation of student behavior. The claim here is that the university enforces a set of socially approved values, or values deemed desirable by the university itself, that constitute the enforcement of a substantive moral view. Although the ending of *in loco parentis* may have reduced the degree to which institutions of higher learning regulate student social life, some core values are still supported and enforced. While these vary from institution to institution, even the most liberal colleges and universities frequently regulate consumption of alcohol and drugs, assign roommates only of the same gender, and in light of the AIDS epidemic and other sexually transmitted diseases, adopt value-laden policies such as making condoms available or urging sexual abstinence.

Colleges and universities can try to avoid the claim that they enforce controversial ethical standards in regulating student life. According to one seemingly attractive line of reply, universities can claim to only be providing the greatest amount of freedom to students. Student choices, not university policy, set values. In other words, the university gives the students opportunity to make their own value decisions for themselves. Opponents of neutrality would rejoin, however, that *laissez-faire* is itself a value-laden policy that requires as much defense as any other. Indeed, to those who think that colleges should be much stricter than they are in enforcing standards of decency, the policy of giving students as much liberty as possible will seem particularly pernicious. Can the claim that colleges and universities ought to be neutral be defended in the light of regulation (or lack of regulation) of student behavior?

While the problem here is a real one, we can see that a reply is possible on behalf of neutrality if we remember that the kind of neutrality we have found to be appropriate for colleges and universities involves neither total value freedom nor consequential neutrality (equivalent consequences for all positions). In particular, since the university's commitment is to critical neutrality, it can promulgate rules governing student life that are compatible with neutrality if the rules themselves are designed to protect rational discourse and promote inquiry. Thus, rules governing the abuse of alcohol and other drugs can be defended as necessary to preserve and promote a campus atmosphere suitable for reflection, study, and debate. Prohibitions of loud partying, drunkenness, and other forms of disruptive behavior surely can be justified by appeal to the very values central to the university's intellectual mission.

Other arguments also apply that can be used to reinforce the neutralist position with regard to regulation of student behavior. Thus, universities have no exemption from legal requirements concerning the use of drugs and alcohol. So even if there were not a neutral justification available along the lines sketched above for regulations on drug and alcohol use, legal requirements would still apply. If those legal requirements were not neutral in an appropriate sense, it would not be the university but the state that violated neutrality.

Moreover, state regulations themselves might have a neutral justification, although not necessarily of the same kind as that applicable to the university. That is, state regulations on the use of alcohol and drugs perhaps are justifiable without reference to a specific conception of the good life, the kind of neutrality that many liberal writers regard as appropriate in the political realm. Rather, regulations arguably are necessary to maintain public order and the rights of others to be free of harm from intoxicated persons and other social evils allegedly attendant upon drug use. In any case, while it is controversial whether acceptable neutral justifications for regulation by the state of alcohol and drug use can be provided, requirements arising from law are the responsibility of the state, not the university. Accordingly, the proponent of institutional critical neutrality within the university has a fallback position, even if the quite plausible case for regulation based on the requirements of critical inquiry is somehow undermined. That is, the neutralist surely would not regard legally required regulations as a violation of the university's neutrality but at most as violations of state neutrality instead. More to the point, however, since critical neutrality is not equivalent to value freedom, it does not prohibit the university from regulating student life in ways designed to protect and promote critical discourse.

Keeping these points in mind, consider university policies that bear on sexual morality. For example, a university may react to the threat of AIDS in a variety of ways. But won't any such policy reflect a view of proper sexual morality and so fail to be neutral? Thus, if the university urges sexual abstinence as the first line of defense, it seems to be reflecting one moral perspective, whereas if it sanctions the distribution of condoms, it seems to be reflecting quite another. Either way, it appears that the university has taken a partisan stand on a controversial moral and political issue.

In response, proponents of critical neutrality should distinguish between two kinds of reasons the university might have for adopting a policy in this area, whether it be distributing condoms, advocating abstinence, or something else entirely. The first kind of reason might be because the university believes the behavior likely to be encouraged by the policy it adopts is *morally* better than the behavior that would be encouraged by other policies. Thus, it might regard abstinence from sex outside of marriage as morally better behavior than engaging in sexual intercourse outside of marriage. In this case, the university is taking a position on a controversial moral issue on grounds unrelated to its educational mission and so is violating critical neutrality. The same conclusion would follow if the university distributed condoms simply because it wanted to encourage sexual relations among students on the grounds that they were a good thing or, more plausibly perhaps, that such relations were not morally wrong and that condoms prevented various social disutilities, such as pregnancy and sexually transmitted disease. So long as the choice of policy is based on a moral principle or ideal, even a utilitarian one, which is unrelated to the educational mission of the institution, critical neutrality is violated.

However, there are other kinds of reasons for adopting a policy in this area that seem compatible with critical neutrality, and also seem a morally appropriate stance for a university to adopt. First, some policies toward sexual relations may better serve the university's educational goals than others. Surely, preserving the health of the student body and an atmosphere in which intense educational efforts can be sustained fall within its sphere of proper authority. Clearly, the spread of sexually transmitted diseases as well as unwanted pregnancies can adversely affect the ability of students to learn and study. Thus, not only is the university remaining true to its mission by adopting policies on such a basis, it arguably has a clear duty to do so.

Second, if there is no policy that is required or even favored by educational reasons arising from the mission of the university, colleges and universities may justifiably leave matters up to the autonomy of the students. Thus, by making condoms available, but leaving it up to students whether or not to use them, the choice has been left to the students rather than being made by the university.

But surely this reply is defective, critics will argue. Autonomy itself is a substantive value. To come down on the side of autonomy rather than, say, authority, is to adopt a substantive and highly partisan moral view. Once again, the critics will maintain, we see the tendency of liberals to adopt a controversial moral stance, one that would be anathema to many religious fundamentalists, and pretend they are only being neutral. A society based on autonomy, however desirable it might be, is still one that reflects a particular normative stance that many people committed to religion or other traditions would unhesitatingly reject.

This criticism may well have force against liberal views of state neutrality, which support policies on the grounds of promoting individual autonomy while at the same time denying that they favor a particular conception of the good life.[1] However, the claim that colleges and universities ought to be critically neutral does not entail the view that they ought not to favor any particular conceptions of the good life. Rather, it implies that universities may (and even may be required to) adopt those conceptions of the good life that are instrumental for carrying out their educational missions. And since critical inquiry presupposes the value of autonomous investigators, the adoption of policies by the university that promote or rely on the autonomy of its constituents do seem to have a neutral justification not available to the state. In this area at least, the liberal case for the neutral state—neutral toward conceptions of the good—diverges from the case for the critically neutral university that should remain neutral not toward conceptions of the good but toward partisan moral and political positions that are unrelated to its educational mission. Since autonomy arguably is so closely related to critical inquiry, the kind of neutrality appropriate to the university would seem to allow and sometimes even require allowing individual members of the university community to make their own autonomous decisions about controversial areas of individual social behavior.

II. Freedom, Racist Hate Speech, and Neutrality

Imagine the following incident. A group of right-wing students at a party shout anti-Semitic and other racist slogans from the windows of their dormitory. These are heard by other students, who ask the university to discipline those responsible. The accused students, however, claim that they simply were exerting rights of free speech. Should the university discipline these students? The problem raised for advocates of neutrality by incidents like this, which unfortunately are not as rare as one would hope on our campuses, is acute. If the university disciplines these students because their speech is offensive, but does not similarly discipline other groups whose speech also is offensive, the university has taken a partisan political stance and is no longer neutral. On the other hand, if the university disciplines all speech found offensive by someone, free discussion on the campus would be radically limited, since almost any controversial claim is likely to be offensive to someone. Apparently, the university is faced with a hard set of choices. The university must be an active partisan of some groups and positions against others, or it must allow any speech no matter how racist or crude, or it must undermine the very framework of free discussion that is necessary for critical inquiry to take place.

In response to a number of incidents of what might be called racist, sexist, anti-Semitic, and homophobic speech, some colleges and universities have formulated speech codes designed to give institutions the right to punish those who engage in such conduct.[2] However, such codes have been perceived as undue limitations on free speech and so far have been struck down by the courts when challenged. Whether newer codes that have been more narrowly drawn to apply only to racist speech associated with active harassment will survive legal scrutiny is still unclear. The legal and moral issues associated with such speech codes will be explored in depth in another volume of this series. Remarks here will be restricted to implications for neutrality.

The first point to note is that the values at stake, rather than being in conflict with neutrality, can be conceived as two components of it. That is, if critical neutrality is a complex set of values, different constituents can come into conflict. That appears to be the case here.

Those who support speech codes that allow for punishment of persons engaging in racist speech do not see themselves as opponents of critical inquiry but as supporters of it. On their view, critical inquiry requires a diverse community of investigators. But if women and members of various minority groups can be made the targets of hate speech with impunity, they can be intimidated and harassed. As a result, they will be less likely to enter the campus in the first place and more likely to be silenced by fear when they do enter. As a result, hate speech, rather than being any sort of contribution to rational discourse and discussion, actually undermines it.

Can offensive hate speech be regulated on the grounds that it promotes fear and harassment within the community so that inquiry itself is threatened? Should the expression of the offending ideas be prohibited on the ground of preserving the kind of diverse community needed for intelligent inquiry? According to a view we can call the *communitarian* perspective the answer is affirmative.[3] Communitarians emphasize that critical inquiry is carried out within a community and that for critical inquiry to be effective the community must be diverse so that different perspectives participate. They argue that protection of hate speech diminishes or destroys the bonds of a scholarly community, so that the framework that makes critical inquiry possible is diminished or destroyed. It does so by limiting the participation of diverse groups within the community, since threatened groups may be intimidated into silence, and destroys the common respect necessary for dialogue among diverse groups to take place.

The communitarian case for regulating hate speech certainly has force, especially when one considers it from the perspective of minorities who may see themselves as surrounded by hostile "others" and who as a result may feel intimidated, isolated, and afraid. Nevertheless, those committed to freedom of expression, while sympathetic to the plight of the victims of hate speech, may remain unconvinced by the case for prohibition. After all, they may argue, the forceful assertion of any controversial position may be threatening to those who oppose it and may silence opposition. If speech is to be prohibited simply because it is controversial, there would be little debate of any real intellectual worth going on in our colleges and universities.

Perhaps the gap between the communitarian prohibitionists and the civil libertarians can be bridged by a third group, the moderates, that believes narrowly drawn speech codes can regulate those instances of hate speech that are threatening to specified individuals and thereby constitute harassment, while leaving the merely offensive statement of controversial positions unregulated as long as specific individuals are not targeted. This intermediate position has some promise, but it would leave disturbing incidents such as our hypothetical case of the shouting of racial epithets untouched, since no specific individuals are harassed. Although we cannot explore the overall merit of each of these different positions here, some of the implications for neutrality need to be emphasized.

First, as noted earlier, the problem arises because institutional critical neutrality encompasses a cluster of related values that, although normally mutually reinforcing, can conflict in some circumstances. Thus, critical inquiry requires free and open debate but also is best conducted by a diverse community of inquirers so that issues can be examined from a variety of perspectives. The problem is that in pursuing one of these values, we may be faced with hard choices about limiting pursuit of the other. Free discussion, for example, may permit the expression of opinion intimidating to some groups and in extreme cases may lead to their withdrawal from the university community.

In other words, critical neutrality has a negative and positive aspect. Negatively, it requires the university to protect those engaging in rational discourse and inquiry from interference with their legitimate activities. Positively, it requires the university to promote an intellectual climate in which rational discourse and inquiry can take place and even flourish. The problem is that the positive and negative aspects of critical neutrality can conflict.

While a hard choice may be called for, the choice is not between neutrality and some other values but rather concerns what weight to give different elements of neutrality itself when they conflict. Thus, the conflict over how universities ought to react to hate speech does not show that neutrality ought to be overridden by other, more important values, let alone that neutrality is impossible, but rather that we must decide which aspects of neutrality ought to take priority over others. Moreover, this point is not a mere verbal subterfuge. Critical inquiry does require open and unrestricted discussion but also does require provision of an atmosphere in which expression of diverse viewpoints is encouraged and welcomed. Silencing of views through intimidation and coercion violates core values of the academic ethic itself.

Any attempt to balance the competing values at stake in this controversy is likely to be controversial, and a thorough examination of it would take us too far from the central topic of neutrality. However, our discussion of neutrality does suggest some guidelines for consideration. Thus, while there may be cases where speech should be limited in the name of preserving community, particularly when the speech counts as a threat or a form of harassment of specified individuals, it is plausible to think the burden of proof should be on those who wish to restrict expression. This is because when one enters the university, one enters an institution the major purpose of which is to engage in investigation and discussion of difficult and often highly controversial issues. It is unlikely that people can seriously engage in such an activity without expecting to encounter views that may offend them or that they find dangerous. In a sense, the risk of being offended, or being exposed to views regarded as dangerous or subversive of one's values, is a risk one should expect to encounter in a university, one that we can reasonably expect members of the university community to bear, just as the risk of being hit by an errant golf shot is one golfers can reasonably be expected to bear when on the golf course. Both are part of the normal context of the activity in question. Therefore, an especially strong case must be made for the necessity of silencing specific acts of expression if restrictions are to be justified. Mere offense to the community or threat to favored views is insufficient. Otherwise, the politically strongest groups would be able to silence dissent simply because they are offended by it or their views are threatened by the arguments of the critics. Accordingly, if speech or expression is to be regulated at all, it must be more than merely offensive or merely threatening in a broad sense, but rather must amount to a specific threat or a form of harassment that undermines the rights of especially targeted victims to function as full and equal members of the university community. The problem of hate speech, then, does raise significant problems for the university community and for the concept of neutrality. But rather than undermine the idea of neutrality, the problem indicates the importance of each of its component elements instead.

III. Whom Should the University Honor?

So far, we have focused on whether or not colleges and universities should act in an overt political manner by taking stands on political issue or on matters of ethical import that arise internally. Other kinds of actions by colleges and universities may covertly violate neutrality as well. In particular, the awarding of honorary degrees and selection of speakers for commencements and other institutional celebrations presuppose a choice by the university about what sort of persons ought to be honored.[4] These choices presuppose that the university uses some set of values in making its selection. Not only is this a violation of neutrality, it might be argued, but it is highly desirable that neutrality be violated in this way. Surely, it is proper and appropriate for the university to honor persons who have achieved greatly or served the society well. But mustn't the university use value-laden criteria of selection in order to do so? Moreover, in deciding what is a great achievement or an important service that is worthy of being *honored,* the university must go beyond simply applying the rules or values of critical inquiry and make a substantive decision about what is a worthy achievement or service.

There are, as might be expected, a number of replies available to the proponent of neutrality, but it is quite debatable whether any are fully adequate. To begin with, the university might adopt a restrictive stance and declare that adhering to neutrality is more important than honoring individuals. In other words, the university might simply stop awarding honorary degrees, selecting commencement speakers, and the like. Individuals and groups within the university might still choose to award honors on a value-laden basis, but the university as an institution would not.

Alternately, the university could moderate the restrictive view by awarding honors only on the basis of contributions to values central to its own mission; for example, for support for education, for preservation of the freedoms necessary for inquiry, or for service to the university itself. Here, the university would be applying certain values, but they would be values internal to its own academic ethic and so would not violate neutrality in the relevant sense of institutional critical neutrality.

Although the restrictive and moderately restrictive stances do preserve neutrality, it is far from clear that they do so at an acceptable cost. The price is that colleges and universities would not be able to honor persons of achievement in areas not directly related to the academic ethic and would not be able to hear their views at important ceremonial functions, such as commencements. Surely, it is important that universities be able to invite interesting and often provocative speakers ranging from Jesse Jackson to Jeane Kirkpatrick and across wide ranges of the political, scientific, and cultural spectrum.

Perhaps, however, a stance other than the restrictive one is available to the neutralist. By adopting what might be called a pluralistic view, honors could be accorded on a wide variety of grounds, so long as the justification for awarding the honors is not to provide political or ideological support for a particular perspective, political position, or ideological framework. That is, the university's stance might not be value free and might not be consequentially neutral, but the reasons for its decisions would not be partisan. For example, a particular winner of the Nobel Prize in a natural science might be a political activist as well, but if the university awards him an honorary degree or invites him to speak at commencement because of his scientific achievements rather than to promote his political goals, it is acting neutrally in the view we are considering.

However, things are not quite so easy. First, in at least some cases, moral and political values may bear on what counts as a scientific achievement worth honoring. Thus, presumably the university should not honor certain sorts of scientific achievements, such as the invention of a deadly new form of germ warfare or results obtained through unethical abuse of human subjects. But if we specify that the scientific or intellectual achievement that is to be honored must contribute to human welfare, or at least must not be on balance harmful or be attained ethically, political and moral judgments will have to be made about what is beneficial, harmful, or unethical. At best, it is not easy to see how institutional judgments of those sorts are compatible with the case for institutional critical neutrality made earlier.

A second and perhaps even more serious difficulty arises if the achievement itself is in the realm of ethics, politics, or social service. Unless we are to disqualify honoring any behavior that is at all controversial, the university will have to make substantive choices about what is worthy of being honored in these value-laden areas as well. Not only does it appear that a neutral stance is impossible, it also seems that if the university ought to honor those who have made worthy contributions to our society, then the university ought not to be neutral in this area in the first place.

While these difficulties are serious ones, however, they may not be decisive. Perhaps the university can remain critically neutral without being unduly restrictive and while honoring worthy achievements and issuing institutional invitations to controversial figures. For one thing, while the university may have to make value judgments, it can make them from the perspective of critical neutrality itself. Thus, the university can extend invitations and award honors in such a way as to further critical inquiry without actively supporting partisan political stances. For example, persons with a wide range of views can be included in selection committees, and efforts can be made to insure that recipients of awards and invitations represent a diverse set of perspectives. Of course, not every perspective can be included, but that is the case with the curriculum itself, as we saw in the discussion of astrology. If a viewpoint is not taken seriously by the community of inquirers, it need not be included, although the exclusion itself may have to be justified in metadebate about the process. But there can be agreement among people of good will that speakers with whom they strongly disagree may have a viewpoint that ought not to be excluded from consideration, or that an achievement in science or the arts is of great intellectual merit although it is debatable whether its social or political importance is of the first rank.

It is at least arguable, then, if the university is trying to recognize and honor contributions to critical inquiry and human understanding, that its intent in other words is not partisan, that a broad range of views are represented among institutional representatives who select recipients, and that the recipients themselves tend not to represent a narrow or partisan range of opinion, the university has acted neutrally. On the other hand, if recipients are overwhelmingly from one end of the political spectrum and those who represent other perspectives that significant elements of the intellectual community and broader society find worth honoring are excluded, neutrality has been violated. For example, if recipients of honors predominantly represent liberal perspectives, and conservatives are not only significantly underrepresented but even deliberately excluded, neutrality has been violated.[5] In such cases, the university can be accused of betraying its trust as guardian of critical inquiry and of covertly supporting a particular partisan view, not because of the strength of arguments, but through the hidden use of institutional power.

Finally, while the university clearly cannot censor speakers it invites to ceremonies such as commencements, speakers may have a moral obligation to respect the point of the occasion and not use their platform for a narrowly partisan address. After all, the point of a commencement is to honor the graduates, not expound one's views to a captive audience that has no formal means of reply. In other words, at a commencement ceremony, the graduates and their guests have a reasonable expectation that the occasion will not be used for partisan purposes. We need to ask, in other words, if people have a right to come together for purposes that are not political. If so, someone who uses a platform provided for one reason for narrow partisan purposes may wrong those who had formed reasonable expectations to the contrary.

It might be objected that the reasonable expectations of the audience can be altered if the commencement speaker simply warns them in advance that the occasion will be used for a highly partisan political speech. However, the expectations in this case are simply not based on the avowed intentions of the speakers or other participants in the ceremony but on the point of the ceremony, which is primarily to honor the graduates. We need to ask then whether persons have the *right,* based on their freedom to associate for purposes they regard as desirable, not to have the event turned into mainly an occasion for protest or for narrowly partisan diatribes.

This does not mean that commencement speeches must be bland and uncontroversial. It does mean that the speaker should show respect for the purpose of the occasion, understand that a wide diversity of views probably is represented in the audience, and that normally the occasion is not one for a stinging attack on the perspectives of some of the guests.

Admittedly, a commencement address is perhaps the one occasion where students and faculty have the opportunity to bring perceived injustices, particularly ones occurring within the university community itself, to the attention of wide constituents of the university, including parents and alumni. Surely, they might respond, it would be wrong for them not to use such an opportunity to bring injustices to the attention of those who may be able to correct them. In such cases, why isn't a stinging attack upon the corruption within the university appropriate? Is silence in the face of injustice what neutrality requires? If so, so much the worse for neutrality.

As we will see in the next section on divestment, the charge that the university itself is committing an injustice raises serious difficulties for the neutrality thesis. However, in the present context, several points must be kept in mind. First, even if the university is involved in commission of an injustice, a commencement may not be the morally appropriate place for a diatribe on the topic. If it is worth honoring the graduates in the first place, real questions can be raised upon shifting the focus from a ceremony to a protest. Here, we need to consider whether members of the university community have the right to come together for purposes that are not primarily political, but that have to do with honoring achievement. If so, such occasions normally may be no more the occasion for narrowly partisan attacks than other ceremonies that have no political purpose, such as a funeral, confirmation, or bar mitzvah. Second, it may be highly controversial whether the university actually is engaged in the commission of an injustice or how the issue in question properly should be framed and evaluated. To present a captive audience with only one side of the issue, especially when they have little chance of learning about alternative viewpoints during their visit to the campus, undermines critical inquiry instead of contributing to it. The use of position to impose a view on others seems to replace the idea of reasoned evaluation of it.

Third, there may be ways to present the issue fairly, with some deference to the viewpoints of others, that counts as a contribution to dialogue rather than a harangue. Given that over time different perspectives may well be represented at institutional ceremonies, perhaps a politically relevant and reasoned speech that is not a diatribe is compatible with critical neutrality.[6] Commencement speeches, therefore, need not consist of bland pieties, but do need to be reasoned presentations made within a framework of respect for the occasion and for the values of guests who have no formal opportunity for reply and who may have reasonable expectations that their values will not be the subject of especially stinging and emotional attacks.

Accordingly, if we combine the pluralist position with the idea that there is a distinction between a presentation that may be political and normative in a broad sense and one that is a narrowly partisan attack upon the values of many in the audience rather than an invitation to question, neutrality may well be possible even in the area of honors, awards, and institutional invitations.[7] If awards represent a reasonable range of intellectual, political, and social diversity, and if the occasion is not misused for narrowly partisan purposes, a case can be made that not only has institutional critical neutrality not been violated but that it has provided a set of useful guidelines for policy as well. This conclusion, if plausible, suggests that a neutral position is not impossible or undesirable even in an area in which at first glance partisan choices seem nearly impossible to avoid.

IV. Divestment: A Counterexample to Neutrality

Is a neutral policy with respect to university investments even possible? Isn't investing in a business a form of support for it? If so, shouldn't universities be governed by ethical constraints in their investing policies? Moreover, by participating in the Western capitalist system at all, don't universities become part of the system, and hence fail to be neutral? From the point of view of a critic of that system, aren't they part of the problem rather than part of the solution? How can they both be a participant in the system and neutral when the system itself is politically controversial?

Issues about the ethics of a university's investment policies often simmer below the surface on many campuses but rise to the top when a specific concern becomes the center of a political controversy. This was the case during the debate over divestment on many American campuses during the late 1980s. At this time, worldwide pressure was being put on the white government of South Africa to end the policy of apartheid that relegated South Africans of color, the vast majority of the population, to legally, educationally, and economically inferior status. Universities were asked by significant numbers of their own students and faculty members to join this struggle against racism by divesting themselves of all investments in companies doing business in South Africa. The point was to join in an economic effort to put pressure on the South African government to end apartheid, as well as to remove the university from what the proponents of divestment regarded as participation in and support of an unjust political regime.

Opponents of divestment joined in the moral condemnation of apartheid but argued that divestment was not an appropriate policy for ending it on a variety of grounds—because it would be ineffective or even counterproductive, or because it violated the neutrality of the university, or because trustees would violate their fiduciary responsibilities by using the endowment for purposes unintended by donors. This led to a series of sometimes bitter protests on many campuses, the erection of shanties symbolizing the plight of the oppressed in South Africa, and confrontation between proponents of and critics of divestment. Before turning to the specific issues for neutrality raised by the divestment movement, however, a brief examination of the implications of our discussion of neutrality for investment policy may provide a useful background for examination of the divestment issue.

To begin with, a proponent of neutrality surely should concede that the act of making an investment (as well as acts of omission such as not making an investment or not changing one's investments) can have politically significant consequences. It does not follow, as we have seen, that lack of consequential neutrality precludes lack of neutrality in all other significant senses. Similarly, a professor's decision to order a particular textbook for her course may have significant consequences. For example, the treatment of a topic may lead students to take certain views seriously that they otherwise might not even have considered. It does not follow, however, that she intended to have students support those views or that her justification for selecting that text was that it would result in students adopting certain views. She simply may have thought that the text was the best and fairest available treatment of the material. Similarly, a university's justification for making a certain investment may not be that certain politically significant consequences will follow. Rather, its justification may be simply that this investment will help the university best carry out its educational mission by yielding the largest possible financial support.

But isn't this neutrality of justification often immoral? How does it differ from the claim of a negligently speeding driver that he didn't intend to hurt anyone; he just wanted to see what it felt like to drive fast? After all, if our acts have terrible consequences, isn't it bad faith to say that our justification for our act was independent of its consequences, especially if the consequences of our behavior were foreseeable by us? Isn't it plausible to think that our moral duty not to commit a serious evil or wrong sometimes overrides the obligation to be neutral?

The answer to this last question sometimes may be "yes," but before turning to such exceptional cases, it is important to understand that there is a general presumptive case in favor of a policy of neutrality in making investments. Neutrality in this context does not mean critical neutrality, since investments rather than critical discourse are at stake, but neutrality in the justification for making the investment. Justificatory neutrality, making the investment because of expected return rather than because of the political consequences, has crucial connections to critical neutrality, however, and it is these connections that provide the justification for a neutral investment policy. In particular, consider whether universities would be more justified *as a general rule* in following a neutral investment policy meant to maximize financial return *or* one in which all major investment decisions were made as to maximize some moral value or combination of moral values, such as utility, social justice, or maximizing the integrity of the environment.

There are at least four arguments against making investment decisions with the goal of maximizing specific moral values that are worth considering. First, it often is unclear or controversial just what investments actually will promote the desired values. University officials, including faculty, may have no special insight into just which investments are morally efficient. Moreover, since the university's own educational mission is also a morally worthy one, priority should be given to the investment that maximizes the university's ability to carry out its goals.

Of course, in some cases, it may be no more clear which investment is best likely to maximize the university's profits than it is which investment will best promote some moral value. Even if that point is conceded, however, a second argument remains. In particular, if the university decides to risk profits to secure moral values, normally it would be using contributions of donors and fees obtained from students, as well as taxpayers' dollars, for reasons that were not knowable at the time the funds were provided. Indeed, many donors, students, or taxpayers may be morally opposed to some of the moral values the university might try to promote in its investments. In a sense, the donors would be used without their consent as mere means for implementing the moral sensibilities of others. Such a policy would not only be all too likely to have the effect of lowering overall contributions to higher education, since donors could not be sure what causes their donations would end up supporting, but arguably would also wrong individuals whose donations were obtained under false pretenses.

Suppose, however, that universities publicized just which values they would attempt to promote in their investment policies. Or suppose that donors simply were informed that on occasion the university might forego the best investment from a financial perspective because of overriding moral concerns, without specifying in advance under just what circumstances this might happen. Although this conceivably might affect the overall level of contributions, it would avoid the charge that the donations had been used for purposes not intended by the donors. Some might argue that the loss of revenues would be outweighed by the moral gains, appealing to the idea that profits are not more important than ethics. However, even if such a policy of openness was adopted, and we put aside the rejoinder that the profits are for education rather than personal gain, significant objections would remain.

At this point, the third argument arises. How is the university to decide just which investment decisions are the moral ones? The problem has to do not just with determining that a particular decision is the moral one but also in deciding how the university as an institution is to make such a decision. In other words, *who decides* is just as much of a problem as determining what should be decided. Who speaks for the university? Is it the faculty that should make the decision, perhaps by majority vote? Is it a special committee composed of representatives of the major constituencies of the university? How do we decide what is a major constituency and how much representation each is to receive? Clearly, the potential for injustice to some constituencies is high and the danger of abuse of power is great. Even if we agree that some representative procedure is the proper one, some groups simply may get outshouted by others. At best, it simply is unclear in most cases who has the authority or right to make moral decisions of the kind in question for the institution.

Perhaps even this objection, which does seem to have considerable force, may be open to reasonable reply. After all, different constituencies of the university may have joint input into certain sorts of decisions, and procedures for securing joint participation of the universities' constituencies in decision making are sometimes recognized as fair. For example, a faculty budgetary committee may participate in the making of budgetary decisions by the administration, since those affect the quality of the educational program. Similarly, administrators sometimes have a legitimate say in curricular debates before the faculty, since the kind of curriculum the university offers may affect its ability to attract students, secure financial support, and conduct critical inquiry in a fair and open manner.

Nevertheless, the creation of a mechanism for making politically and morally loaded investment decisions raises special difficulties. For one thing, it is unclear that such decisions should be made by simple majority vote, even if all constituencies of the university are fairly represented.[8] Even if we agree on some sort of majority principle, which in itself is morally questionable, how are the problems of justice and fairness involved in creating such a procedure to be solved? Thus, in view of the difficulties involved, the idea that investment decisions of universities normally should be made on moral and political grounds seems exceedingly difficult to justify.

However, even if all these problems are left aside, perhaps the most important difficulty of all remains. That is, if universities were to adopt a general policy of making all investment decisions on moral and political grounds, institutional critical neutrality would likely be threatened in the ways outlined earlier. To carry out such an investment policy, the university would have to take stands on a great number of moral and political decisions, ranging from environmental issues to animal experimentation to national defense and even abortion. By becoming identified as a political agent operating on behalf of specific causes, the university would not only become the target for opponents of those causes but, even more important, would undermine critical inquiry itself. Opponents of the university's position would be less likely to want to be associated with such an institution, threatening the intellectual diversity of faculty and students. Those who remained would have the burden of arguing from a view that already has been labeled as politically incorrect by the very institution for which they work or at which they study. Accordingly, it is at best exceedingly questionable whether such a politicized university also could be a center of free debate and critical inquiry—these are activities that require the testing of views by exposure to rigorous argument and objection from those who disagree.

However, even if there are good reasons for a *general* policy of neutrality in the making of investment decisions, there also may be grounds for making *exceptions*. In some cases, an injustice may be so unambiguous that virtually all reasonable people recognize it as such and so serious as to amount to a moral catastrophe.[9] In such cases, for the university to invest in a way that contributes to the injustice constitutes a serious wrong. While its educational mission may be a noble one, surely the university has no more right than any other agent to commit or aid in the commission of an injustice or to violate the rights of others. For example, if a university is the only landlord in a poor neighborhood, it has no right to gouge the tenants and exploit them. So although the university may not have an obligation to do good, or even to avoid doing any evil altogether, a standard no fallible agent could reasonably be expected to meet, it surely has a duty not to commit gross injustice or aid in the commission of a moral catastrophe. Finally, if the university alters investment decisions to avoid aiding in the commission of a gross moral wrong, donors have no right to complain that their generosity was abused. Since the donors themselves have no right to aid in the commission of a moral wrong, their claims are defeated in this kind of context.

Thus, proponents of divestment seem to have a sound case when they maintain that the university cannot legitimately claim that it should be neutral when its investments actually constitute or contribute to the commission of a serious, extensive, and clear case of injustice or wrongdoing. In such cases, the normal case for neutrality can be trumped by the principle that no moral agent may knowingly commit a gross injustice or wrong. Moreover, it surely is true that the oppression of people of color by the system of apartheid in South Africa is a clear, significant, and extensive case of wrongdoing or injustice, perhaps the greatest systematic injustice perpetrated by a government in the world today. Does it follow, however, that colleges and universities should divest their holdings in businesses doing business in South Africa?

Before turning to that issue, it is worth emphasizing that proponents of divestment have a strong point when they warn that we cannot simply *assume* that the normal case for neutrality is a good defense against their position. Trustees and other opponents of divestment are not entitled simply to take for granted that since divestment would violate neutrality they simply ought to be neutral and not divest. There are at least two reasons that count against the normal presumption in favor of neutrality. First, the presumption in favor of neutrality can be overridden by the principle that the university should not contribute to the commission of clear, gross, and extensive injustice. Although it may be the case that violation of neutrality involves an even greater injustice, this needs to be argued and not just assumed. (See the selections by Steven M. Cahn and Martin Trow in Part II for arguments relevant to this point.)

Second, colleges and universities *already* may have violated neutrality by adopting policies with respect to investment in companies doing business in South Africa that are not neutral. Many colleges and universities already have pledged only to invest in companies doing business in South Africa that endorse and implement the Sullivan Principles, a set of rules requiring fair and nondiscriminatory treatment of employees regardless of race in South African subsidiaries. Proponents of divestment can argue, also with force, that it is disingenuous to appeal to neutrality as a bar to divestment when by adopting the Sullivan Principles, which set moral limits in investment decisions, the university already had adopted a nonneutral policy in this area.

But while these arguments in favor of divestment do have force and must be seriously considered, it is by no means clear that they are determinative. First, even among those who accept the principle that the university is prohibited from committing clear cases of gross and extensive injustice, there may be sharp disagreement over whether investment in companies doing business in South Africa constitutes such an action. That is, while there is widespread moral agreement that apartheid is a clear case of injustice amounting to a moral catastrophe, there is extensive disagreement over whether divestment is a morally required (or even morally allowed) response.

As a matter of fact, many thoughtful and morally sensitive opponents of divestment have argued that the university would be committing an injustice *by divesting*.[10] According to one line of argument supporting such a view, divesting would lead American and other foreign investors to leave South Africa, leaving control of the South African economy in the hands of white South Africans (and perhaps less scrupulous foreign investors), the very group least likely to promote reform and most likely to mistreat workers. According to a second line of argument, the nondiscriminatory practices of foreign companies that endorse the Sullivan Principles serve as important examples of racial equality, undermining the case for racial segregation and oppression.

Therefore, it is controversial whether divestment is the morally appropriate response to racial injustice in South Africa, in that we can see how morally sensitive individuals might reasonably disagree over the issue. Accordingly, opponents of divestment can argue that the decision to divest would be a partisan political act. (See the selection by Martin Trow in Part II.) Moreover, they would add that since exactly what is controversial is whether failure to divest is commission of or participation in an injustice, the injunction against causing injustice does not automatically trump the neutrality principle. Just as trustees cannot legitimately assume that appeal to neutrality frees them from the need to debate the divestment issue, proponents of divestment cannot simply assume that investment in companies doing business in South Africa is commission of or participation in gross injustice.

Finally, opponents of divestment can argue that endorsement of the Sullivan Principles is uncontroversially required by the prohibition against causing or contributing to injustice, and so is in a different moral ballpark than the much more controversial policy of divestment. In fact, it is adherence to the Sullivan Principles, in this view, that blocks the charge that all companies doing business in South Africa are participating in an unjust system, since the principles arguably block participation in the system to begin with.

Whether or not divestment is required if the university is to avoid commission or participation in injustice is indeed an arguable issue, the resolution of which would go well beyond the discussion of neutrality. Our discussion is not an attempt to support either side but only to examine the relationship between the divestment issue and the case for neutrality. In any event, proponents of divestment clearly have the right and perhaps the duty to try to persuade the university community that divestment is morally required. Our examination suggests, however, that a significant element of the dispute between proponents and opponents of divestment is not about neutrality at all, but about a complex set of other issues including whether or not investments in companies doing business in South Africa always is unjust and about what the consequences of divestment would be.

In fact, opponents of divestment may do themselves a disservice when they allow appeals to neutrality to function as a rationale that obscures the need for debate on other aspects of the issue. They also need directly to address the charge that by not divesting, the university is actively participating in the commission of an injustice. On the other hand, proponents of divestment may distort the issues at stake when they suggest that all their critics care about is profits, as if there were no moral concerns that might lead people to disagree in this area. Even given moral consensus on the evils of apartheid, there is considerable room for disagreement on whether divestment is a morally required or even morally allowed response to that evil. As long as that issue is itself controversial among informed and reasonable people of good will, the neutrality principle still stands as a significant bar to divestment. Thus, proponents of divestment are quite right to insist that the neutrality principle does not shield the university from moral examination of its investment policies. Nevertheless, they do a significant disservice not only to the university but to critical inquiry and reasoned discourse when they dismiss all talk of neutrality in this area as a crude rationale for the pursuit of profit, and reject neutrality itself as nothing but a sham and illusion.

V. Divestment and Overriding Neutrality: Sorting Out Some Principles

Earlier, we asked whether the requirement that universities ought to be critically neutral was absolute or presumptive. An absolute requirement is one that is overriding, while a presumptive one is overriding unless outweighed by competing moral considerations. Our discussion of divestment implies that the requirement to be critically neutral is presumptive. In particular, it can be overridden by the contrary requirement that the university should not commit or participate in the commission of clear, gross, and extensive injustice. Neutrality does not permit the university to wrong others, at least when the wrong is serious and apparent to virtually all reasonable people of good will.[11]

Are there any other moral requirements that might override the obligation to be neutral in specific contexts? One principle, often appealed to by proponents of divestment, is that the university not only should not participate in the commission of injustice but also should not *profit* from the commission of injustice by others. In their view, a second line of argument in favor of divestment is that if universities do not divest, they profit from participation by others in the system of apartheid, even if they do not directly support it themselves.

Two separate issues need to be distinguished here. The first is whether it is always wrong to profit from injustice committed by others. The second is whether such a principle is sufficiently weighty to sometimes override the requirement to be critically neutral. Let us briefly examine each in turn.

Consider the principle that it is wrong to profit from injustice (or wrongdoing) committed by others. First, we need to consider whether that principle is always justifiable. Suppose the profit gained is minimal, the wrongdoing is not directly connected to the profit, and is not particularly serious. For example, suppose my friend, unknown to me, cheats in a poker game, wins an extra five dollars that she would not have won if she hadn't cheated, and lends me the money, which I bet at the race track. If my horse comes in, is it wrong for me to take the winnings, since in a sense I have profited from my friend's wrongdoing? If it is wrong, isn't wrongdoing virtually unavoidable in an interdependent world? What is the point of a principle that is virtually impossible to live up to?

However, if we manage to draw a line and say that profits from wrongdoing under some circumstances is wrong but in others is permissible, we need to be careful not to draw the line in a biased way. It is all too easy to say that it is evil for the university to profit from its grossly immoral investments, but that our own profits from similar entanglements in the real world are simply the unavoidable by-products of life in a complex society.

Perhaps a reasonable line can be drawn here, but the attempt to do so would take us far beyond the topic of neutrality. Instead, let us assume, if only for the sake of argument, that it is wrong to profit *in morally illegitimate ways* from injustice or wrongs committed by others, leaving open just what is to count as morally illegitimate. We can then go on to discuss the application of this principle to the divestment controversy.

To begin with, although proponents of divestment may argue that universities that do not divest are wrongly profiting from injustice, their opponents may reply, as we noted above, that the university's profits do not derive from the apartheid system. Rather, they can argue as explained above that so long as the companies in which they invest distance themselves from the system through nondiscriminatory treatment of their own employees, they are opposing injustice rather than profiting from it. Again, that argument may or may not be ultimately convincing, and I myself have serious doubts about its force. Be that as it may, the point is that it is not self-evident that universities are profiting from injustice in this case; the point needs to be supported and not just stated.

However, even if this point is conceded to proponents of divestment, another difficulty remains. Does it follow that the university ought to divest rather than profit from injustice? To see the difficulty here, consider the situation at the individual level. Consider the students who presumably profit from their education. If their institution does not divest, are they morally obligated to divest from it? If a college divests from corporations doing business in South Africa, does that mean it cannot also accept gifts from them, even those that provide financial aid to students? Should students accept such aid? May they accept employment from companies doing business in South Africa even though their universities may not invest in those very same companies?

While proposed answers to these questions may be controversial, we at least need to make a principled, coherent response to them. Once again, it is all too easy to apply one set of strict standards to the university and much looser standards to the individual. Can the proponents of divestment fairly view university officials who do not order divestment as wrongdoers while accepting benefits from the university, or even from the very same companies that do business in South Africa? Whatever response we make to these questions, surely a double standard should be avoided.

Proponents of divestment might reply that the issue is not one of "clean hands" but rather is one of consequences. The consequences of universities and other powerful institutions divesting are likely to be much greater than that of individual action. Therefore, there is a much greater case for institutional than individual divestment. There is no double standard; rather, it is a matter of the far greater effects of institutional action. (For a consequentialist case for divestment, see the contribution by Richard Werner in Part II.)

In this view, the university should take political action when the consequences of doing so are sufficiently beneficial. Some consequentialists may advocate political action whenever the expected consequences of doing so are better than the expected consequences of remaining neutral. This kind of consequentialism, which we call the extreme version, runs head on into the arguments for a general policy of neutrality, and in my view is defeated by them. However, what about a more moderate consequentialist policy, one that advocates overriding neutrality only when the consequences of not doing so are extremely bad?[12] In this moderate consequentialist view, a general policy of neutrality is justified but can be outweighed by the need to prevent moral disasters or catastrophes. Proponents of divestment would add that the continuation of apartheid in South Africa is a moral catastrophe and so the university should do what it can to prevent or alleviate this moral disaster, presumably by divesting its holdings from companies doing business in South Africa.

Unless we are prepared to defend the position that the preservation of critical neutrality outweighs all other values, and that we should adhere to it regardless of the consequences, some form of moderate consequentialism must be accepted. However, because the values protected by adherence to institutional critical neutrality are crucial, neutrality can be overridden only in exceptional circumstances. A clear case might be opposition to a vicious totalitarian regime that itself would stamp out critical inquiry and reasoned discourse within the university to preserve its hold on power. (See the conclusion of Robert Holmes's contribution in Part II for a discussion of this point.)

Whether the moderate consequentialist case for divestment goes through is more controversial. For one thing, there is considerable disagreement about what the consequences of divestment would be. As we have seen, opponents of divestment sometimes argue that the consequences of divestment would be harmful rather than helpful to the cause of racial justice in South Africa; some of the moderating agents who can help promote change simply would be removed from the scene. In addition, divestment may involve other moral costs, including those flowing from a loss of neutrality on the issue in a highly divided university community. (For discussion of another kind of moral cost, see the debate between Steven M. Cahn and his critics in Part II.)

We need not attempt to resolve these complex issues here. The main point for our purposes is that much of the debate over divestment is not over neutrality at all, but over other difficult factual and moral issues. These include such questions as what the consequences of divestment would be, whether failure to divest constitutes participation in wrongdoing and injustice, and whether profits from companies doing business in South Africa are illegitimately obtained. The doctrine of institutional neutrality is neither a logical bar to divestment nor a shield preventing criticism of investment policies. In fact, properly understood, it can be appealed to by proponents of divestment as well as opponents if, for example, proponents could show that failure to divest was not neutral, or that the conditions for overriding neutrality were met.

On the other hand, the doctrine of institutional neutrality creates a logical framework within which debate should take place. It promotes reasoned discourse on the issues rather than victory through the use of power and intimidation and sets out guidelines and burdens of proof for debate. Opponents of divestment may do themselves a disservice when they hide behind the banners of neutrality to preclude discussion of the moral responsibility of universities. However, proponents of divestment also may distort the issues when they speak as if all their critics care about is profits and as if there were no moral concerns that might lead people to disagree in this area. Moreover, they do a great disservice to the university itself, and to the need for a neutral framework in which their own views can be testd and justified, when they jump from the premise that neutrality does not shield the university from moral examination of the divestment issue to the conclusion that neutrality itself is but a sham and an illusion.

Notes

1. For an extended discussion of this sort of line of criticism against some liberal theories of state neutrality, see Patrick Neal, "The Liberal Theory of the Good," *Canadian Journal of Philosophy*, Vol. 17, No. 3 (1987), pp. 567–82.

2. For a discussion of speech codes in the context of the law and the ethics of academic freedom, see Judith Wagner DeCew, "Free Speech on Campus," in Steven M. Cahn, ed., *Morality, Responsibility, and the University* (Philadelphia: Temple University Press, 1990), pp. 32–55.

3. Communitarians, in this sense, need not have anything else in common with those nonliberal theories of justice known as communitarian approaches except an emphasis on the importance of background institutions and practices in shaping individual behavior and on the need to promote certain background community structures so as to protect virtuous action.

4. The importance of this point was suggested to me by Steven M. Cahn.

5. Of course, conservatives or moderates can be favored as well and liberals and those further to the left excluded. The danger is that only proponents of "safe" views will be selected as recipients of honors so that all controversy can be avoided. This itself may even be a defensible policy, since the point of a commencement or similar institutional ceremony is to honor the achievements of students and faculty, not to provide a platform for the expression of a controversial point of view.

6. In my own experience, the use of platforms at commencements or other institutional ceremonies to express a narrow political position in such a way as to detract from the point of the ceremony is (apart from the ethics of such behavior) often counterproductive since the captive audience resents the undermining of the purpose for which they attended in the first place.

7. Does this mean that a commencement speaker should not attack racism just because some members of the audience might be racists? Here, we might distinguish positions that are controversial within the broader intellectual community, such as the relative weight to be assigned to personal liberty when it conflicts with attempts to promote more economic equality, and views that are not controversial, such as the view that racism is wrong. (This is not to

deny that it sometimes is controversial to decide that some forms of action or belief are racist.) Again, we also need to keep in mind the purpose of a commencement address and remember that even if a view is wrong, not every occasion is the proper one for a stinging and angry attack on it.

8. One problem with the majority procedure is that it may be unfair to the minority view. Thus, if 60 percent of the universities' constituencies favor divestment at a particular time, does that make it appropriate or fair to say the university as an institution favors divestment or should divest? Second, there is the problem of shifting majorities. What if six months later, only 49 percent favor divestment?

9. I owe the expression "moral catastrophe" and its application to this issue to discussion with Rick Werner.

10. See, for example, Robert L. Payton, "Tainted Money: the Ethics and Rhetoric of Divestment," *Change,* Vol. 19 (May–June 1987), pp. 55–60.

11. Proponents of neutrality may differ among themselves about whether the injunction against the commission of serious and apparent injustice automatically overrides neutrality or whether the two requirements must be balanced against one another in different contexts. Some but not all proponents of neutrality may want to argue that the violation of neutrality itself can be a serious instance of wrongdoing, which can only be permitted to prevent an even more serious wrong or injustice.

12. One can adopt the moderate view either on nonconsequentialist grounds or because one believes the consequences of adopting it are better than those of adopting the more extreme view. That is, the arguments for neutrality presented earlier can be accepted at least partially on consequentialist as well as on nonconsequentialist grounds. Thus, one might think the consequences are better in terms of respect for autonomy and the use of critical inquiry to detect harmful errors if the university generally remains neutral than if it does not. In other words, the consequences of pursuing a policy of moderate or rule consequentialism may be better than those of pursuing a policy of extreme consequentialism, and judging each case on its apparent merits. So adherence to institutional critical neutrality is not incompatible with all forms of consequentialism but may well be supported by some of them.

CHAPTER 5

Neutrality, Politicization, and the Curriculum

I. Introduction

We began our examination of neutrality by considering the claim that universities should "save" students from various forms of error. If this claim means that students should be taught to value and participate in the examined life, through utilization of the tools of critical inquiry and reasoned discourse, it surely is correct. As we have seen, however, it becomes problematic when taken to mean that a university education, as a matter of institutional policy, should promote particular ideological stances when such stances or perspectives are not elements of critical inquiry themselves.

More recently, many have argued that significant revision of the college curriculum, particularly in the humanities and social sciences, is necessary if students are to be saved from the cultural blinders allegedly imposed by the dominant groups and traditions within their society. Indeed, the curriculum of colleges and universities has become a contested area in the various ideological and cultural disputes currently being waged about higher education in America. Concerns about multiculturalism, the debate about political correctness, and demographic shifts in the ethnic composition of student bodies and the American workforce all have or are claimed to have significant implications for the curriculum of colleges and universities. In this family of debates and controversies, proponents of more traditional conceptions of the curriculum have tended to accuse opponents of politicizing the curriculum, in effect, of trying to "save" students by inappropriate and unjustified means. The reply of those in favor of revision frequently has been that the curriculum was always politicized anyway. In this section, certain issues that arise from the charges about politicization of the curriculum, especially issues having to do with the meaning and justification of such claims, will be explored. These issues are directly relevant to the debate about institutional neutrality, since they concern whether politicization of the curriculum is unavoidable, whether it is objectionable, and whether it is incompatible with the ideal of critical inquiry our examination has found at the heart of concern for neutrality itself.

According to many of those who wish to fundamentally restructure the curriculum, whom I will call revisionists, the charge of politicization functions only ideologically.[1] The function of the charge of politicization, on this view, is to allow proponents of the traditional forms of the curriculum, whom I will call traditionalists, to unfairly accuse the revisionists of importing politics into what had previously been a politically free zone devoted to objective scholarship, appreciation and understanding of great works, and the pursuit of truth. Many revisionists would reply that the curriculum always has been politicized. Since past politicization involved values taken for granted by the traditionalists, traditionalists were able to see educational choices as free of political bias, even though such choices simply reflected the values of dominant groups.

According to many participants in the debate about multiculturalism, the debate is primarily a political one about power. As one advocate of multiculturalism maintains in a passage cited in Chapter I, on "both sides the advocates are partisans in an intellectual struggle . . . pious pretense to the contrary. The curriculum that we have today in American society is a by product of power. The effort to change the current curriculum is an effort to destroy the political orthodoxy which has established itself through power."[2]

But are curricular debates over Afrocentrism, multiculturalism, and revision of college and university curricula only disputes about power, or are there genuine intellectual conflicts about the merits of conflicting positions? Do claims about the politicization of the curriculum function only ideologically or do they sometimes raise issues of substance? If all such disputes are ultimately political, doesn't neutrality fall by the wayside since any curriculum the university adopts in fact expresses a political position? Perhaps the best way to make a start at dealing with these questions is to separate some of the issues raised by the whole topic of politicization of the curriculum and its application to the neutrality debate.

II. Politicization: What Are the Issues?

Claims about politicization clearly raise a host of conceptual and normative issues.[3] For example, what does the charge of politicization amount to? What counts as politicization? Is politicization of the curriculum good or bad? Is it avoidable or unavoidable? Is politicization incompatible with objectivity and concern for intellectual merit? Is it incompatible with institutional critical neutrality? Would an unpoliticized curriculum necessarily be committed to traditional subject matter—to what has been called the "canon" in literature and the humanities?

We can begin by asking what function the charge of politicization serves. Clearly, it often is used as a conceptual weapon to discredit rival approaches to the curriculum. Revisionists are accused of making the curriculum into an ideological tool, which presumably it is not supposed to be. Traditionalists are accused of failing to recognize their own ideological blinders, and thereby failing to appreciate not only that the curriculum always was politicized but couldn't help but be politicized in the first place.

But why does the claim that the curriculum is politicized function as a criticism of other views? The charge of politicization does not function purely as an epithet. On the contrary, it can only function critically precisely because it makes some claim about the curriculum to which it is applied. But what is that claim? Unfortunately, as we will see, it is unlikely that all those who speak about the curriculum being politicized have the same conception of politicization in mind. As with other important concepts in political philosophy, such as equality, justice, fairness, ideology, and neutrality itself, different conceptions or theories of each notion exist in the field.

Although all of these different conceptions cannot be discussed here, at least some of the parties to the debate over the curriculum are advancing the view that what is politicized is neither neutral nor fully objective—perhaps not rationally justifiable at all.[4] Thus, by claiming that the more extreme revisionists are politicizing a previously pure curriculum, traditionalists are charging the revisionists with departing from the ethics of objective scholarship to engage in political action. By responding that the traditionalists ignore their own past politicization, many revisionists are implying not only that the curriculum never was objectively defensible to begin with but that any choice of curriculum is more a matter of power politics than rational educational choice. When pressed to the limits, this account of politicization undercuts the claim that curricular decisions ever can be defended in terms that impartial people of good will, reasoning from diverse political perspectives, would find defensible. In this extreme interpretation, rational discourse itself becomes an ideologically contested notion, interpreted differently by those from different political, cultural, or socioeconomic backgrounds.

Let us begin to examine the family of conceptions that tend to characterize politicization in terms of lack of neutrality, objectivity, or impartiality by considering the charge that politicization is unavoidable. That curricular struggles are really political battles in which claims of objectivity and neutrality play only an ideological role is at least suggested by the authors of the American Council of Learned Societies report "Speaking for the Humanities" when they assert that

> traditional claims to disinterest, to the humanities as the realm of "sweetness and light," reflected unacknowledged ideologies. . . . The best contemporary work in the humanities strives to make clear both its critique of the ideologies of previous work, and its own *inevitable* ideological blindspots.[5]

Is politicization unavoidable? Is it a necessary element of contemporary political debate between traditionalists and revisionists? In considering such questions, we can also begin to distinguish at least some of the different conceptions of politicization employed in current discourse about the curriculum.

III. Is Politicization of the Curriculum Unavoidable?

As we have seen, if a politicized curriculum is unavoidable, then traditionalists who object to what they regard as revisionist politicization of the curriculum just don't get it. If the unavoidability thesis is true, the revisionists are simply replacing one politicized or ideologically loaded curriculum with a different, equally politicized and ideologically loaded one.

What reasons can be given for thinking the curriculum is unavoidably political? Perhaps by distinguishing the different reasons that can be given in support of such a view, we can also distinguish the different conceptions of politicization at work in this area.

According to one argument, the curriculum is inevitably political because it cannot be value free. Thus, Henry A. Giroux, speaking to a conference of what has come to be called "the cultural left," asserts

> the institutions of higher education regardless of their academic status represent places that affirm and legitimate existing views of the world, produce new ones, and authorize and shape particular social relations: . . . The university is a place that is deeply political and unarguably normative.[6]

Arguing along similar lines, Henry David Aiken has also maintained that "to depoliticize the university would require the exclusion of all normative social and political studies."[7]

On these views, the curriculum is unavoidably normative as long as it contains normative studies (Aiken) or, more broadly, as long as it legitimizes certain worldviews and shapes social relations (Giroux). Although it is not entirely clear what Giroux means by "legitimatizing worldviews" and "shaping social relations," he seems to be suggesting that at a minimum, the curriculum endorses some positions rather than others as worthy of examination and debate and so is value laden. Since a value-free curriculum is no more possible than a four-sided triangle, and since a value-laden curriculum is unavoidably political, an apolitical curriculum is impossible as well.

Can the curriculum be value free? Probably not. Values can inhere in what is taught, how it is taught, and why it is taught. Clearly, a curriculum devoted solely to the classic texts, explored in an attempt to find universal truths or principles, is just as much committed to values as is one focused solely on texts critical of the classical tradition and skeptical of the existence of universal truths or principles. Surely the goals of searching for truth and promoting study of the classical curriculum are as much values as hostility to what some call "the canon" and skepticism toward traditional ideas of truth and objectivity. Values, as Giroux maintains, are unavoidable in education. But what are the implications of this conclusion? In particular, is Giroux's inference from "the university is unarguably normative" to "the university is political" valid?

Clearly, if lack of value neutrality implies the curriculum is politicized, and the curriculum unavoidably is value laden, the curriculum cannot avoid being politicized. But what is the significance of this conclusion? Thus, as we have seen, the clause of the U.S. Constitution forbidding an establishment of religion is value laden, since it places a value upon religious liberty, but that does not prevent it from requiring government neutrality toward specific religions. Similarly, a good referee at a basketball game is enforcing the norms laid down in the rules of basketball, but this does not preclude the referee being impartial toward the contesting teams. A stance of value commitment, then, while perhaps "political" in the broadest possible sense, does not preclude lack of politicization in narrower and perhaps ethically more significant senses as well.

In particular, although any curriculum must be permeated with values that guide decisions about what is taught, how it is taught, and why it is taught, all values may not be equally *partisan*. Some values may be more narrowly partisan than others and perhaps less justifiably employed in educational contexts. Thus, traditionalists who claim that revisionists are politicizing the curriculum may agree that any curriculum is value laden but also go on to argue that what they object to is the particularly partisan nature of the values they claim the revisionists are employing.

In a sense, then, to say that the curriculum is unavoidably political because it is value laden is trivial, because it obscures the need to make important distinctions among the kinds of values at stake. Like the claim that the university cannot be neutral because it cannot be value free, the claim that the curriculum is necessarily politicized because it is not value free is in danger of stretching the concept of the political so broadly that it makes no useful contrast and hence obscures narrower senses in which politicized and nonpoliticized curricula can be contrasted. Aiken's claim that the curriculum is inevitably politicized as long as it deals with normative topics is open to similar sorts of objections. One might as well argue that basketball referees are inevitably partisans of one specific team or another simply because they engage in discussion of how the rules ought to be interpreted or changed.

Perhaps more to the point, there is a large gap between showing that a curriculum is normatively loaded, on the one hand, and demonstrating that it is narrowly partisan, biased, or in some other way cognitively defective on the other. The premise that the curriculum is inevitably value laden does not imply that it should be structured or presented so as to support a particular partisan ideology, whether on the left or right. Rather, among its normative goals may be acquainting students with enough critical tools and knowledge of major works that they are in a good position to make intelligent ethical and political choices for themselves. Accordingly, the jump from the normative character of the curriculum to the conclusion that it therefore is inevitably political, in any nontrivial sense of that term, seems far too quick and is at best highly suspect.

Perhaps a second view of politicization of the curriculum has more to offer. It suggests that politicization has to do not with the mere presence of value judgments but with the particular value judgments that are included in the curriculum. In this view, traditional forms of the curriculum are political because they express, include, or support a particular selection of values: namely, those endorsed by dominant social groups. The curriculum is politicized, in other words, when it is value laden in a biased manner. Revisionists claim to broaden the traditional curriculum by broadening the selection of values it supports, perhaps by including the perspectives of those held to be excluded by more traditional approaches, particularly the voices of women and racial minorities. The politicized curriculum in this view is the biased or unrepresentative curriculum; one that favors the outlook of dominant social groups.

This approach may have more promise than those considered earlier, perhaps because it is plausible to think the content of the curriculum has been affected more by the values of the relatively powerful than by those of the relatively powerless. However, it too needs to be considered with care. In particular, in what way does it show that the curriculum is unavoidably political? In fact, rather than supporting the claim that the curriculum is unavoidably political, it conflicts with it. That is, if revisionists claim to be replacing a curriculum that was originally biased toward a particular and presumably not fully adequate set of values with a less biased, more adequate substitute, then surely it claims to be replacing a more politicized curriculum with a less politicized one. If so, that claim needs to be defended in critical debate by appeal to acceptable standards of justification and not presented simply as the replacement of one ideology by another. In particular, which changes in the curriculum ought to be considered improvements rather than simply the replacement of one highly politicized perspective by another?

Surely revisionists as well as traditionalists only lose if they view curricular arguments merely as power struggles for representation in an unavoidably politicized curriculum. If new curricular proposals cannot be plausibly presented as better educationally than others for all concerned, what reason have those who are skeptical about the new proposals been given for changing their minds? Moreover, if power is all that is at stake, why should traditionalists change their minds at all? The critique of traditional political values itself becomes simply another political technique that, while perhaps effective, cannot claim to be rationally superior to the position it is critiquing.

Accordingly, then, if the claim that the traditional curriculum is politicized can best be understood as asserting that the traditional curriculum is biased in favor of the values of dominant social groups, that claim does not cohere easily with the claim that all curricula are unavoidably politicized, particularly when that claim is interpreted in turn as undermining the possibility of objective rational discourse about curricular choice. It gives us no rational basis for choosing among the many curricular options open to us. Rather, it is best understood as presupposing that an unbiased, apoliticized set of curricular options is available to us. That claim may be true or false, justified or unjustified, but it can be debated and examined by critical standards accessible to both traditionalists and revisionists alike.[8]

A second set of problems with this conception of politicization concerns the idea that the curriculum ought to *represent* the value of all groups. For one thing, it surely is unclear what is to count as a group in this context. Are white males a group, for example? If so, what values do theorists as different as Plato, Mill, Nietzsche, and Derrida all represent? Are justice, fairness, and equality, which have been discussed extensively by writers ranging from Plato through Mill to Rawls, white male values, or are they of more universal import? Is there room in the curriculum for all groups to be represented, even assuming that we can define groups in a narrow and thoughtful manner?

If our goal is the *representative* curriculum, these issues need to be thought through in depth. Indeed, as I suspect, such an examination might show that group representation is suspect if intended as the basic principle of curricular organization. Be that as it may, those who do argue that the new curriculum should be more representative than the old are presupposing a distinction between what counts in their own terms as a less biased and more biased curriculum, and hence are undercutting, however, unintentionally, the claim that all curricula must be equally politicized.

But while it may be plausible to think that charges that the present curriculum is biased presuppose the concept of an unbiased curriculum, advocates of the unavoidability thesis may claim that matters are not so easily resolvable. For although we may have the concept of an unbiased curriculum, each and every particular conception of it may be controversial. (Similarly, although we may share a common concept of justice, no one conception of justice may be shared by all those who share the common concept. Thus, we may agree that justice requires treating everyone fairly but disagree about what constitutes fair treatment in particular cases.)

Thus, we need to consider a third account of why politicization of the curriculum is unavoidable. According to this "perspectivist" approach, traditionalists who speak of the need for objectivity, impartiality, and disinterested scholarly pursuit of truth ignore the degree to which criteria of objectivity, impartiality, and truth are embedded in the contexts of particular cultures, traditions, or socioeconomic perspectives. Thus, a "Eurocentric" education takes for granted conceptions of objectivity, impartiality, and truth that may be challenged from other perspectives. In a more complex view, such as that suggested by Alasdair MacIntyre in *Whose Justice? Which Rationality?*, Western culture itself is fragmented into diverse traditions, each with its own criteria of rationality, objectivity, and justice.[9] In some cases, criteria of objectivity, for example, may even be linked to gender. In her widely discussed book, *In A Different Voice*, Carol Gilligan reinterprets the empirical surveys conducted by psychologist Laurence Kohlberg and suggests that the impartiality perspective, often identified by theorists with the moral point of view itself, tends to be associated more with male than female reasoning, while women tend to reason from what has been called the perspective of care.[10] Although the exact relationship between the perspective of impartiality and that of care is controversial even among those sympathetic to Gilligan's views, in some interpretations what may count as objective reasoning from one of these points of view may be defective moral reasoning from the other.

The idea that criteria of objectivity, rationality, impartiality, and the like are embedded in specific perspectives or traditions suggests a third way in which the curriculum inevitably is politicized. In this view, the curriculum inevitably includes materials from specific traditions or perspectives, and so is biased in favor of the criteria of objectivity, rationality, and the like that they contain. Such a bias is political because the criteria of some groups, traditions, or perspectives is given status, even canonical status, through inclusion in the curriculum, while the criteria of other traditions or groups are denied such status through exclusion.

In its crudest form, the criticism is that the standard curriculum embodies a "white male point of view." More sophisticated theorists, such as MacIntyre, recognize the radical diversity of traditions that make up Western culture, but their analysis still suggests that conceptions of impartiality, rationality, and objectivity must be understood within specific contexts, perspectives, or traditions. This lends itself to the thesis that the curriculum is inevitably politicized, and therefore fails to be neutral, since the choice of traditions or perspectives to be taught invariably includes some conceptions of objectivity, rationality, and the like while excluding others. This view is more radical than the less extreme claim that the curriculum is unrepresentative. What it suggests is not simply that different groups have different values that may be given different status in the curriculum, but also that the standards of reasoning and evaluation, the structure of rationality itself, may differ from culture to culture or group to group.

While this analysis is of considerable interest, this kind of perspectivism does not fit easily with much of the critique of the traditional curriculum. After all, the critics of the traditional curriculum presumably want to say that their suggestions for revision improve the curriculum, make it better than it was, and therefore that their suggestions are justified. But perspectivism, at least in its less sophisticated forms, implies that judgments of better or worse, more or less justified, objective or unobjective, can only be warranted locally within a particular perspective or tradition. Thus, in a perspectivist analysis, what reason is there for those from other traditions or perspectives to accept the revisionists' critique of the traditional curriculum? According to perspectivism, no universal or interperspectival reasoning can be provided that is normative for all of those who approach the curriculum in a multiperspectival society.

Perspectivism, at least in its cruder forms, seems to leave us with a model of the debate over the curriculum as at best a sort of Tower of Babel. The disputants engage in a debate in which adjudication or even mutual understanding seems impossible. In other words, this view of the unavoidability of politicization of the curriculum seems self-defeating. It undermines the claims of the revisionists themselves to have justifiable and well-reasoned objections to the traditional curriculum, which should be plausible to well-intentioned people from a wide variety of perspectives.[11] The trouble with perspectivism, at least if it is crudely understood, is that it seems to imply a self-defeating form of curricular relativism.

Perhaps, however, some forms of perspectivism do not lead to the kind of curricular relativism criticized above. Consider briefly MacIntyre's attempt to avoid the kind of relativism to which perspectivism seems committed. According to MacIntyre, although all criteria of rationality are embedded in particular perspectives, some in virtue of their survival and development in the face of epistemological crisis prove better than others over time. As MacIntyre argues, every tradition,

> whether it recognizes the fact or not, confronts the possibility that at some future time it will fall into a state of epistemological crisis recogniz-able as such by its own standards of rational justification. . . . The adherents of a tradition which is now in this state of fundamental and radical crisis may at this point encounter in a new way the claims of some particular rival tradition. . . . They may find themselves compelled to recognize that within this other tradition it is possible to construct . . . a cogent and illuminating explanation . . . by their own standards of why their own intellectual tradition had been unable to solve its problems.[12]

In developing this point, MacIntyre argues valiantly that commitment to perspectivism, the view that all standards are embedded in particular cultural, intellectual, or social perspectives and traditions, does not entail either skepticism or relativism. Even though standards are not universal, it does not follow that they are all equally good. Some traditions respond to intellectual crises better than others. If successful, MacIntyre's defense allows perspectivists to make justified evaluative judgments. In making this point, however, MacIntyre may smuggle in universal criteria of evaluation, and thereby reject a robust perspectivism. This point has curricular implications and is worth exploring further.

Indeed, it is far from clear that MacIntyre himself holds a full-fledged form of perspectivism. For one thing, he insists that the criteria of objectivity, rationality, and justice of different traditions are mutually intelligible. Members of one tradition can learn to understand other traditions. Indeed, his own analysis of different traditions would be impossible if it were not possible to understand traditions different from our own. This leads to a broader interpretation of MacIntyre in which we can reach an overarching or encompassing perspective from which different traditions can not only be understood but evaluated by criteria that apply to both. Thus, the statement "Tradition A has responded to intellectual crisis better than tradition B, even when each is evaluated in their own terms" seems to be made from a perspective that, if not entirely independent of A and B, seems vastly different and more encompassing than that of an isolated adherent of either. That is, the evaluator must be able not only to understand the different traditions involved but also to make a comparative judgment about which has done better in meeting the intellectual crisis it has faced.

What are the implications of these comments for the debate over the curriculum, and for the broader question of institutional neutrality? They suggest that even if some curricular revisionists and some curricular traditionalists approach the curriculum from different perspectives or from within different traditions, rational evaluation of both outlooks by common criteria of evaluation, or at least from a common perspective, is far from impossible. In this broader conception of perspectivism, then, it does not follow that all curricular discussion is unavoidably political in the sense that no independent perspective for making justified claims can be found. This further suggests that curricular decisions do not have to be made from a partisan perspective that others cannot share but that more neutral points of debate, which encompass multiple perspectives, can constitute the framework for discussion.

On the other hand, if we interpret MacIntyre as a robust perspectivist, no commitment to universal principles of evaluation, or even to a common transperspectival point of view, is implied. Suppose, for example, that we accept the assumption (an oversimplification of MacIntyre's view) that the traditional curriculum is based on a "Western" worldview, which contains its own internal standards of rationality, truth, and objectivity.[13] In this interpretation, external criticism of the traditional "Western" perspective is impossible, since all criticism, in the narrow interpretation of MacIntyre's view, is internal only, made from within the perspective being examined.

Our discussion suggests, then, that the argument that the curriculum is unavoidably political because it expresses the limited perspectives of dominant groups is defective. Either such an argument embraces the narrow kind of perspectivism that makes objective curricular criticism impossible, or it must acknowledge the possibility of acceptable standards of curricular evaluation and transperspectival points of view that are not partisan or applicable only within the limited perspectives of particular groups. The belief in such independent standards or viewpoints is compatible both with the broader form of perspectivism I have attributed to MacIntyre and with rejection of perspectivism in favor of more explicitly nonperspectival epistemologies.

This is not to deny that what counts as justification, impartiality, or objectivity often is controversial. Radically different theoretical accounts of these notions exist in the field. Neither is it to deny that conceptions of rationality and objectivity sometimes function ideologically as rationalizations for partisan political agendas. However, it is to suggest that any account that regards all such notions as merely representative of a limited point of view makes rational debate over the curriculum impossible.

So far, we have examined three conceptions of what might be meant by the claim that the curriculum is unavoidably political. According to the first, the curriculum is unavoidably political because it is unavoidably value laden. According to the second, the curriculum is unavoidably political because it is unrepresentative, giving too much weight to the values and standards of dominant groups. According to the third, the curriculum is inevitably politicized because the very standards of evaluation it contains—the very notions of rationality, objectivity, truth, and impartiality employed—reflect the limited points of view of particular cultures, groups, or perspectives. While we have not considered all possible conceptions of politicization of the curriculum, perhaps enough has been said to show not only that the concept of politicization is complex, but also that the charge that politicization is unavoidable is questionable. What are the implications of this for discussion not only about the curriculum in higher education but for institutional neutrality as well?

IV. Nonpartisanship and Curricular Discussion

One implication is that it is counterproductive for revisionists to embrace the more extreme forms of normative or epistemological relativism and skepticism. After all, the revisionists themselves are making claims that are critical not only of more traditional forms of the curriculum but sometimes of the broader social and political order as well. Since these claims are presented as justified, those who make them are committed to some sort of criteria for evaluating claims over and above those that just happen to be accepted by a particular group at a particular time. At a minimum, such standards include a renunciation of coercion and manipulation, since the goal of the debate is not simply to win, but to find which of the contesting views is more reasonable or more justified.

This in turn suggests that critical neutrality can apply to debate about the curriculum as well as to the stance the university should take on external controversial political issues. That is, curricular debate is not necessarily politicized and can and should be governed by the same standards of critical inquiry that apply to debate in other areas. While individual faculty and students may take strong positions on curricular issues, debates should take place in a climate of reasoned exchange, governed by concern for evidence, good scholarship, and willingness to face and examine objections. Critical inquiry should not stop where curricular waters run deep.

Of course, as we have seen, there is considerable room for debate over how we should conceive of critical inquiry.[14] Debate and metadebate about the standards that ought to govern rational discourse and inquiry is not only permissible but highly desirable, as long as it is realized that all such standards cannot be up for revision all at once and, most important, that everything need not be at stake all at once in each debate about particular issues.

This suggests a second implication of our discussion: namely, that the notion of an "academic ethic" or ethic of inquiry should be a major component of our approach to the curriculum. Much of the discussion about multiculturalism has expressed concern over the lack of social and intellectual unity that overemphasis on pluralism might promote. Perhaps part of a common core of any curriculum might be an emphasis on critical standards of inquiry, including not only noncoercion, but respect for evidence, obligations to consider criticisms, and willingness to test one's view against those of others. These surely are values, but they seem to be core values that should be acceptable to all views that claim to be open to reasoned examination. As such, they are normative but nonpartisan, and so can be the core of an approach to a nonpoliticized curriculum. In a sense, they supply part of an academic "overlapping consensus" in that they are not only part of the overall perspective of those groups committed to rational inquiry within the university but also in that they have normative force as presuppositions of such inquiry as well.

If a commitment to standards of rational discourse and critical inquiry should be common to defensible forms of both revisionism and traditionalism, the idea that the university itself ought to be politically neutral deserves consideration from both perspectives. Rather than dismiss the doctrine of institutional neutrality as just another guise for imposing a traditional education perspective on the university, revisionists as much as traditionalists may have reason for supporting it. At the very least, if they reject institutional neutrality, they need to show why they are not rejecting a concern for autonomy and intellectual diversity along with it. Even more important, if they reject the framework that protects and promotes reasoned discourse, how can they claim that their own views have passed the test of reasoned examination? Traditionalists, on the other hand, are more prone to favor neutrality, but need to realize that a neutral framework may often protect challenges to traditional scholarship and that such challenges needed to be met in intellectual debate rather than be excluded from the discussion *a priori,* perhaps because some group or other does not consider them sufficiently "correct" from its own political perspective. (See the contributions from Laura Purdy and David Paris in Part II for more discussion of this point.)

This point leads to a third implication of our discussion that concerns how disputes over the curriculum might be handled within the curriculum itself. Thus, few traditionalists would disagree with the proposition that in the course of a university education, students should become (or even be required to become) familiar with a culture other than their own. Dispute breaks out between traditionalists and revisionists over what counts as another culture, whether traditional studies of Western civilization should be given any special priority, and over what traditionalists see as a political slant or bias in much revisionist teaching. Many revisionists, on the other hand, would reply that they are merely countering the political slant in the teaching of traditionalists, and that it is a political move to give special priority to traditional courses.

One model for resolving this kind of dispute might be called the feudal model, in that each side is given its own fiefdom over which it has control. Sometimes feudalism is combined in an uneasy alliance with free markets, as when students are given the choice of which fiefdoms they will enter. For example, students might be told that they must take a certain amount of credits in traditional areas and a certain amount on study of a culture other than their own. They might then be given the choice of just which departments they enter to fulfill each requirement. For example, courses in Asian studies or African studies or Islamic studies or feminist studies may be among those that satisfy the requirement for knowledge of a culture other than one's own for many students.

Although this approach has considerable merit, there are three reasons for thinking it ought not to be the only curricular reaction to the debate between traditionalists and revisionists. First, it leaves unclear not only what is to count as culture, and what is to count as a culture other than one's own, but also just which cultures "other than one's own" are to be represented on the list of courses satisfying the requirement. For example, may courses in feminist studies, as well as those in say Africa, Islamic, or Asian studies, be used to satisfy requirements that white male students learn about another culture? Should there be a different list for white females, as well as for representatives of other groups? What courses go on the list for each group?

Second, since, in the feudal model, the proponents of radically different approaches to issues of methodology and justification never have to engage one another, there is a risk of generating a kind of uncritical relativism about such issues. Students learn to think using one kind of framework in one area and another somewhere else, but never attempt to reconcile conflicts between the two. As a result, a quite understandable but also unexamined tendency to relativize standards or ways of thought to areas of study would be expected to develop.[15]

Finally, and most important, direct debate over the deeper methodological, ethical, and epistemological issues dividing different approaches would be compartmentalized with little direct engagement among the parties. Not only would this deprive students of appropriate models of scholarly disagreement on fundamental issues, but it is unlikely to make the debate intellectually profitable either.

An alternate approach, which need not be incompatible with the feudal one, is to build the dispute between revisionists and traditionalists into the curriculum at appropriate points. Thus, as Nalini Bhushan has recommended, "We can expose our students to some problems of confrontation that commitment to cultural diversity brings so they can wrestle with the difficulties themselves and come to realize that a serious accommodation of another culture is hard work and involves conflicts that are not clearly resolvable to everyone's satisfaction."[16] Philosophy, as a discipline, might be especially suited to examine such intellectual disputes, just as a course in ethical theory might attempt to adjudicate between the impartiality and caring approaches to our moral life. In other areas, institutional criteria could be developed to ensure that somewhere during their education, students were exposed to persons of different viewpoints who examined fundamental questions underlying curricular debate in some depth.

By placing the emphasis on process rather than on trying to "save" students from bad ideas, we would have a better chance of avoiding both the preaching to the already converted that is a pitfall facing the feudal approach and the sniping and name calling that too often replaces real debate within the academy. Moreover, it goes without saying that using the classroom as a political platform, to the extent it involves ignoring or distorting important evidence, is prohibited, whether done by traditionalists or revisionists.

Of course, genuine debate also carries real risks, for if debate is genuine it is unclear what views will ultimately emerge as successful. Thus, one avowed aim of many multiculturalists is to have the curriculum teach appreciation and respect for different cultures, but critical inquiry might well lead to greater moral and intellectual criticism of some cultures than others. For example, treatment of women in many non-Western cultures may come to be regarded as morally deficient when compared to recent changes in many Western societies.

To conclude, nothing said here determines whether the traditionalists or revisionists have the better case in curricular debate. Rather, what our discussion implies is that to deny that curricular argument is possible, and to regard rational discussion itself as a purely persuasive practice ideologically inseparable from specific partisan traditions, is to abandon the very framework of inquiry in which curricular proposals can be justified in the first place. Debate about the curriculum, then, is an entirely legitimate and often educationally valuable contribution to critical inquiry. However, it is important at least to attempt to distinguish arguments that appeal to educational benefits of curricular issues from those that are more partisan or narrowly ideological in character. This distinction may be often difficult to make in practice. Partisanship is not the exclusive property of just one side of the political spectrum. However, to insist that all debates about the curriculum are really only ideological rationalizations, that all curricula are political in some partisan sense, and that rational evaluation of curricular proposals is a myth, is to pay a heavy price. To avoid even the attempt to distinguish the partisan from the nonpartisan in the mistaken belief that all education is intrinsically politicized, and that hence all curricular debates are only over power, is to fail to do justice to the values of critical inquiry that should be at the heart of the educational enterprise itself.

Notes

1. The use of the term "revisionist" is not meant to deny that there are significant differences among those, such as multiculturalists, who recommend such fundamental change. Thus, revisionism is a term for a family of positions, not just one position. Moreover, the use of the term is not meant to deny that its scope is unclear. How much change must one advocate to be properly termed a revisionist is itself a difficult question, but is one that need not be explored here since nothing in the discussion depends upon the truth of a particular resolution. Similarly, "traditionalism" is a name for a family of often-conflicting positions as well.

2. Ronald Walters, "A Different View: 'Afrocentrism' Means Providing the Neglected Black Perspective," *American Educator,* Vol. 15, No. 3 (Winter 1991), p. 26.

3. Politicization, whatever it is, can pertain not only to what is taught but to how it is taught, and to why it is taught (i.e., the reasons for teaching it). Clearly, traditionalists would regard even the teaching of the most classic texts as politicized if the reason for employing them was only to discredit anything Western and if the method selected for accomplishing that aim was indoctrination of students.

4. Although I develop a different line of argument in what follows, I am heavily indebted to the general approach of John Agresto in his article, "The Politicization of Liberal Education," *Academic Questions,* Fall 1990, pp. 69–73, particularly his insistence that liberal education "lives on the prospect that there can be knowledge over opinion" (p. 73).

5. George Levine et al., "Speaking for the Humanities", American Council of Learned Societies Occasional Paper #7 (New York: American Council of Learned Societies, 1989), p. 11, italics my own. For a different reading of *Speaking for the Humanities,* see Laura Purdy's contribution to Part II of this volume.

6. Henry A. Giroux, "Liberal Arts Education and the Struggle for Public Life: Dreaming About Democracy," *The South Atlantic Quarterly,* Vol. 89, No. 1 (1990), p. 114.

7. Henry David Aiken, "Can American Universities Be Depoliticized," *Philosophic Exchange* (Summer 1970), reprinted in Sidney Hook, *Convictions* (Buffalo: Prometheus Books, 1990), p. 256, and included in Part II of this volume.

8. The claim that the curriculum should be representative raises a host of problems itself. Who gets represented and how much representation is due? Is the goal "a curriculum that looks like America" and, if so, how is that to be implemented? Should groups be represented in the curriculum in rough proportion to the percentage of the community they constitute? If qualitative standards of representation are to be applied instead, what standards are likely to be justified?

9. Alasdair MacIntyre, *Whose Justice? Whose Rationality?* (Notre Dame: The University of Notre Dame Press, 1988).

10. Carol Gilligan, *In a Different Voice* (Cambridge, Mass.: Harvard University Press, 1982).

11. Indeed Gilligan, who appears not to be an epistemological perspectivist, explicitly rests her case in *In a Different Voice* for the existence of different gender-linked moral perspectives on empirical evidence open to and presumably persuasive to anyone.

12. MacIntyre, *Whose Justice? Whose Rationality?,* p. 364.

13. Of course, MacIntyre himself seems to regard "Western thought" as itself made up of diverse and sometimes conflicting traditions.

14. In fact, these sorts of controversies among different conceptions of epistemic and moral justification call into question the overdrawn picture of a monolithic "Western culture," which underlies some of the criticism of the traditional curriculum. The study of Plato, Nietzsche, Hume, Mill, Kant, Marx, Rawls, and MacIntyre surely is the study of an extraordinarily diverse group of theorists.

15. Here I draw heavily on the discussion by Nalini Bhushan in "The Real Challenge of Cultural Diversity: Clarifying the Boundaries of Legitimate Philosophical Practice," *Teaching Philosophy,* Vol. 14, No. 2 (June 1991), pp. 169–70.

16. Bhushan, "The Real Challenge of Cultural Diversity," p. 175.

CHAPTER 6

Institutional Neutrality and Political Correctness

I. The Controversy Over Political Correctness

In the late 1980s and so far for much of the 1990s, controversy has arisen over "PC," or alleged pressures for political correctness, that according to critics are stifling free inquiry in many disciplines on American campuses. To the critics, the pressures toward conformity arising from the PC movement have transformed some colleges and universities into "islands of repression in a sea of freedom."[1] The conformity allegedly generated by pressures for political correctness has been attacked in a variety of widely discussed books and criticized in national publications, including those with a generally liberal perspective.[2] However, other prominent academics have replied that the extent of PC conformity has been grossly exaggerated by its critics, who themselves are claimed to have a political agenda they wish to impose on the university.[3]

How is PC thinking to be characterized? It is doubtful if there is one characterization that can capture what different participants in the debate over PC have in mind, since it is unlikely they all are working with the same conception to begin with. Rather, different conceptions seem to run through the debate. In its broadest sense, PC seems to stand for "pressures to conform," regardless of the source on the political spectrum. In a narrower sense, critics of PC seem to regard it as emanating largely from what might be called the cultural left, itself a broad spectrum of perspectives generally associated with at least some of the following: suspicion of hierarchy in any form; criticism of traditional ideas of objectivity, impartiality, and truth; support for multiculturalism; criticism of the traditional canon as "Eurocentric";

belief that race and gender are major and perhaps the predominant categories for understanding human behavior as well as works in the humanities and social sciences; and a commitment to fight against racism, sexism, and homophobia, which are in turn broadly understood and viewed as characteristic of much of American society.

Although the extent and influence of PC thinking is controversial and widely debated, and the facts of reported incidents sometimes are in doubt, some of the more extreme cases that have been reported are frightening to friends of open inquiry and rational discussion. Allegations run from charges of harassment of professors who do not endorse what they regard as politicized versions of new multicultural curricula, overly strict speech codes that limit "hate speech" only at the cost of stifling free discussion, the use of terms like "racism" and "sexism" to silence those who dissent from PC thinking, and a double standard of conduct that seems to exempt minorities from behavioral requirements that apply to others. Thus, to cite one of the incidents often cited by critics of PC, when in 1993 a group of African-American students at the University of Pennsylvania destroyed copies of a campus paper that contained a column they disagreed with, the university's president, rather than denounce the action, merely issued a statement saying that "two university values, diversity and openness, seem to be in conflict."[4]

Another not-atypical allegation describes an incident claimed to have taken place at a midwestern university. Although it is as yet unclear whether this particular allegation is accurate, the fact that it seems believable to many is itself a significant comment on the atmosphere on many campuses. According to reports, at a session for faculty led by a facilitator from outside the university, apparently hired to raise faculty sensitivities toward multiculturalism, each woman present was asked to stand and describe her intellectual background.

> Those with degrees from prestigious universities were required to remain standing. This procedure was then followed for men and then again for both men and women as regards their graduate degrees. At the conclusion of this elimination process, one young woman alone possessed the qualifications which kept her standing before her colleagues. She had earned all three of her degrees from prestigious private schools—the bachelor's degree from Wellesley, and the graduate degrees from Harvard and New York University.[5]

Was this woman praised as an example of an academic overachiever? Quite the contrary, according to reports. Rather, she allegedly was singled out by the facilitator as a "member of the privileged white elite." Again, according to reports, she was forced to remain standing while being instructed by the facilitator that because of her blond hair, white skin, and blue eyes, she was the most likely to succeed. Critics of this event also charge that the same woman, later in the session, was singled out for criticism as a member of the privileged class because of her physical beauty and was reduced to tears, while no other member of the faculty present either spoke in her defense or criticized the proceedings.[6]

While one would hope not only that reports of these incidents are exaggerated but also that cases like them are few and far between, such reports illustrate what critics find frightening about extreme forms of PC thinking; namely, a kind of self-righteousness mixed with a willingness to use the university as an institution to propagate a particular and highly controversial political perspective. In reaction, it has been charged that extreme forms of PC thinking are much less extensive than the critics of PC allege, and that reports of many incidents, perhaps including the ones referred to above, are inaccurate. Moreover, as we have seen in the preceding section, traditionalists often are accused of having their own political agendas that, because they are compatible with dominant ways of thought, have covertly infiltrated the university and constitute a kind of "reverse PC" of their own.

Many of the most important issues in the PC debate are empirical. How dominant are extreme forms of PC on most college and university campuses? Are reports of apparently outrageous incidents accurate? Is PC producing greater surface conformity and fear to dissent on our campuses? Other sorts of issues, such as the debate over the politicization of the curriculum and the legitimacy of university codes against hate speech have been discussed already and will be treated in greater depth in other volumes in this series. However, the dispute over PC raises issues having to do with university neutrality that, although they also have been touched on earlier, merit some examination now as well.[7]

II. Political Correctness and the Neutral University

Perhaps the key implication of neutrality for the debate over PC has to do with the distinction between positions taken by individual faculty members and those taken by colleges and universities as institutions.

Individual faculty, as we have seen in Chapter 3, have the right to advocate positions in class that are relevant to their academic expertise and the course material with which they are concerned, as long as they do so in a manner compatible with canons of critical inquiry. That is, at a minimum, they must be open to objection, consider contrary positions and evidence fairly, and provide to the best of their ability a fair and accurate account of alternate views. Thus, students and faculty whose views might be seen as revisionist or PC have as much right as traditionalists to argue for their views in appropriate forums, and may make at least as valuable a contribution to the intellectual life of the university.

However, what worries critics of PC is in part what they regard as the illegitimate appropriation of categories such as race and gender to silence opposition on controversial topics, especially when the university as an institution enforces this appropriation. In other words, critics fear that extreme proponents of PC, who in their view often dominate university campuses, stretch the meaning of terms like "racism," "sexism," and "discrimination" so that controversial but arguable positions that are not PC are placed on the moral defensive. As a result, opponents are intimidated by fear of being called racists or sexists and hence never enter the debate. The PC position then wins by default.

If what is at stake here is simply the actions of individual faculty members and students, perhaps the proper response might just be to advise others not to be intimidated and join the debate. After all, in the view of the university defended here, colleges and universities are supposed to be forums where issues like this are discussed and debated. (On the other hand, critics of PC rejoin that at least some of their colleagues seem more interested in silencing opposition than in joining in mutually profitable debate.)

However, the issue becomes more complex if the university itself employs such tactics as an institution. Then, the very institution that is supposed to enforce the rules of critical inquiry so as to protect open debate has, at least according to some of the critics of PC, abused the rules to insure the dominance of one side in the political life of the university. Whether and how often this has actually happened, and whether revisionists are more prone to the use of such tactics than traditionalists, are, as we have seen, empirical questions, but we can profit from consideration of the underlying principles that can be used in *evaluating* the facts, whatever they turn out to be.

In particular, it is important to distinguish between positions the university may take precisely because of its intellectual mission and positions that, although they superficially resemble the permissible ones, are positions on which the university ought to remain silent.

Consider, for example, the value of opposition to racism, or antiracism for short. Antiracism has been a major theme of many multiculturalists and, in addition, has frequently been appealed to against the critics of PC. According to this defense, conservative academics, who are timid about pressing the fight against racism, label as PC what are in reality legitimate steps in the fight against racism on campus (e.g., codes against hate speech and training to sensitize academics to work with culturally diverse students). In this view, while some incidents on campus that have been labeled PC are extreme and outrageous, they are few and far between and should not be allowed to obscure the larger and more moderate movement against various forms of discrimination and prejudice.

Indeed, there is a sense of antiracism that we can call the core sense in which colleges and universities as institutions clearly ought to be antiracist.[8] Thus, such institutions have an obligation to ensure that all students and employees are free from invidious discrimination, and that institutional policy does not reflect any racist or prejudiced beliefs about the differential moral worth of individuals based on their group identity (the core sense of "racism"). Indeed, insofar as the academic ethic requires adherence to rational discourse, and racism requires demeaning the contributions of some not because of their intellectual worth but because of the ethnicity of their source, the two inherently are in conflict.

However, it is one thing to claim that universities as part of their educational mission should be antiracist in the core sense and quite another to stretch that into an institutional stance against antiracism in what I will call the ideological sense. The term "racism" is used ideologically when the term "racism" is used to carry the emotional charge of racism in the core sense although it is highly controversial whether the elements that are the basis for that moral force are actually present.

Positions that have been called racist but in which it is plausible to think that charges of racism function ideologically include the following:

Racial preference in college admissions is invariably racist (or alternately, affirmative action is invariably racist).

Opposition to racial preference in college admissions is invariably racist.

The belief that some cultures should not be respected as much as others is racist.

Theories that economic or social factors rather than individual or institutional racism best explain group economic differences in America is itself racist.

Such claims clearly are controversial, and it is conceivable that argument could establish links between some of them and racism in the core sense. On the other hand, people of good will are found on different sides of these issues, and arguments of some force are available to proponents that do not rest explicitly on expression of prejudice for members of specific racial, ethnic, religious, or other groups.

In any case, the point from the perspective of institutional critical neutrality is not only that arguments for various views on these issues may have little to do with racism in the core sense but also that the taking of an institutional position on such issues is not directly related to the institution's educational mission. In fact, open and free discussion of such issues, protected within the framework of institutional neutrality, seems to best serve desirable institutional goals.

Part of the trouble with stretching the notion of core racism to cover one or another group's version of ideological racism is that it runs the risk of trivializing the notion of racism by blurring the distinction between the core meaning and ideologically contested views. For example, someone who questions whether the treatment of women in some Islamic countries is morally acceptable and is told she is a racist because she is not regarding all cultures as moral equals may then question whether racism is so bad, never noticing the shift that has been made from core to ideological forms of racism in the discussion.

More important for our purposes, however, although there are neutral reasons for colleges and universities to oppose core racism, reasons related to their educational mission, it normally would be improper for them to adopt one or another ideological version of racism. That is because such an institutional commitment on an intellectually contested issue will most likely stifle free debate on that issue within the institution, lending institutional force to one side or another and making autonomous choice more difficult.

Thus, there is a major difference, for example, between an institution adopting an affirmative action policy on contested but *educationally relevant* grounds, and declaring as institutional policy, on the other hand, that opposition to its decision is itself racist, not to be tolerated, or not to be taken seriously.[9] For example, an example of a neutral justification for affirmative action or racial preference in recruiting students and appointing faculty might be the promotion of diversity within the academic community. Racial, gender, and ethnic diversity would be held to contribute to intellectual diversity and so enhance critical inquiry. Although such a rationale is controversial, it is compatible with critical neutrality in that the reason presented in favor of racial preference has to do with the enhancement of critical dialogue, a goal clearly within the university's proper domain of responsibility.[10] On the other hand, for the university simply to stipulate that criticism of racial preference is itself a kind of racism—or at best a demonstration of insensitivity to racism—is to shut off debate on a controversial public topic. Accordingly, although the line may be difficult to draw in many cases, it seems that often we can draw distinctions between relatively politicized or ideological approaches to curricular debates and at least relatively less partisan and ideological ones.

Proponents of critical neutrality, then, make a plausible distinction between value-laden perspectives that are so intimately related to the educational mission of the university that the institution may endorse and act upon them and those that are not so related. Commitment with respect to the first set of issues may well be not only compatible with critical neutrality but sometimes may be required by it. However, in the second kind of case, political commitment does violate critical neutrality and therefore, if the defense of neutrality presented here is sound, is presumptively wrong.

Some more radical critics of the prevailing political climate may still be unpersuaded by all that has been said so far. Some may feel that the university, as part of the status quo, is so elitist, sexist, homophobic, or racist that so-called critical inquiry is either a sham or persuasively defined so as to support dominant views. In their view, the proper thing to do is transform the university into an agent of political change, not engage in "critical dialogue" with representatives of the very society they hope radically to change.

At some point, at least in extreme cases, there may be no common ground left between such critics and proponents of the neutral university.[11] The commitment to neutrality, as we have seen, is not totally value free and hence it is not compatible with every conceivable political or ethical position. However, the proponent of neutrality can argue against those who would reject neutrality that they pay a heavy price. Since they have opted out of critical dialogue, they have not exposed their position to the challenges, criticism, and objections that perspectives that are defended within critical discourse must meet. Since such challenges have not been met, the proponents lack the basis for claiming their views have been adequately justified. While they themselves simply may not care about justification of this sort, or perhaps have merely subordinated it to allegedly higher goals, the price may not seem too high from their own perspective. But unless others have been given good reason to adopt that perspective, they have both the right and the duty to protect the neutral university and the framework of reasoned discourse it protects and represents.

Whether opponents of PC have exaggerated the extent and effects of PC thinking certainly is debatable. However, they have raised an important issue when they raise an issue of principle about how far colleges and universities may go in enforcing values that appear to be highly controversial and not directly tied to their educational mission. There certainly is room for debate about how broadly that mission should be construed. But the danger of stretching the university's mission to include promotion of more and more values that we may regard as highly desirable is that of stretching it so far that the university may fail in its charge of protecting reasoned critical discourse and helping it to flourish.

Notes

1. See, for example, Chester E. Finn, Jr., "The Campus: 'An Island of Repression in a Sea of Freedom'," *Commentary,* Vol. 48, No. 3 (September 1989), pp. 17–23, and Dinesh D'Souza, *Illiberal Education: The Politics of Race and Sex on Campus* (New York: The Free Press, 1991).

2. See, for example, *The New Republic,* special issue on "Race on Campus," Vol. 204, No. 7 (February 18, 1991).

3. See, for example, Catharine Stimpson, "Big Man on Campus," *The Nation,* September 30, 1991.

4. This incident is likely to attract increasing public attention as the then-president of Pennsylvania is being considered at the time of this writing as a nominee for the chairmanship of the National Endowment for the Humanities. For discussion and summary of reactions to the incident, see "When a University is Forced to Examine its Very Soul," *The Pennsylvania Gazette: Alumni Magazine for the University of Pennsylvania,* Vol. 91, No. 7 (May 1993), pp. 15–18, as well as the editorial, "Don't Burn Hackney at the Stake," *The New York Times,* June 10, 1993, p. A26. For discussion of other alleged

incidents of PC, see *The New Republic,* op. cit., and Finn, "The Campus: 'An Island of Repression in a Sea of Freedom'," op. cit.

5. For a report of this incident, see Nino Langiulli, "When It Came to 'That' at the University of Cincinnati," *Measure,* No. 114 (March 1993), pp. 2–3.

6. Langiulli, "When It Came to 'That' at the University of Cincinnati," pp. 2–3. While spokespersons for the university involved apparently deny that this incident happened, or happened as reported, others claim to have witnesses available and to have interviewed the victim. In any case, the report, whether accurate or not, illustrates the fears of traditionalists about the PC movement. For a defense of the claim that the incident happened as reported, see Walter E. Williams, "UC 'Sensitivity' Session Did Involve Nazi Tactics," *Measure,* No. 117 (June 1993), p. 8.

7. See also the discussion by John Searle, Laura Purdy, and David Paris in Part II. Purdy in particular expresses skepticism about the veracity of reports of some of the more extreme instances of PC behavior.

8. Here, I borrow from Lawrence Blum's account of core racism in his article "Philosophy and the Value of a Multicultural Community" from *Teaching Philosophy,* Vol. 14, No. 2 (June 1991), pp. 127–28, although I do not know if he would be sympathetic toward my account of ideological racism.

9. See, for example, Fred Siegel's discussion of an alleged policy at Smith College in his article, "The Cult of Multiculturalism," *The New Republic,* op. cit., pp. 34–38. In his article, Siegel claims that

> Through a combination of sensitivity training sessions and the ideological weight of a document issued by the college president called "The Smith Design," the administration has made it clear that no criticism of racial quotas in admission and student life, no matter how thoughtful, will be taken seriously. The students, Smith English Professor Eric Reeves told me, are subtly intimidated. "They censor themselves in class out of a fear of both peer pressure and the possibility of sanctions."

10. For some skeptical doubts about this sort of rationale for racial preference, see Robert L. Simon, "Affirmative Action and the University: Faculty Appointment and Preferential Treatment," in Steven M. Cahn, ed., *Affirmative Action and the University* (Philadelphia: Temple University Press, 1993), particularly pp. 74–82.

11. David Paris has made me appreciate the importance of this point.

CHAPTER 7

Institutional Neutrality and the Academic Ethic: A Summary

Concerns about institutional neutrality are deeply entangled in many important controversies that arise on college and university campuses, including those about the legitimate scope and limits of protest, the ethics of divestment, and disputes about the content of the curriculum. Critics of neutrality argue that it should have no role in discussions of such issues, since if neutrality is not an outright sham and illusion, it is at best an abdication of moral responsibility and the obligation to operate in a morally appropriate manner. What the critics may have failed to see, however, is that in some circumstances there is a moral case for neutrality itself.

Our discussion suggests that while colleges and universities cannot be neutral in some senses of neutrality, there are other senses in which institutional neutrality is possible. The kind of neutrality that might be most appropriate for colleges and universities is what we have called institutional critical neutrality. The claim that universities ought to be institutionally critically neutral amounts to the assertion that they ought to provide a framework in which critical inquiry can take place such that the outcome is the result of the dynamics of rational discourse and scholarly argument rather than institutional policy or predisposition. In this view, there is a presumptive case for institutional critical neutrality; colleges and universities ought to be neutral in this sense unless the case for neutrality is outweighed by conflicting values of the greatest moral significance (e.g., the principle that the university should not commit a serious injustice).

Concern about neutrality is closely tied to concern for the process of critical inquiry and reasoned discourse that is at the heart of the traditional conception of the university as a center of rationality and learning, which investigates and tests not only "the best that has been thought and known" but tries to transmit and extend that knowledge as well. Indeed, this traditional role of the university is so central that it is difficult to concede the efficacy of any justificatory process without some similar kind of institution taking some role in the process. For the university is the institution par excellence where objections are raised, criticisms dealt with, and debate joined. Without such activity, could we have good reason to believe that our beliefs could survive criticism and merit adherence?

It does not follow, however, that institutional neutrality is only a guise supporting predominantly traditional views on substantive issues. As we have seen, curricular revisionists would do far better intellectually to make their case within a reasoned framework of neutral debate than to present their curricular views as pure assertions of power in a struggle for political control of the university. As Robert Holmes argues in his contribution to Part II, neutrality does not necessarily favor conservative over liberal or radical views in all contexts.

It is of course possible that critical inquiry itself is a sham and that there is no conception of reasoned discourse that is neutral to all parties to debate. Perhaps the idea of reason itself is only a weapon in the ideological wars, appealed to by different sides, but really only a verbal sword with which to skewer opponents devoid of genuine normative force.

If such an extremely skeptical view toward reasoned discourse and critical inquiry can be supported (but how can it be justified if the process of justification is itself illusory?), then of course the case for the neutral university collapses. But there is a heavy price that critics of neutrality would pay for such a victory. Since, in their own view, the conception of reasoned discourse is only an ideological tool empty of content, their own views on education, politics, and social change cannot be justified either. All becomes a war of power against power in which they not only have no guarantee of winning but no basis for claiming they *ought* to win either. We are left with emptiness; all political dialogue is sound and fury valuing nothing since values themselves, like all claims, are simply unsupportable prejudices.

Since such skepticism is likely to prove unattractive once it is brought into the open, it becomes important to explore the scope and limits of critical discourse and the role of institutions that should serve as its protectors. In Part II, the topics raised in the preceding discussion of neutrality are explored from conflicting points of view. While that discussion itself must meet the test of critical inquiry and must be tested itself by critical fire, it does indicate that the related values of neutrality and an academic ethic of critical inquiry should indeed be central to our academic institutions and the life of the mind they should be protecting and promoting.

The essays in Part II begin with articles written in the 1960s and 1970s, reflecting then current and often bitter disputes over the university's role in protesting the Vietnam War and its reactions to the often vigorous protests of others. They continue with a series of exchanges on the university's external entanglements, especially demands for divestment and the university's response to them, and conclude with contributions on contemporary disputes about the neutrality of the curriculum.

PART II

Selected Readings

CHAPTER 1

Neutrality and Its Critics

The Myth of the Neutral University
Robert Paul Wolff

In the dialectic of charge, response, and confrontation which domi-
nates the campus these days, one of the most familiar disputes revolves
about the role of the university as supporter or opponent of government policy. Characteristically, the interchange proceeds something
like this:

1. The university is engaged in a variety of extra-educational activities, such as contract research, the scheduling of job interviews,
transmission of class standing to draft boards, and so forth. These
activities accumulate haphazardly without deliberate university control
and in the absence of a coherent policy.

2. Radical students and faculty focus attention upon some few of
the extra-educational activities as evidences of the university's positive
support for a controversial and evil government policy. Transmission
of class standing to draft boards supports the Vietnam war. Acceptance
of contract research on counterinsurgency supports the reactionary
imperialism of the United States abroad. The university's real estate
dealings discriminate against the poor and the Black in the surrounding community.

3. The university defends its activities on the grounds that it takes
no position with regard to social or political issues. It leaves its faculty
free to teach what it likes, and to do research as it chooses. It opens
its doors to speakers of all persuasions and recruiters for virtually any

From *The Ideal of the University* (Boston: Beacon Press, 1969).

enterprise which is not illegal. Individuals within the university may engage in whatever political activities they like, but for the university as an institution to take an official political stand would be in violation of its fundamental principles of value neutrality and academic freedom.

4. The radicals reply that the university *is* endorsing positions and policies by its actions, but that it is endorsing the *wrong* positions and the *wrong* policies. What is needed is an about-face, so that the university will throw its considerable prestige and power into the fight against a reactionary establishment.

This debate, in all the many forms it takes from university to university, revolves about one of the oldest tenets of the liberal tradition—the myth of the value-neutral institution. Just as the state, in classical liberal economic theory, is expected to stand clear of the competitive battles waged between firm and firm, or capital and labor, merely maintaining the freedom and order of the market place of commodities, so the university is expected to stand clear of the intellectual battles waged between doctrine and doctrine, dogma and dogma, in the market place of ideas. Its sole function is to regulate the contest, ensuring a place in the debate to every position and every party. The university administration is charged with the responsibility of protecting those within the academy from the repeated assaults by outside critics, while at the same time guaranteeing that absolute freedom of debate reigns within. From this freedom in the market place of ideas, it is confidently believed, the greatest possible advance in truth and wisdom will flow.[1]

As a prescription for institutional behavior, the doctrine of value neutrality suffers from the worst disability which can afflict a norm: what it prescribes is not wrong; it is impossible. A large university in contemporary America simply cannot adopt a value-neutral stance, either externally or internally, no matter how hard it tries. This obervation is scarcely original with me; indeed, I should have thought it was a commonplace of social analysis. Nevertheless, it is so often and so willfully forgotten that a few lines might profitably be spent demonstrating its truth.

Let us begin with the university's relation to society. A large university, in respect of its employees, faculty, students, land holding, endowment, and other material and human resources, is in many ways comparable to a large corporation. Columbia University, for example, is one of the largest property owners in the city of New York; the University of California must surely be one of the major employers in the state; and cities like Ann Arbor, Cambridge, and Princeton have somewhat the air of company towns. Now, one of the first truths enunciated in introductory ethics courses is that the failure to do something is as much an act as the doing of it. It is perfectly reasonable to hold a man responsible for *not* paying his taxes, for *not* exercising due care and caution in driving, for *not* helping a fellow man in need. In public life, when a man who has power refrains from using it, we all agree that he has *acted politically*. Omissions are frequently even more significant politically than commissions in American politics, for those in positions of decision usually rule by default rather than by consent.[2] Hence, acquiescence in governmental acts, under the guise of impartiality, actually strengthens the established forces and makes successful opposition all the harder.

For example, let us suppose that a university cooperates with the Selective Service System, motivated in part by a simple desire to be helpful to legitimate government agencies and interested students, and in part by the conviction that deliberate refusal to cooperate would constitute an institutional opposition to the draft which would violate the principle of political neutrality. Obviously, the university strengthens the draft system, positively by its cooperation and negatively by its failure to take the deliberate step of opposition which was open to it. To be sure, public refusal would have a greater political effect against, than quiet cooperation would have for, the government. Hence there must be better reasons for opposition than there are for cooperation. But the reasons need not be overwhelming or apocalyptic, and, in any event, the action, positive or negative, is a *political* act based on *political* considerations. No major institution can remain politically innocent in an open society.

When pressed with such obvious arguments, the administrators frequently retreat to the claim that they merely follow the law. Dow Chemical is permitted to recruit because it and its activities are legal. No moral or political judgment is superimposed on the accepted law of the land.

Now, in actual fact, this defense is false, for the CIA recruits freely on campuses even though it admits to repeatedly breaking domestic laws and violating international treaties. But even when true, the defense fails, for we live in a society which pursues policies by enacting laws. Hence, mere obedience to law is at the same time support for established policy. Suppose, to take a case which is presumably no longer possible, that a school in a state which legally forbids marriages between whites and blacks refuses to hire a white scholar on the grounds that he is married to a Black woman. It thereby lends its great institutional weight to the enforcement of an evil social policy, even though it does so merely by obeying the law. There is no difference between this hypothetical case and the case of defense research or cooperation with the draft, except of course that all good white liberal professors and administrators are opposed to the wicked segregation in the South, while many of the same people feel quite comfortable with America's foreign policy or with their own university's behavior in the surrounding neighborhood.

When we turn to the internal organization of the university, we find the same unavoidable evaluative bias. I have already rehearsed the radical complaint that American capitalism prepares young men for the rigors of the corporate world by the lockstep character of education. Whatever one thinks of this view, it is obvious that an institution imposes some set of values on its students merely by requiring that they maintain a passing grade average, attend classes regularly, take examinations on time, and leave after completing an appropriate assortment of courses. To be sure, the vehicle for the imposition of values is the *form* rather than the *content* of the educational process, but the effect is imposition nonetheless.[3]

An analogous bias is built into the free market place of ideas, which usually pretends to be neutral among competing dogmas and doctrines. By permitting all voices to be heard, the university systematically undermines all those doctrines which claim exclusive possession of the truth and seek therefore to silence opposed voices. By permitting a Catholic to preach his faith only so long as he allows others to preach theirs, one quite effectively repudiates precisely the central thesis of the Catholic Church. This fact is perfectly well understood in countries like Spain, where opposition to the censorship of the Church is a *political* act. It is also understood in Czechoslovakia, or Russia, or China. For some strange reason, American intellectuals cannot perceive that their own commitment to free debate is also a substantive political act, no more neutral than the prohibition of dissent in religiously or politically authoritarian countries.

Finally, every university expresses a number of positive value commitments through the character of its faculty, of its library, even through the buildings it chooses to build. Astronomy departments ignore astrology, psychiatry departments ignore dianetics, philosophy departments ignore dialectical materialism. Universities build laboratories for experimental research, thereby committing themselves to the importance of the scientific enterprise; libraries devote scarce resources to the accumulation of rare and ancient manuscripts; whole faculties are organized to teach and study social welfare, veterinary science, law, or business. Each of these institutional decisions embodies an evaluation which can easily become the focus of a political dispute.

The conclusion is obvious. No institution can remain politically neutral either in its interaction with society or in the conduct and organization of its internal affairs. To pretend otherwise is merely to throw up a smokescreen; it is a way of rationalizing the value commitments already made, by attempting to remove them from the area of legitimate debate. Students for a Democratic Society speak of the need to *politicize* the campus. Moderate professors and students oppose this *politicization,* which they protest would alter the character of the university for the worse. But the truth is that every campus is now politicized, necessarily and unavoidably. The radicals do not wish to inflict politics on a realm which once was happily apolitical. They only wish to force an awareness of the already political character of the university, as a first step toward changing the policies which the university embodies or pursues.

On the basis of this analysis, it might appear that the university should drop the mask of impartiality, openly acknowledge the political biases implied by its policies and educational practices, and confront the problem of deciding how its political orientation should be determined. That would, indeed, be the honest and consistent course to follow. To be sure, any system of majority rule or collegial decision would still leave members of a dissident minority unhappy at being associated with an institution whose avowed policies differed from their own; but that must inevitably be true in any case, and at least the policy would be openly and fairly arrived at.

However, the honest and consistent course is not always the best; and I am persuaded that in the United States, at the present time, such a course would have reactionary rather than progressive consequences. There are two reasons why radicals would be ill-advised to expose the incoherence and hypocrisy of the doctrine of institutional neutrality. In the first place, faculties and student bodies tend, by and large, to be conservative in their leanings; and once the university is forced to bring its policies out into the open, the majority is liable to move the direction of those policies even farther to the right. Students are always surprised to discover the melancholy facts of faculty-student conservatism. Since the liberals and radicals on the campus make most of the noise and grab most of the headlines, it is easy to be fooled into thinking that the campus is a hotbed of radical conviction barely contained by a manipulative and repressive administration. Inevitably, the day of disillusion arrives when a faculty vote or student referendum reveals the radicals to be in a distinct minority.

I confess that during the tumultuous events of Spring 1968 at Columbia, I permitted myself to hope that the forces of progress had acquired sufficient support to carry a meeting of the faculty. Each time we were convened, however, the pro-administration bloc defeated the challenges of the rebels by a two-thirds majority. Even in the faculty of Columbia College, a number of whose members had been beaten by the police during the two raids, there was not even a large minority for motions of censure or expressions of opposition to President Kirk's actions. In the end, we had our greatest effect through informal channels of discussion and pressure, where intensity of concern could in part compensate for lack of numbers.

It would be tactically unwise, therefore, to push to an open vote such matters as university acceptance of defense research or the policy of open recruiting. But this is hardly the greatest danger which the politicization of the university invites. Far worse is the ever-present threat of pressure, censorship, and witch-hunting by conservative forces in society at large. The universities at present are sanctuaries for social critics who would find it very hard to gain a living elsewhere in society. Who but a university these days would hire Herbert Marcuse, Eugene Genovese, or Barrington Moore, Jr.? Where else are anarchists, socialists, and followers of other unpopular persuasions accorded titles, honors, and the absolute security of academic tenure? Let the university once declare that it is a political actor, and its faculty will be investigated, its charter revoked, and its tax-exempt status forthwith removed. How majestic and unassailable is the university president who protects his dissident faculty with an appeal to the sanctity of academic freedom!

It is a bitter pill for the radicals to swallow, but the fact is that they benefit more than any other segment of the university community from the fiction of institutional neutrality. For the present, therefore, I would strongly urge both students and professors to hide behind the slogans "lehrfreiheit" and "lernfreiheit," and give up the attempt to politicize the campus. If this advice is too cautious to satisfy their revolutionary longings they may look on the universities as those protected base camps which, Mao Tse-tung tells us, are the foundation of a successful protracted guerrilla campaign.

Notes

1. For a critical analysis of John Stuart Mill's famous defense of this thesis, see my *The Poverty of Liberalism,* Chapter One.

2. I am referring here, of course, to the well-known theory of "veto groups." For a general defense of this anti-power-elite view of American politics, see *The Poverty of Liberalism,* Chapter Three.

3. Let me say that I *approve* by and large of the values thus imposed. I am personally very strict with regard to lateness of papers and the like. But I recognize that I must *justify* such requirements with an argument and not claim to be neutral on the issues involved.

Can American Universities Be Depoliticized?
Henry David Aiken

In his inaugural address a year ago last autumn, Morris Abram, the second president of my own university, Brandeis, called for a general "depoliticizing" of our universities and colleges. Many others, both inside the universities and out, are making similar appeals. The hope, it seems, is for a return to a golden age of higher education when professors professed, and administrators, delighted to leave well enough alone, spent their time passing the hat, balancing budgets, acting as substitute parents, and performing such ceremonial acts as presiding at faculty meetings and commencement exercises. Of course such a golden age is long gone. It hasn't existed at private colleges for generations; at public colleges and universities, many of which evolved out of the old land-grant colleges, it never existed. In fact, another university president (or rather ex-president), James Perkins of Cornell, has argued approvingly that American institutions of higher learning generally have combined in a unique way the three "missions" of teaching, research, and service. By "service," however, Perkins seems originally to have had in mind primarily service to the state and to the national society over which the state presides. In times past, such services have often grudgingly been performed; indeed, faculties and students alike have frequently debated whether they do not compromise the integrity of the American scholar. And even when members of the university have accepted the principle that the college should also include a service station, they have rarely agreed among themselves as to the proper nature or extent of the services to be rendered. But such disagreements, like the services themselves, are inescapably political.

For example, long before the Vietnam war made the ROTC such a bone of contention on our campuses, many academicians, old as well as young, insisted that this conspicuous tie between the academy and the military be severed. Occasionally, moreover, they prevailed, thereby saving their colleges energies for better ways of showing patriotism. Another example may be mentioned which is more interest-

From *Philosophic Exchange* (Summer 1970): 3–18.

ing and important. As some of you may recall, it was during the First World War, at Columbia, and during the Second, at Harvard, that programs which now go by the name of General Education were respectively initiated at those distinguished universities where recently there has been so much turmoil. At the outset, the purpose of such programs was undisguisedly political: their function, quite simply, was to awaken the minds of hitherto indifferent or misguided students to the transcendental virtues of our American system and to the wickedness of all systems that oppose it. To be sure, this great awakening should be accomplished in a suitably genteel and roundabout way, by searching out the fountainheads of freedom in the works of such ancient masters as Plato (the greatest of all exponents of the aristocratic ideal who reserved the higher forms of learning for the guardians of his ideal Republic) and Aristotle (the first pragmatist who preferred a mixed polity in which nonetheless some men, being slaves by nature, cannot be allowed to participate since they are unable to grasp the meaning of political obligation). From the beginning, of course, General Education was widely opposed. Some opposed it on the grounds that so obviously politicized an educational venture demeans the university, whose modes of political indoctrination should be less conspicuous; others (in their own way perhaps anticipating educationist such as President Abram) opposed it on the ground that any form of politicking on the campus should be excluded since it diverts institutions of higher learning from their proper business, which is advancement and dissemination of learning. Were they consistent, such purists, who do not pause to examine the varieties of human learning, would have to go much further. In America, however, where even purists are pragmatists, few have questioned the prerogatives of established departments of political science and sociology, in which much time and energy are spent in ideological and hence political controversy.

Several lessons may be drawn from this example: one is that politicized activity on the part of members of the so-called academic community is generally acceptable if it is sufficiently concealed, indirect, learned, and firmly established; it is below the salt only when it becomes open and direct, formally unlearned and boldly innovative. But another and happier lesson may be learned from the example of General Education. For it was through the efforts of highly politicized academic patriots that great educational movement was launched whose function has been to revive the spirit of what used to be called liberal education in an age of rampant specialism, professionalism, and scientism. The failures of the movement, alas, are all too plain. But in nearly all cases they are owning to the fact that its exponents have been too timid and too concessive, too limited in their demands for educational reform, too conventional in their conception of the forms of education that are necessary for free men in a really free society.

Here it should be emphasized that purists who oppose such existing politically-oriented educational programs as the ROTC or General Education are politicized by the very act of opposing them. In fact, the only way a scholar can avoid the trap of politics is by shutting the door to his study, pulling down the shades, and sticking, despite hell and high water, to his own neutral researches and to courses of instruction related exclusively to them. President Abram's presidential address, whether he realized it or not, was a political act, in the same way that the actions of committed anarchists, who yearn to dispense altogether with politics, employ political means to achieve their post-political ends. The state, as we have learned, never does its own withering away. But of course the depoliticizers (if "depoliticize" is a word then so is "depoliticizer"), like the anarchists, cannot succeed. History, human nature, not to mention existing versions of the American dream, all conspire against them. In one direction, the Pentagon and the great scientific-technological establishments that are themselves so closely intertwined with government, will continue to find their way into the universities and colleges, in part because they have an insatiable need for the products of the "knowledge factory." In the opposite direction, even the most servile university, in bringing together exceptionally lively and imaginative individuals, also brings into existence what I call a "shadow university" where free men find ways of instructing and advising one another about the social and political conditions of a more fully human life. In Russia, in Spain, in Czechoslovakia, and in the United States, the university has always served in spite of itself as a breeding ground for the education of political dissenters, reformers, and revolutionists. The only way to disperse such dissidents, and so to prevent them from enlightening one another, would be to disband the universities. But this is precisely what the state and its functionaries, academic and otherwise, cannot afford to do. Hence, since politics, like nature, abhors a vacuum, the educationally absorbing question is not whether the universities and colleges can be depoliticized, but rather what forms of political activity they may properly encourage or tolerate. And it is to this question that we must presently address ourselves.

Still, granted that efforts to depoliticize the academy are, to put the point least offensively, quixotic, it is an instructive exercise in the philosophy of higher education to perform the imaginative experiment of considering what the educational as well as human results would be, were our colleges actually to succeed in eliminating every form of political activity from the academy.

In the first place, liberal education would disappear. For liberal education is intended by definition for free men, and free men, by definition, are political beings, concerned not with their own self-government only, but with the liberation of all their kind from every form of human bondage, including those forms of bondage by which men in societies enslave one another. Clearly, liberal education is committed from the outset of the study of institutions, including the state, and this not merely as they have been and are, but as they ought or ought not to be. In a word, to depoliticize the university would require the exclusion of all normative social and political studies. But it would also entail the abandonment of ethics, since, as Aristotle long ago pointed out, ethics and politics are ultimately inseparable. And since ethics, broadly conceived, is the heartland of philosophy, it would have to exclude philosophy too, or at least those parts of it that are not purely analytical. Neither Aristotle nor Plato—nor, above all, Socrates—could get a job in the depoliticized academy.

Indeed, as we ponder the matter we are driven to the conclusion that a depoliticized academy could not tolerate any educational program nor any sort of sustained speculation and criticism aimed at the radical reformation of human personality. "Know thyself," said the oracle. But what would be the point of trying to know oneself, with the help of enlightened teachers, unless one were determined to change one's life? And how could one think of undertaking such a task if one were not prepared to entertain the possibility or necessity of actions which, if they succeeded, might revolutionize all our social institutions, including of course the colleges and the state themselves?

I am bound to say also that a fully depoliticized academy could not permit any form of religious study which aimed at something more than the external examination of historical religions, their creeds and rituals, and churchly paraphernalia. For active religious reflection, as Paul Tillich used to say, has to do with matters of ultimate concern to us as human beings, with what is worthy of our profoundest loyalty and love. But the awakened religious consciousness, as all great religious leaders, from the Prophets and Jesus to Gandhi and Pope John XXIII, have demonstrated both in their teachings and in their lives, is always a threat to the established order, including the political order. Indeed, great religious geniuses, like great philosophers, and artists—*by their very existence*—endanger the established orders, and the dominations and obsessions of their governing elites.

What then would be left to the higher learning were all significant political thought and activity excluded from the university? We are driven, I think, to the conclusions that if our academies were systematically depoliticized, many traditional and humanly important parts of the humanities and the so-called social sciences, even in their present-day confused and emasculated forms, would have to be dropped from the curriculum. Moreover, many researchers now conducted under the more austere auspices of natural science departments would have to be abandoned, since their results, devoid of theoretical interest, have value only for governments committed to the deadly business of power politics. To be more concrete (and I shall continue to play our little game as even-handedly as possible), one cannot imagine that cathedrals of pure scholarship would tolerate such political activists as Professor Marcuse or (at the other extreme) Professor Sidney Hook; no doubt Chomsky would have to go, but so too would Professors Schlesinger and Galbraith, to say nothing of such eminent newcomers to the academic scene as Professors Humphrey and Johnson. But these are not all. For thousands of indentured technological scientists, along with their multitudes of graduate assistants, would also have to find new jobs in the great industrial laboratories where there is no quibbling about the aims of higher education.

What about the student activists, who are currently such burrs in the saddles of our academic administrators? Surely there would be no place for them, even if they stopped carrying arms and rifling the files of deans of the faculty. For they would still be politicized. So it would be necessary to proscribe such student organizations as the SDS and (were the authorities consistent) the Young Republican Clubs. And if the reply were made, which is not without merit, that one can get an education of sorts by engaging in such extra-curricular political activities, the reply, in this instance, would fail, for a political education is still a part of the political life of men in societies.

Nor have I forgotten here the distinction between forms of political education that are topical and directly activistic and those concerned more abstractly with the critique and formation of general ideological principles which serve their political ends more indirectly. And to those who concede that the higher learning *should* have a place for studies of the latter sort (and I fully agree with them) the reply must be that they are forgetting the game we are playing. I cannot see how an academy, depoliticized in any depth, could tolerate a William James, a John Dewey, or a Bertrand Russell, and any more than it could tolerate a Marcuse. For again, all forms of political reasoning, whether abstractly ideological like Plato's *Republic* and Rousseau's *Social Contract,* or concrete and topical, like the *Declaration of Independence, The Emancipation Proclamation,* or the *Communist Manifesto,* have a practical intention: that is to say, they are aimed, whether for the longer or shorter run, at the modification of active political-social attitudes. In fact, they defeat their own purposes if, when the time is ripe, they fail to move us to action designed to reform or, if necessary, revolutionize the existing order.

In sum, a thoroughly depoliticized academy, were it ever actualized, would not be an institute for all the forms of advanced study necessary to the progressive enlightenment of mature human beings, but instead would be learned mandarins lost finally both to the world and to themselves. No doubt an affluent society like our own, which presumably can afford anything that takes its fancy, could afford such an institution, and for a time at least it might even be willing to tolerate it, just as it now tolerates religious retreats and sanctuaries. What is more doubtful is that the internal purity of the academy could be maintained. How could it make certain that a few whole men—whether students or professors—might not get into it by mistake? And how could it guarantee that such impure spirits, like our own campus rebels, would not in the end become so alienated from it that, despairing of further argument with their uncomprehending superiors, they would not be disposed at last, like all other alienists, to take matters into their own hands? Surely it is not hard to imagine in these troubled times that beginning with teach-ins and sit-ins, they might be tempted to seize the administration building by main force and hold the president and his deans incommunicado until their "non-negotiable" demands for a more liberal conception of higher education were met.

Suppose they did. In such an event, we may well imagine, a depoliticized college president or board of trustees would be exceedingly reluctant to make use of the strong arm of the state. For in so doing they would of course be responding in kind—that is to say, politically—to the actions of the rebels. Still, one must suppose that in the end they would feel obliged, necessarily in uneasy conscience, to call in the police in order to protect the integrity and the freedom of the academy. But what sort of freedom would this be? Not, surely, the freedom to discuss in a critical spirit the nature and limits of science, whithersoever the argument might lead. For anyone who starts asking limiting questions about the proper aims and functions of scientific inquiries may well find that such limits are extremely unclear or else that they are in need of radical revision in an age like our own in which governments, with the indispensable help of scientists, can destroy mankind. No matter how paradoxically, it is doubtful whether a depoliticized academy could tolerate active and open debates about the aims of the higher learning as a whole, since these would almost certainly result in disagreements whose implications are inescapably political. Indeed, the whole problem of academic freedom would become so stylized, so touchy, that discussions of it would be permitted only in cases of specific violations, and then only by safe men who have accepted in advance the ground rules established by academic authorities who understand the limitations of a politicized academy.

Suppose, however, that some overly-conscientious professor raised questions about the wisdom or the good faith of his superiors? Would he not also have to be put down in one way or another, thus further compromising the purity of the guardians of the depoliticized academy? What then? Here plainly the road becomes exceedingly slippery. But compromise, as usual, leads to compromise. And one may as well be hung for a sheep as for a lamb. In the real world, as Plato himself foretold, intelligent purists must also be realists, and even the depoliticized academy needs guardians who are willing and able to sustain it. Physicists and mathematicians, as well as poets, must eat and their studies and laboratories must be decently provided for. Hence donors must be solicited, foundations appealed to, legislatures and governors of states placated and cajoled, congressmen begged, and presidents of state exhorted. Thus in practice even the purest institutions of advanced study and higher learning require their front men, who know how to wheedle funds from those who possess or control them: lobbyists, public relations men, and sober-sided presidents like Mr. Pusey, who know how to talk to congressional committees that might otherwise not be able to understand the non-political aspirations of the academies. But this is not all. For academicians, no matter how chaste their intentions, are invariably misunderstood by the hoi polloi that live in the slums that surround the precincts of the academy, and in many cases are owned—in trust of course—by the academies for purposes of future expansion and for the housing of their own less affluent members. Let us face it. The hoi polloi do not understand, nor care to understand, the purposes of the academy; what they see are oppressive landlords, indifferent and condescending professors, students who raise hell on Saturday night. So the academy must either maintain its own praetorian guards, which invariably prove inadequate to the demands made upon them, or else be willing to call upon the armed services of the city or the state in order to protect its privacy and its property against intruders who mean harm to the members of its community. Extraterritorial rights are not honored save at a price. And the price, as we may as well recognize, is a price whose name is politics.

Is this picture overdrawn? Then merely by an inch. Does it also ring a bell? I believe it must. Can the deep inconsistencies which it involves be overcome? Short of utopia, I am sure they cannot. The conclusion is inescapable: The managers of our academic establishments, like their allies in our legislatures and state houses, in the congress, and the White House, who tell us that the proper business of the universities and colleges is not with politics but only with the advancement of neutral learning, are either disingenuous and hence guilty of bad faith or else so self-deceived that they are incompetent and deserve to be removed from office.

These, I realize, are harsh terms; nor do I use them lightly. Let me explain. Such men act in bad faith, or else are self-deceived to the point of madness when they invoke the image of the academy as a haven and repository of pure learning, itself completely at variance with the actual practices of their own institutions, and then condemn, or else—as the English put it—send down obstreperous student activists who give them the lie direct and the countercheck quarrelsome. They act in bad faith, or are self-deluded, when they accept government or foundation money, which commonly has political strings attached, yet pretend that they are free, and are outraged when dissident students and faculty members point this out to them and then, in their own turn, take steps, not always genteel, to see that those strings are cut. They are disingenuous when they represent themselves as agents of law and order, yet never raise deep questions about the justice of that law or order, nor acknowledge that there can be no law or order without government and hence politics.

They are particularly disingenuous, let me add, when they argue, as McGeorge Bundy and others do, that university administrations and governing boards possess merely formal power and that the actual power and authority in the academy resides in the faculty, when they know that our faculties are chock full of careerists who have no interest in its governance so long as they themselves are left alone to do their work according to their own flickering lights. As they very well know, faculties are nearly always self-divided and usually incapable of independent and decisive action to rectify either educational wrongs or administrative malpractices. They also know how clever and determined administrators, with their own informal ties to government, industry and business, can and do manipulate their faculties to secure their own frequently political ends. Finally, these apologists for faculty authority cannot fail to know, especially in this time of troubles, that formal power can always be reconverted into actual power by university presidents and by the governing boards at whose pleasure all presidents enjoy their tenure.

They speak and act in bad faith when they pretend to be votaries of reasonableness, yet reserve for themselves the peremptory authority to determine for students and faculty members alike the standards and limits of reasonableness, and times and places where their critics may foregather to present their reasons for opposing existing academic practices and policies. Above all, they are either appallingly naive or again are guilty of bad faith when they angrily condemn those dissidents who, disillusioned by arguments that get them nowhere, resort to force, yet in the clutch react—and overreact—in kind.

But here I myself may have been a bit disingenuous. For I concede that gentlemen like the presidents of universities such as Columbia and Harvard do not react in kind to students who unceremoniously eject academic deans from their offices, occupy administrative buildings, rifle files, and sip presidential sherry in order to quiet their nerves. For as they well know, the force employed by the students is informal, personal, and usually intramural and poorly organized, whereas the force upon which they themselves rely is extramural, highly skilled, well armed, and sublimely confident in the assurance of its constituted authority. Of course such administrators know full well that when the chips are down, as they have so often been of late, this majesterial power is always incomparably greater than that of their youthful opponents, with their obscenities, sticks and stones, pop bottles, their occasional pistols (for we must be fair), most of them unused, and their bare hands and unshielded bodies.

These last comments may be misleading. Let me then emphasize that it is not part of my own argument to condone acts of gross violence, whether on the part of the university authorities and the governments that offer their moral and military support, or on the part of misguided students—black as well as white—that jeopardize the very existence of *liberal* learning (and mind you, I emphasize the word "liberal"). Cowardly arsonists who come in the night to burn books and manuscripts, studies, libraries, are not exponents of freedom, their own included. On the contrary, from the point of view which I defend, the destruction of any constructive and liberating work of the human mind is always appalling. But if a burned book or study is something forever to be grieved over, broken heads or backs are far more lamentable, especially when they are the heads and backs of innocents who are always sacrificed when men in groups resort to violence.

But this is not the place to undertake a general discussion of violence and its legitimate (or illegitimate) issues. It is my conviction that in most situations, thoughtful but sparing use by academic administrators of the legal device of injunction is justified in order to protect scholars and students, as well as the legitimate fruits of their labors, against marauding hoards whose only purpose is to terrorize the academy and to destroy the materials and records necessary to its proper work. This conviction commits me, accordingly, to the view that the university as a corporate body is entitled to perform legal and political acts in its own defense. By the same token, however, I am obliged to consider whether the university, as such, may also be entitled to take other political positions when its own integrity is threatened.

As it happens, Professor Hook and I found ourselves in at least partial agreement some years ago when a number of distinguished colleagues proposed, at a business meeting of the American Philosophical Association, that the association, as a corporate body, condemn the government's policies in Vietnam. And I, for my part, contended that a purely professional organization, concerned exclusively with its own professional business and ends, was not entitled to take political stands not closely germane to that business and those ends. This, so I argued, in no way denied the right of members of our association, speaking not only as private persons but also, if they wished, as individual members of the group, to condemn the Vietnam War (which I myself have always heartily opposed). And I agreed to sign any sensible memorandum or petition deploring the war, not only in my own person but also as a member of the association. (I should add in passing that the American Philosophical Association, if one could judge by its annual programs, seems to me to have long since given up any common concern with the pursuit of wisdom and has become as narrowly specialized and professionalized as, say, the American Association of Morticians.)

The fact is that I am less certain now than I was then of this position. For I now see that even a fairly narrow professional association, dedicated to a small part of the advancement of learning, may find its own work undermined, or even rendered impossible, by policies and actions of the state. However, I shall waive this question here. For the sake of argument, I am prepared to reaffirm the position I took in 1967 regarding the provenance of the American Philosophical Association, viewed simply as a professional society. And I do so because I want to free myself for independent scrutiny of the situation of the university in matters of this sort.

Now, most academicians, including not only students and professors but also administrators, generally agree that the university is not and cannot be understood as a mere galaxy of professional associations. To be sure, its task includes the advancement of learning, by research and teaching, in a wide variety of subjects. And this task has its important professional side, which includes the granting of degrees to student apprentices that will qualify them for more advanced work in particular fields, as well as the creation and maintenance of conditions necessary to the researches of established professional scholars. But the university is much more than an institute for the training of pre-professionals and the support of professional scholars. It is also the great unifying institution of higher learning whose difficult task, above all, includes the education of free men. Because of this, the educational heart of the university is, or should be, its college, not its professional graduate schools.

Thus, unlike the professional society, the university has educational responsibilities which cannot be defined in purely professional terms. As we know, professional societies can sometimes function tolerably well under governments which are repressive and warlike. The university, however, by its nature is threatened by any social or political policy which diminishes the freedom of ordinary citizens. More positively, because the university bears such a heavy responsibility for the full intellectual, moral, and human development of all its members, professors as well as students, it has a corporate obligation to protest, and in some circumstances even to defy or obstruct, social practices or political policies which undermine or constrict its comprehensive educational purposes.

Given the organizational principles which at present obtain in the American university, I for one am loathe to support, without qualification, any and all corporate decisions affecting the relations of the academy to the national society or its government, which the university's existing governing boards and administrative officers may come to. Many such boards and officers lack a clear notion of the extensive freedom necessary to the university. But the faculties and student bodies of the university whose primary concerns are educational, in the wide sense I have here in mind, do seem to me to have the right, after full and open debate, to speak and act against certain social and governmental policies and practices as corporate bodies. Thus, I should argue, the faculties of universities in the South have the right, and perhaps the obligation, to adopt corporate principles and to express corporate attitudes which are at variance with the segregationalist and racist policies of existing state governments. I should also argue, in the same vein, that faculties, perhaps in concert with students, have the right and at times the obligation to condemn, and on occasion to obstruct, policies and practices of the federal government which are inimical to their own educational purposes.

I am not a formalist. Student bodies and faculties, as well as university presidents and boards of trustees, are liable to error and confusion. Indeed, I can imagine circumstances in which wise administrators may be obliged to make decisions at variance with those adopted by their faculties and students. In every institution, in my judgment, no man or group of men is, or should be, sovereign. Yet this does not, I think, affect the point at issue. Universities, and especially their faculties and students, have rights and responsibilities which entitle or indeed require them to make corporate decisions of a political nature when national or state governments adopt policies which undermine the conditions of liberal learning. Of course such decisions should be thoughtfully made, and even when thoughtfully made they may still be mistaken. And it is the duty of minority groups within the university to point out such errors when they occur. Indeed they themselves may be obliged to obstruct or to defy decisions which, in their view, are academically as well as politically unwise. But these qualifications do not impugn the principle: the university, and especially its faculty and students, have the right to take corporate political action when such action is necessary in order to protect the wide and deep aims of higher education.

In bringing this part of my paper to a close, let me emphasize that every institution, if only in its own defense, is involved in politics. The church-state problem, for example, necessarily involved the churches in corporate political action. The same holds, as Leslie Fielder has discovered, even of the family. Politics is an inescapable dimension of every form of institutional activity. And those who refuse to involve themselves in it must, if they are responsible, foreswear participation in every form of institutional life. To my mind, however, this is platitudinous. The great and ineluctable fact is that no institution, given its ends, is more profoundly involved in problems of politics and government than the university.

Thus, as I have tried to show, the question before us is not whether the university can be depoliticized. Rather it is the question of how and to what ends the university should engage in political activity, and what forms of political activity are proper to it.

To this question my answers must be brief. I shall proceed from those problems which are more topical and hence debatable to those that are more enduring.

To begin with, the university must be free to call in question and, on occasion, oppose any form of service to the nation-state designed primarily to enhance the state's military power. Here I have in mind not only such forms of military instruction as are conducted by the ROTC [Reserve Officer Training Corps], but, far more important, research projects supported by federal grants-in-aid whose basic purpose is to increase our national capacity for nuclear warfare. Beyond this, the university is entirely within its rights if it refuses to countenance forms of research designed to explore means of degrading or maiming human beings or of destroying natural resources upon which they are dependent for life. For the university, as an institution of higher learning dedicated to the religious, moral, and political enlightenment, defeats its own ends and undermines the conditions of its own existence when it, or the members of its faculties, engage in such activities as a matter of course. Moreover, the forms of enlightenment fostered by the university are by their very nature public. Hence the university is entitled to deny, and in my judgment should deny, the use of its facilities to academicians involved in the work of such secret governmental services as the CIA and the FBI. And of course the same applies to similar services to industry or other social institutions or societies. In a word, academicians cannot also be secret agents. Finally, the university must be free to criticize, or on occasion actively oppose, both particular public policies and private practices which create an ambience inimical to its own broad educational purposes. And it must make available the use of its facilities to members of the academic community who are concerned to criticize and to oppose such policies and practices.

At the level of ideology, I should deny no member of the academy the right, in the proper circumstances and under proper auspices, to defend any form of thought, religious, ethical, or political, no matter how heterodox, so long as he does so in a manner which is appropriate to it. It is sometimes argued that the only forms of inquiry which are proper to the university as the primary institution of higher learning are those that aim at scientific truth. In another way, it is argued that the only studies which a university should support, or tolerate, are those which are "neutral" or "value free." As I have already suggested, such a principle is educationally pernicious, since, among other things, it precludes the possibility of philosophical investigations whose task is to provide critiques of all forms of putative knowledge. Without begging basic philosophical questions, it simply cannot be assumed that the scientific method is the one and only method of achieving human understanding. A philosopher, not to mention a theologian, a moralist, a literary critic, or an artist, must be free not merely to consider what forms of study are property to his activity, but also to employ the methods and procedures which upon reflection he deems appropriate. If he is mistaken, then it is the business of his colleagues and students to expose his errors.

What concerns me here, above all, are these pervasive but frequently unformulated philosophies, or ideologies of higher learning, that regard liberal education, which is concerned with the development and enlargement of the whole life of the mind, to be a dispensable or peripheral luxury. On another level, such philosophies are deeply suspicious, or even fearful, of liberal education precisely because it is not and cannot be neutral in the scientific sense. From the latter point of view, liberal education, owing to its active concern not merely with scientific study but also with the appraisal and advocacy of religious, ethical, and political attitudes and institutions, automatically involves the teacher and his students in controversial issues which can and do create an atmosphere of dissension which is inimical to that basic congeniality of mind which a community of scholars seems to require.

In reply I must take the bit in my teeth: liberal education does indeed lead to controversy, and undoubtedly its exponents and participants are given forms of dissension that frequently go very deep. The liberal mind is inherently non-conformist, and nonconformity usually has a political aspect. In my view, however, controversy, dissension, and nonconformity are indispensable to intellectual and hence educational development. Accordingly, the price in terms of conflict, both within the faculty and the student body, simply has to be paid. And if this reduces the sense of community among the members of the university, we must make the best of it. The business of higher education is not to make those engaged in it comfortable with one another, but to advance all the basic forms of human understanding.

In short, I do not deplore conflict on the university campus, I applaud it. Nor in saying this do I commit myself to an uncritical or flaccid acquiescence in all the forms of turmoil which now beset our universities. Physical violence on the campus is nearly always to be deplored. And the same holds not only for student "revolutionaries" but also for administrative "reactionaries."

Let me close by making some positive proposals which, if adopted, would greatly reduce the wrong sort of tension which has now become endemic to the contemporary American university. A great part of this tension, which reflects analogous tensions within the wider society, is owing to the obsolete organization of the academy. I do not deplore academic leadership, and certainly such leadership must come, in some part, from the university administration. But this requires that university administrators and, behind them, the governing boards, be educators and not merely arbiters and fund raisers. And they cannot be, or remain, educators unless they also study, teach, and go to school. To this end, I propose a principle of rotation that will close the profound intellectual, moral, and political gaps that presently divide the various academic classes. Administrators must be given, or obliged to take, leave from time to time so that they may renew, in a more concrete and intimate way, their understanding of the work, the attitudes, and the problems of their faculties and students. They must be obliged in a more-than-ceremonial way to participate in the life and work of both faculties and students. Administration, in short, must no longer be treated as a full-time job, and, again, if we all will have to pay a certain price for the change, then so be it. Faculty members must be enabled to participate fully in the governance of the university. Thus, faculty members should be elected by the governing boards in whose hands, as we have learned, to our sorrow, great actual as well as formal power still resides. In some degree the same holds with respect to students. For example, able and enlightened students must not only be permitted but encouraged to participate in the instruction of their classmates and in the formation and revision of departmental curricula. And, in sum, through these and other entirely practicable changes, actions can and must be taken to convert what is now merely an institution into a truer community of self-respecting and mutually understanding scholars.

Beyond this, valuable forms of educational and political activity that are now conducted exclusively within the shadow university should be encouraged to come out of the shadow and to be recognized, not as extracurricular alternatives to football or Saturday night parties, but as relevant educational activities designed for the improvement of the understanding of all members of the university community. Specifically, dissident and radical groups, whose aim is the reconstruction of the whole society, must not merely be tolerated with a grimace, but invited to meet in the light of day with those who disagree with them so that meaningful and continuous dialogues may be established concerning the problems and jobs of work to be done in our confused and faltering social system.

Nor is this all. More enlightened head-start, upward- and outward-bound programs should be established in order to bring into, and so to enrich, the intellectual life of the academic community, many more gifted but disadvantaged students whose deprivation, real as well as imagined, are owing to poverty, inadequate secondary school education, and racial prejudice. These students must be provided with ample scholarships that may enable them to live and to study on equal terms with their classmates. Further, the colleges and universities must be prepared to invite to the campus, whether on a full or part-time basis, knowledgeable and enlightened laymen who have so much to tell us about the possibilities, educational and otherwise, of reform and reconstruction throughout the national society. And sustained programs of adult education need to be established which are no longer marginal and conducted by disadvantaged professors in need of another honest buck.

But all these, of course, are no more than approach shots. What is necessary, above all, is a massive return to the ideals and practices of liberal education itself, properly updated for contemporary men and women who have something more to do in the world than acquire forms of professional and vocational training that may enable them to move upward in the social and economic hierarchy. These ideals and practices must also be reintroduced into the graduate and professional schools. We need and must have forms of liberal education that are relevant to the lives of human beings in an age of unprecedented social and cultural crisis, in an age in which there are problems of life which human beings have never had to face before: the massive consolidation of power in the hands of elites responsible in practice to no one but themselves, the contests for ideological and political control by great states, all of them, including our own, increasingly repressive and totalistic, and, most important of all, the uncontrolled employment of weapons of destruction that, in an instant, can convert this planet into a [scene] of lunar desolation where the life and work of civilized human beings is completely blotted out.

This is the great and difficult work that lies before us. In an era in which as never before the academy is the state's most important institutional auxiliary, we must again make sure that what we call higher education is an education, not for technicians and specialists only, but for autonomous men, enlightened and unafraid. Ours is the responsibility to make certain that the advancement of learning includes the improvement of our understanding of what it means to be a man and a human being. And this task, once again, imposes responsibilities whose meanings are through and through political.

From the Platitudinous to the Absurd
(A Response to H. D. Aiken)
Sidney Hook

Henry Aiken's gush of impassioned rhetoric has carried him from a position that he himself suspects is "platitudinous"—the word is his—to one that will strike others as positively mischievous in its absurdity. How is this remarkable feat achieved? Very simply. First he disregards the specific historical context in which certain campus groups, both students and faculty, are explicitly calling for the politicalization of the university, demanding that the university as a corporate entity become an agency of political, even revolutionary, political change. He then proposes an arbitrary conception of the term "political" so broad that it has no intelligible opposite in human affairs, according to which "to be is to be political"—so that by definition, the university, the church, even the family and kindergarten are political institutions. Thereupon he gradually slides or slips into a more specific, conventional conception of political behavior that in effect would make the political functions and concerns of the university almost coextensive with that of a political party. There is a complete and irresponsible disregard of the overwhelmingly likely consequences of such a program, viz., opening the floodgates to a political reaction that would destroy existing academic freedoms and the relative autonomy of the university which have been so precariously won in the last sixty-odd years against earlier conceptions and practices of politicalization.

On top of all this, he scandalously misstates the position of those whom he is ostensibly criticizing, including President Abrams. He stuffs figures with straw, burns them with gusto, and, sheltered by the resulting thick smoke, charges that those who oppose politicalization *of* the university therefore are, or must be, opposed even to the study of politics *by* or *in* the university, and that they cannot consistently defend the principles of academic freedom when such defense has political implications. This semantic obscurantism makes it easier to blur the distinction between the study of politics and commitment to political action.

Let me illustrate Aiken's method by a reference to some episodes of

From *Convictions* (Buffalo: Prometheus Books, 1990).

American higher education of whose history, to put it most charitably, he is egregiously innocent, for he seems to believe that there was what he calls a golden age of freedom in the American college. (I assure you that those he thinks he is criticizing believe no such thing.) There was a time when American colleges were completely denominational—so much so that no one who was critical of Christianity could teach in them. As Professor Gildersleeve once put it: "The teachers were either clergyman or men who, having failed to make good in foreign missions, were permitted to try their hands on the young barbarians at home." In some colleges no one could teach unless he was a Baptist, and in others unless he subscribed to some specific dogmas and techniques of Baptism. When the proposal was made to de-religionize or secularize the colleges, everyone understood what this meant. It didn't mean that religion wouldn't be studied but only that the college as a corporate institution would take no religious position, that instruction would not be geared to any Christian dogma, that faculty and students would be free to believe or not to believe, and that if they were Baptists the college would not be concerned whether they chose to dip or sprinkle to achieve salvation.

What would we say to some spiritual forbear of Henry Aiken who objected to the proposal that colleges as institutions be neutral in religion, and addressed us in the following words: "It is absurd to demand that the colleges not take a religious position. For our real choice is between one religion and another. The very refusal to take a religious position is itself a religious position. Even those who urge the colleges to reorganize their curriculums to permit students to seek the truth for themselves about religion or anything else—are they not making a religion of the truth?"

What, I ask, would we say to this kind of retort, that parallels Aiken's view that the refusal of a university to take a political position is itself a brand of politics? I think we would say with Charles Peirce that there is such a thing as the ethics of words in given contexts, and that Aiken has manifestly violated it. We would say that he has missed the whole point of the controversy, which is whether it is appropriate for the college to make a *specific* religious or political commitment when its members differ widely in their religious and political views.

The illogic of the retort obfuscates political thinking, too. I believe, for example, that we should tolerate in the political marketplace the expression of any ideas. Consequently, I must also believe that we cannot suffer those who are actively intolerant of the expression of ideas, who prevent those of whom they disapprove from speaking by force. Along comes someone inspired by Henry Aiken's logic who charges me with intolerance, too. "You, too, are intolerant," he says, "just as much as the intolerant Nazi Storm Troopers and Red Guards who break up the classes of their professors. Everyone is intolerant—only about different things. In claiming to be tolerant *you* are guilty of bad faith! For if you were *truly* tolerant, you would tolerate intolerance. Since you are intolerant of intolerance—you are a hypocrite!"

What does it mean when we say that the university should be depoliticalized? Nothing so absurd as Aiken pretends to believe in most of his paper. There are perfectly clear contexts in which we understand and have used the expression without difficulty. I shall give two illustrations, one from this country and one from Germany.

As everyone knows or should know, American higher education has never been free from political controls of the most blatant kind. When I began my academic career, no one who was known as a Socialist and, in many places even as a progressive, could be hired. I could cite instances galore of a political, religious, racial, and social bias that violated the principles of academic freedom. As Council Members of the AAUP [American Association of University Professors] during the thirties, fighting to establish recognition of these principles, we meant by "depoliticalization of the university" that the university was not to penalize faculty members or students for exercising their rights as citizens, that the universities were not to make allegiances to capitalism or to any other social or political ideology a condition for membership in the academic community. These principles of academic freedom—reversing the whole course of educational history—gradually began to win acceptance. For example, in 1935, together with A. J. Muste and some left-wing labor leaders, I organized the American Workers Party with a militant socialist political program. Whereupon the Hearst Press launched a national campaign demanding my dismissal. To everyone's surprise, New York University refused to yield. That was a great step towards the depoliticalization of the university in America—Roger Baldwin thought it was a turning point!—for other institutions rapidly moved in the same direction. There are, of course, still abuses. But how far acceptance of academic freedom has gone is evident in the failure to unseat Professor Eugene Genovese, a public supporter of the Viet Cong, despite a gubernatorial campaign in which his right to teach was the chief issue. Aiken claims that if the American university were depoliticalized, Marcuse couldn't teach, Chomsky couldn't teach, nor could I. On the contrary: the fact that all of us, and even individuals far more extreme politically, teach is evidence of the degree to which depoliticalization has gone. *The American university is far less politicalized today than at any time in the past.*

Here is the second illustration. In the late years of the Weimar Republic, the Nazis attacked the professional integrity of the German universities because of their failure as corporate bodies to condemn the Versailles *Dictat*—the peace treaty which unfairly asserted that Germany was solely responsible for the First World War. This was denounced as a betrayal of *das deutsche Volk* [*the German people*]. It was charged, with a logic and language much like Aiken's, that the refusal to take a political position, to become politically involved, was itself a political act hostile to the German community, German education, and to German youth who were branded as the offspring of war criminals in the eyes of the world. And when Hitler came to power, his minions purged those who had urged the German universities to remain politically neutral. That action was properly called "politicalizing" the university.

Those of us who oppose politicalization contend that teachers should be free to make whatever political choices or commitments they please as citizens, but that the university as a corporate body should not make partisan political commitments. What Aiken contends is that it is partisan to be nonpartisan. (The same silly logic would prove that there are only nouns in the English language because when I say that " 'And' is a conjunction," " 'From' is a preposition," etc. they are really *nouns* because they are subjects of the sentence.)

In short, the "depoliticalization" of the university means the growth, defense, and vitality of academic freedom. The "politicalization" of the university means threats to and erosion of the principles of academic freedom. By academic freedom is meant the freedom of professionally qualified persons to inquire into, to discover, to publish, and to teach the "truth" as they see it—or reach "conclusions" in fields where the term 'truth' may be inapplicable, as in the fine or practical arts—without interference from ecclesiastical, political, or administrative authorities. The only permissible limits on the academic freedom of any teacher would flow from evidence established by qualified bodies of his peers or profession that he was clearly incompetent or had violated the standards of professional ethics. These are the current rules of the AAUP, which now are almost universally accepted.

Today it is a fact ignored by Professor Aiken that these principles of academic freedom are being threatened more by extremist students than by fundamentalist bishops, economic royalist tycoons, and political demagogues. For these students presume to determine who should speak on campus and who shouldn't, break up meetings of those with whom they disagree, disrupt the classrooms of teachers of whom they disapprove, demand the cessation of research *they* regard as not in the public interest, and clamor for the dismissal of teachers whose views they denounce as racist, reactionary or imperialist. On campus after campus, as the *New York Times* editorially declared when Dr. Hayakawa's meetings were shamelessly disrupted, these students acted just like the Nazi Storm Troopers whose hob-nailed boots and clubs broke up the classes of the Socialist and Jewish professors.

A depoliticized university is one in which all sorts of political positions may be studied, defended, and criticized, so long as the ethics of inquiry are not violated. It is one in which the university as a corporate body may take a stand on public political issues that threaten the existence and operation of the principles of academic freedom. It is or should be jealous of its relative educational autonomy of the state even when it receives the support of the state. But this does not make it a political institution any more than a church which protests a measure that would restrict its freedom of religious worship therewith becomes a political institution. As an institution, the function of the university is not to exercise political power but to clarify and test ideas.

This conception of the university, as I shall try to make plain, differs from Aiken's not only in degree but in kind. But before developing these differences I want to say something about his descriptions of American higher education, past and present. He tells us he is no formalist. I don't know what he exactly means by this, but if all he means is that he is indifferent to formal logic, it is apparent enough. I am not a formalist either, but I believe that a little respect for formal logic would not be amiss. It would enable him to distinguish more clearly between a contradictory and contrary, which he obviously confuses.

If Aiken is not a formalist, is he an empiricist taking his point of departure from concrete historical fact? Unfortunately not, because on critical matters he makes up his facts as he goes along. Here are three major examples.

1. He states that the programs of General Education introduced at Columbia and Harvard were "quite simply to awaken the minds of students to the transcendental virtues of our American system and the wickedness of all systems that oppose it." This is sheer invention. I know something about the Columbia system and the men who devised and taught it. Almost to a man they were critics of contemporary society. The program grew out of John Erskine's "great books"

course in the humanities and was broadened to include social studies which were actually basic critiques of the students' assumptions about the American society. For the first time in the history of American education, Marx and Engels's *Communist Manifesto* was required reading. Many of the teachers and students in that program became the architects of the New Deal. For many years it was a genuine liberating educational experience. It received the approval of John Dewey. The major criticisms of it were not that it was political but that it wasn't specialized enough, and this criticism came from the scientists because of the great difficulties encountered in developing General Education courses in science.

2. Or take Aiken's charge that government and foundation grants have "political strings attached" to them. Just a few years ago, when Aiken was still at Harvard, a Report of a Special Faculty Committee appointed to supervise the operation of grants, declared that no political strings were attached to any grant, that no government or foundation financing had subverted research. It is interesting that some research grants to Chomsky and other ardent critics of American foreign policy have come from the Navy and other government institutions with absolutely no political strings attached.

The subject is very complex but three things are clear. No one compels a university or a faculty member to undertake any research of which it or he disapproves. The faculty as an educational body has the right to lay down guidelines governing the use of its facilities, the time of its members, the limits of secrecy, et cetera. No accredited university I know of accepts grants to prove a point of view in advance, or to inculcate opinions or conclusions specified by the donor. Subject to these conditions it is perfectly permissible for a person passionately concerned for the education of free men in a free society to accept research bearing on the defense of the free society, without which academic freedom and the free university cannot survive. To leave the free *society* defenseless and vulnerable to totalitarian aggression is to imperil the survival of the free *university,* too. Defense-related research initiated by Einstein in this country and other scientists in England enabled the Western world to turn back the threat of Hitler, whose victory would have meant the end of all basic freedoms—in the academy and out. Neither Aiken nor I would be talking here tonight if universities had been forbidden to engage in any research "designed to enhance the (democratic) state's military power" during the years when totalitarianism threatened to engulf the Western world.

3. Finally, take Aiken's charge that faculties have no real academic

authority over curriculum or conditions of tenure, that overnight "the formal powers can always be reconverted by university presidents and governing boards into actual power." This is wrong about things that matter most. Aiken is simply ignorant that in most legal jurisdictions in the United States today, the tenure rules adopted by the AAUP and the AAU [the American Association of Universities] have the force of law. President Abrams holds his post at the will of his board but happily for us Professor Aiken cannot be deprived of his tenure either by the will of [the] President or the Board of Brandeis. And if he doesn't believe that this represents real progress and power for the faculty, I recommend that he read Hofstadter and Metger's *The History of Academic Freedom in American Higher Education* or Upton Sinclair's *Brass Check*.

There are many things wrong with American colleges and universities and you will find my criticisms detailed in my book *Education for Modern Man* and *Academic Freedom and Academic Anarchy*. But Aiken's picture or map of academic reality is way off base. He himself says it is overdrawn by an "inch." But on some maps drawn to scale an inch represents a hundred miles or more. Actually his is the wrong map of the wrong country. It tells us more about him than about the university. It proves that he is not a formalist, not a sober empiricist but—what shall we say?—a fantasist! And although hc confesses—in an attempt to disarm criticism—that he may be "a bit disingenuous" he is obviously no judge of size or distance.

Basically, the great and unbridgeable difference between Aiken's position and the view he misrepresents is that, whereas the latter recognizes the right and sometimes the obligation of the university as an *unpolitical corporate body* to take a stand on issues that threaten the integrity of academic freedom, Aiken would convert the university into a political action organization taking corporate decisions on anything which affects "the condition of liberal learning" or "the wide and deep aims of higher education." This takes in the whole range of politics from the income tax, housing programs, interstate commerce, to defense, foreign policy, and disarmament measures.

Listen to this: "The great and ineluctable fact is that no institution, given its ends, is more profoundly involved in problems of politics and government than the university (note: not even our Courts, Congress and Legislatures! S. H.) . . . Ours has become for better or worse a kind of Platonic republic whose crucial institution is the academy."

This gives the whole case away: We are *not* a Platonic republic but a democratic republic whose crucial institutions in political matters are not the academy but a Congress and executive responsible to the electorate. This is the worst form of elitism, and smacks of Marcuse, not of James or Dewey. This university is founded by the democratic community not to engage in politics or influence legislation but to provide opportunities for the free exploration and critical study of all ideas, political and nonpolitical, in the faith that this quest will lead to clearer ideas, more reliable knowledge, and indirectly to more enlightened policy. The university should be the locus of competent and disinterested investigation of human problems, a source and resource for the entire community, dedicated not only to the teaching and testing of known truths and accepted values but to winning new truths, broaching fresh perspectives and values on the open frontiers of human experience. The community does not look to the university as a political action group or political corporate body engaged in a struggle for political power by influencing legislation or laying down Platonic mandates for the masses of ignorant citizens. It looks to it, to be sure, to *study* political ideas, among others. But to study political ideas does not make the university a political institution, to study religious ideas does not make it a religious institution, any more than to study crime makes it a criminal institution.

To politicalize the university in the manner Aiken suggests is to invite educational disaster. First of all, it would lead to the loss of its tax exemption. Legal actions even now are pending against some universities which officially endorsed the Vietnam Mobilization Day by dismissing classes! Secondly, it would turn faculties into warring political factions, each of which would seek allies not only among students but among outside political groups—at the cost of genuine educational activity. Intellectual controversy, of course, is to be welcomed in the universities. But the kind of political controversies generated by concern with all the political issues that are construed by some faculty members as having a bearing on "the wide and deep aims of higher education" is sure to plunge institutions into educational chaos. The results of such politicalization are evident in some South American and Asian universities, and manifest also on some embattled campuses in this country.

Finally—and this is the greatest danger of all—the attempt to politicalize the university along Aiken's lines is sure to inspire a reaction from the larger political community resentful of the political intrusion of a publicly subsidized educational institution. Political majorities, local, state, and national, will themselves move to politicalize the universities to prevent educational resources and opinions from being mobilized against them. There are some evidences of this at hand already. Colleges and universities will be politicalized with a vengeance. The first casualities of this vengeance will be the principles of academic freedom and tenure themselves, won after such bitter battles, and among the victims will be not only the Aikens—who know not what they do when they needlessly rouse by their provocations the sleeping furies of American vigilantism—but those of us who wish to preserve the autonomy of the educational process at its highest levels.

Aiken is blind or reckless about the educational direction of his policy of politicalization. What he proposes is to set back the clock to the days when the cultural Babbits and the economic Bourbons declared that scholarship and teaching must be kept in leading strings to good citizenship—except that his conception of good citizenship differs from theirs.

The view I oppose to his is that the university does not have to choose between one conception of good citizenship or another, that what makes a man a good citizen is no more the affair of the university than what makes him a good husband, that its primary concern is whether he is a good teacher and scholar. Just as I have no right when I take a political stand as a citizen to commit the university, so the university as a corporate body of which I am a member, except on matters of academic freedom, has no right to take a political stand that in the eyes of the public commits me.

CHAPTER 2

Applications of Neutrality

University Neutrality and ROTC
Robert L. Holmes

American universities face an identity crisis. No one is quite sure what they are anymore, much less what they ought to be. Looked at through different lenses, they are overgrown high schools, knowledge factories, corporations, employment agencies, farm clubs for professional football, or servants of the military-industrial complex. Sometimes, last if not least, they are also educational institutions. As such their primary purpose is not to make a profit, win games, improve the government, instill moral rectitude, or even teach. It is, rather, to encourage learning. Teaching is one way to do this, and for that reason teaching has an important role to play in the university. But learning can be fostered by research, discussion, independent study, and through countless other activities which do not, or need not, take place in the classroom. And these have a place in the university as well.

The problem of identity reflects the pluralistic character of American universities. Influenced in their fledgling years by both the European tradition of scholarship for its own sake and the American spirit of everything for the sake of utility, they sought to combine scholarly studies with practical training.[1] This was especially true of the land-grant colleges which sprang up largely in the rural areas, and whose purpose was to provide education for the working classes. The people they served, however, were accustomed to a life of toil and sweat; for them the "learning, poetry, and piety" promised to the community by President Eliot of Harvard at his inauguration was hardly enough.

From *Ethics* 83, no. 3 (1973): 177–195.

They had cattle to feed, crops to plant, machinery to repair; they wanted training geared to their way of life. Responding to this early demand for "relevance," the universities gave birth to a tradition of service to society, service which was at once more practical than skill in Greek or Latin and more immediate than the rewards of philosophy.

Long regarded as one of the strengths of the American university, this dual emphasis upon education and service today is at the root of its most critical problems. For it is an open question in a society wracked by controversial foreign and domestic problems whether a university can both serve outside interests and at the same time be neutral on the issues in which so many of those interests are implicated, and even more of an open question whether it can fulfill its primary educational purposes *unless* it is neutral.

I

There are two questions here. The primary one is whether universities *ought* to be neutral. There is a growing conviction among many students and faculty that the problems that confront us today are so serious that it is irresponsible if not downright immoral, to fail to bring the full weight of the university's power and prestige down on the side of peace and social justice (and note that it is the neutrality of the university as an institution that we are discussing, not the propriety of individual members of the university community taking stands on issues, either as citizens or, say, in their capacity as students or faculty). This question, however, is ambiguous. It may be asked whether the university ought morally to be neutral, or whether it ought to be neutral from an educational standpoint or, if you like, from the educational point of view. In the latter case the relevant criteria would be whether or not neutrality is required for the promotion of the university's primary educational aims. The moral question is ultimately the decisive one, but we can limit ourselves to the educational question if we make the assumption that only morally defensible policies will be educationally sound in the long run. For then one can assume that in making a sound educational decision he will have covered (though not necessarily expressly considered) the relevant moral issues.[2]

The second question concerns what constitutes institutional neutrality. This needs clarification before the first question can be answered. The fervor with which neutrality has been both attacked and defended is often matched only by a lack of clarity about what it is.[3] During campus crises, administrators often spoke as if the universities were now neutral and that to accede to the demands of protestors would be to compromise that neutrality. They assumed both that the status quo was neutral and that neutrality is desirable. Protestors, on the other hand, charged that the problem was precisely that the universities are *not* neutral and are serving immoral causes. Their view was that neutrality is undesirable and should yield to the service of good causes.[4] With both sides thus starting from different conceptions of what constitutes neutrality, as well as from different premises about what the university should be and different perceptions of its current status, the stage was set for the typical confrontation.

Without intending any political connotations, I shall call the above views, respectively, the conservative and liberal views. Complicating the debate is a third position, which may be called the necessitarian view, which says that the university *cannot* by the nature of the case be neutral; that whatever it does, say, with regard to issues like ROTC, inevitably constitutes "political acts," and hence that all that is open to us is to get on with the business of deciding in which ways the university is going to be nonneutral.[5]

The problem in general, of course, is to define the university's proper role in society at large. More specifically, it is to determine the university's proper position with regard to social, political, and moral controversies. This undertaking must be a major part of the former enterprise. It requires distinguishing the question of whether the university should take a stand on such issues from the question of what the correct stand is *on* those issues. For sometimes whether to take a stand on a set of moral issues is itself a moral question and has to be assessed in the light of the consequences of action or inaction in the same way as the issues over which it initially arises. This makes the question of neutrality the prior question, inasmuch as whatever a university does with regard to these other controversies presupposes an answer to it.

II

Let us therefore begin by considering first how a plausible principle of university neutrality might be formulated. We may start by noting that neutrality can be assessed in light of both what a university says and what it does. Let us call these, respectively, official and de facto neutrality. The former is determined by the official pronouncements of the vested authorities of the university and can be expressed by a principle like the following:

1. A university ought not to take official stands on controversial social, political, and moral issues.[6]

Most universities are neutral by this criterion. They only rarely commit themselves officially and explicitly in this manner. But as important as principle 1 is to an overall conception of neutrality, it is obviously too weak a principle if taken by itself, for it places no limits whatever on what a university does and what causes it supports as long as it carefully refrains from officially confirming what it is doing. It would, for example, allow a university to sponsor a program, say, to train Republican county chairmen (a program, let us suppose, financed, staffed, and controlled by the Republican party and—to make the analogy even more obvious—after graduation from which students were under contract to spend so many years in the service of Republicanism) and yet to claim neutrality on the grounds that it took no official stand on Republican policies. In the absence of similar services to other political parties, such a claim would be hardly credible. Taking an official stand suffices to violate neutrality, but refraining from taking such a stand in no way ensures neutrality.

This means that what is needed in addition to 1 is a principle to take account of a university's policies as well as its pronouncements, its implicit as well as its explicit commitments. It is tempting, in light of this, to think in terms of a principle like:

2. A university should do nothing which supports one side or the other on controversial social, political, and moral issues.

But this would be too strong a principle. It is one which a university could not help but violate in the normal course of performing its educational functions. If a university educates one student who joins the marines and another who joins the draft resistance, it contributes indirectly to the respective causes they serve. And there is no way to ensure that it will not contribute more to one cause than to another in the process. But educating students could not for that reason plausibly be called a political act.

Principles like 1 and 2 have often been tacitly appealed to in campus disputes. When administrators represent the university as neutral when it sponsors recruiting by the military, the CIA, or Dow Chemical, or trains officers for the armed services, they frequently do so simply on the grounds that the university (meaning, in this context, themselves as its official spokesmen) has taken no official position on the policies of any of these agencies. When students, on the other hand, have charged the university with complicity in immoral acts, they have often done so on the grounds that it was in fact supporting the efforts and activities of these agencies. Even granting the correctness of the factual elements in their respective claims, it is evident that the two were at cross-purposes right from the start, each opting for the conception of neutrality which most supported their more general positions.

What is needed is a principle that is stronger than 1 but not as prohibitively strong as 2. The following, for example, would meet that condition:

3. A university ought not to adopt policies whose intention is to favor one side or the other on controversial social, political, and moral issues.

Like 1, 3 captures a necessary feature of any full-blown conception of neutrality. But also like 1, it is insufficient. The drunken driver may have had no intention of killing the pedestrian, but he is culpable nonetheless as long as he knows (or is accountable for knowing) the likely consequences of drunken driving; the point being that we are accountable in our actions for more than just what we intend, a fact which should be reflected in an account of neutrality. This suggests a principle which embraces 3 but goes beyond it:

4. A university ought not to adopt policies whose expectable consequences favor one side or the other on controversial social, political, and moral issues.

According to 4, a decision or policy would fail to be neutral if it in fact had foreseeable consequences of this sort, even if it were no part of the intention of the formulators of the policy that it do so.

But even this has a shortcoming. For it might be argued that the pursuit of a university's proper educational goals might sometimes have consequences of the sort described, and yet that in such cases we should be reluctant to characterize them as neutrality violating, particularly on the assumption noted earlier that sound educational policies will not in the long run contribute to unsound or immoral social or political causes. One might even argue that an official university stand on certain issues like free speech would be consistent with neutrality, the grounds being that free speech is an essential and integral part of the educational process without which the aims of education simply cannot be effectively pursued. To take account of this qualification to 4, let us propose:

5. A university ought not to adopt educationally nonessential policies whose expectable consequences favor one side or the other on controversial social, political, and moral issues.

This draws together the preceding considerations and yields a principle of de facto neutrality. Principles 1 through 5 represent varying degrees of neutrality. Principle 1 is the weakest, 2 the strongest, and the others fall between the two.

The preceding line of reasoning is not unattended with difficulties, however. Two objections in particular might be advanced against the qualification just introduced into 5 (as well as against the grounds for rejecting 2): first, that it arbitrarily rules out possible cases in which a university cannot help but violate neutrality, and hence begs the question against the necessitarian; and second, that because the survival of the nation is no less a necessary condition of the pursuit of educational goals than is, say, free speech, it makes virtually every major issue of foreign policy and national defense the proper business of the university, a state of affairs which if alleged to be consistent with neutrality reduces that notion to absurdity.[7]

On the first point, since much of the campus debate we have been trying to clarify has centered around whether the university *ought* to be neutral, we have indeed been guided partly by the desire to frame a plausible principle according to which a university *can* be neutral. But this need not be question begging against the necessitarian. His position, as we have stated it, implies that there is no meaningful sense in which a university can be neutral. And that view is clearly false with regard to official neutrality and probably false with regard to de facto neutrality. There are many issues on which a university can be neutral: it can refrain from supporting candidates for city council, mayor, the U.S. Senate, or the presidency, or from passing judgment on welfare reform, local dog-leash laws, coastal fishing rights, or abortion legislation. At most there are only certain respects in which a university cannot be neutral.[8] This means that even if the necessitarian view be conceded, a whole host of normative issues regarding whether or not the university should take certain stands will remain to be dealt with, and how they are dealt with will make an important difference to the overall character of the university. It is just that, contrary to the necessitarian position, it seems plausible to view these as involving neutrality.

But should even that much be conceded? Is it clear, that is, that there are *any* respects in which it is impossible that a university should be neutral? Without attempting to deal with this question at length, let me suggest only that arguments to this effect risk placing a greater burden on the concept of neutrality than it can bear. When any social consequences of education are taken to count against neutrality, or when a commitment to any values whatsoever—even if they are ones like learning, truth, or knowledge—is taken to be incompatible with neutrality, then surely we should have to agree that no university can or should be neutral. Neutrality has been ruled out by definition of the university and its purposes.[9] But is there any good reason to define neutrality in such a way? Not, I think, if we are to take our point of departure from the sorts of issues which have in fact most often given rise to the question of neutrality. For those issues have not arisen over the consequences of education and learning, but over the pursuit of educationally nonessential ends. And with regard to such issues, it is not at all apparent why a university cannot be neutral. A university does not *have* to sponsor recruiting by the marines, the CIA, or business-industrial firms; it does not *have* to do classified research for the Department of Defense; it does not *have* to train officers for the military. Nothing in the nature of the values of learning or the purposes of higher education requires it to do any of these things.[10] . . .

But even if neutrality were understood . . . so as to render the university practically or even logically incapable of attaining it, nothing whatsoever would follow with respect to the remainder of the necessitarian's argument. For that argument as often expressed says essentially that *because* universities cannot be neutral, they should take stands on a variety of other issues (being those of most concern to the persons advancing the argument). But if the premise of this argument means only that a university cannot by the nature of the case help but have a concern with education and its distinctive values and that education has social consequences, nothing follows regarding what the university should do with respect to noneducational matters. If it means more than this, and means that a university cannot help but address itself to noneducational issues,[11] then this claim in all probability is false and in any event has to be supported. And if it could be established, it still would not settle the question of what to do regarding the many respects in which a university can be neutral. So whether we characterize neutrality in such a way that universities cannot be neutral, and then ask independently what we should do about the many issues whose solution is not dictated by that observation, or characterize it as we have here in such a way that they can be neutral and then ask whether they should be, is ultimately of little consequence. Precisely the same normative questions remain to be answered either way. But as I have indicated, the latter focuses more clearly the issues which in fact have generated the problem, and for that reason seems a less misleading way of framing these questions.

The second objection to principle 5 is in many ways a more important one and deserves more attention than I can give it here. Let me simply indicate the general direction in which I think an appropriate reply to it can be framed. It involves distinguishing between conditions which are necessary to the very existence of a university and those which, additionally, are inextricably bound up in the educational process itself. To say that the pursuit of educational goals warrants taking a stand on all issues relating to the former conditions would indeed so attenuate the notion of neutrality as to deprive it of any real meaning. To say, however, that it warrants taking a stand on the latter issues (assuming for the moment that we are talking about official neutrality) would not similarly dilute it. For there clearly are certain values, particularly in the form of rights and freedoms pertaining to teaching, research, publication, and so forth, which are closer to the heart of the whole educational enterprise than others, even if some of the others are no less necessary in the last analysis to the existence of the university. The promotion and maintenance of these values is one of the specific functions of the university. There are many other issues of a political and foreign-policy nature which have nothing to do with education, even though they may have a bearing upon the circumstances under which education takes place, or even upon whether it continues to take place in any particular context. Their resolution—calling as it does for concrete action of various sorts—is the proper business of society at large, as is the promotion and maintenance of many other values like peace, economic prosperity, and political freedom. All of these are proper subjects for research, study, and debate within the university, and the university at its best should exemplify certain of them; but it is not the university's job qua university actively to promote them in society or the world at large.[12]

While the preceding are not the only objections to this line of analysis, they are among the more important ones. But neither of them, if I am correct, is decisive, and I would therefore propose as a principle of institutional neutrality the combination of 1 and 5:

6. A university should neither take official stands nor adopt educationally nonessential policies supporting one side or the other on controversial social, political, or moral issues.

While there is room for refinement of such notions as what is educationally essential, or what constitutes a "controversial" issue,[13] there do not seem to be any insurmountable problems here, and I submit that 6 embodies the essence of any plausible conception of institutional neutrality. . . .

III

Should neutrality so conceived be aimed at? I believe that it should and must, not because neutrality is itself an academic value like learning, truth, or academic freedom, but because it is necessary to maintaining the conditions under which these other values can flourish. For they can flourish only in an atmosphere of mutual confidence that they are prized to such a degree that no person or group will seek to transform the institution which sustains and nourishes them, and whose sole rationale is to do just that, into a vehicle for the promotion of other causes. Such confidence cannot exist if the time and energy of students, faculty, and administrators alike are consumed in an incessant struggle to prevail in the determination of the university's position with regard to the many non-academic causes which may compete for its allegiance. Nor is there any way to create the mechanisms for supervising such a contest and adjudicating the differences it will bring to a head in a fair and equitable way and on a continuing basis without virtually transforming the university into a political institution. To try to have it both ways, as some universities have done, and to implicate the university deeply in controversial noneducational issues while at the same time withholding the full range of democratic rights and guarantees in the decision making that determines the nature of that involvement, is to court disaster. Our country from its inception has expressly taught people to demand and if necessary to fight for just such rights in their political institutions.[14]

This means that if one takes neutrality seriously, he must be prepared to deny the relevance of some of his most fervently held convictions to the determination of institutional policy, and be prepared to see the character of the university shaped as nearly as possible by academic considerations alone. It also means that departures from the university's central educational goals in the interests of "public service" should be made if at all only when it is clear that they will not jeopardize neutrality.

All of this presupposes, of course, that the universities are worth preserving. There may be a point in the deterioration of a society, whether owing to domestic or to international causes, beyond which the objectives of an institution of higher learning are no longer attainable or even desirable. At that point the principle of neutrality for which I am arguing is no longer binding.[15] For then, among other things, the assumption of the coincidence of the moral and educational points of view will no longer hold. I would argue that this is true in some Latin American countries and that it was true in Nazi Germany. It is for this reason that I am not persuaded by those arguments against neutrality which point to the case of Hitler's Germany and maintain that it is indefensible for universities to remain neutral in those contexts. One can only agree with the latter part of this claim, but not because nonneutrality is a sound and defensible position for an institution with an ongoing commitment to learning to take but, rather, because some situations are so bad, and some evils so great, that it is manifestly immoral for anyone to continue to occupy himself with teaching, study, and research, that is, to maintain that commitment at the expense of a wholehearted commitment to oppose that evil. To argue as though it were desirable to continue the so-called life of the mind in such situations, but just to do so in a way which at the same time leads the fight against the world's evils, seems to me wrongheaded. At times like that, universities should close down, or transform themselves into something other than educational institutions. What one cannot defensibly do, in my judgment, is to hold that universities should both continue to function as institutions of higher learning and at the same time serve political causes. In short, if there are to be institutions of higher learning, they should strive to be neutral; but sometimes the maintenance of such institutions is neither possible nor desirable.

IV

While virtually all of the problems arising from the relationship between the military and the universities raise in one way or another the question of neutrality, ROTC brings the issue into sharper relief than do most of the others.

ROTC has its roots in the Morrill (or Land Grant) Act of 1862, according to which the purpose of the land-grant colleges is to teach agricultural and mechanical arts "without excluding other scientific and classical studies, and including military tactics." While it was unclear for many years precisely how this latter provision was to be interpreted, it has come to be expected that such schools will provide military training as part of their programs. Since the National Defense Act of 1916 establishing the Army Reserve Officer Training Corps (with Navy and Air Force programs appearing in 1926 and 1946, respectively), ROTC has been the vehicle by which this provision has been met. Its various programs, revised and expanded, and ranging far beyond the original land-grant schools, are currently administered under the ROTC Vitalization Act of 1964. Like other ties with the military—most of which developed during and after World War II— ROTC was largely taken for granted until the United States became deeply involved in Vietnam. After that time it came under heavy fire, and was forced out of many of the country's leading universities.

Since universities do not as a rule officially endorse military policies, the question of neutrality with regard to ROTC hinges upon the issue of de facto neutrality, specifically upon whether ROTC is educationally essential and represents de facto institutional support of an agency deeply committed on controversial social, political, and moral issues.

The answer on both counts seems clear. To provide on-campus military training is not, and has probably never been claimed to be even by advocates of ROTC, a central part of the educational function of a university. The chief arguments for ROTC have been its benefit to the armed services, its contribution to national security, and its sup- posed moderating influence upon the military.[16] There is rarely any claim of benefit to the university or attempt to justify the training of officers for the military (as distinct from justifying credit for individual courses) on academic grounds. That ROTC benefits the military, moreover, no one disputes . . . and that the military is deeply embroiled in controversial social, political, and moral issues is incontrovertible.

If so, then for a university to contract to supply the military with officers is to compromise its neutrality, not because it entails *saying* that the university approves of this or that policy of the military, or even because it necessarily signifies an intention on the part of decision makers to do so. Rather, it compromises neutrality because it *in fact* places the university in the service of a powerful outside agency which perhaps more than any other is at the center of the major moral, political, and ideological issues of the day. If, further, our reasoning about the importance of neutrality is correct, then ROTC should be discontinued.

V

Such a conception of the university may strike some as too high-minded. Universities train nurses, field football teams, and sponsor glee clubs, as well as host rock concerts, beer blasts, and political rallies—none of which is clearly any more central to the main purposes of a university than ROTC, and some of which have no conceivable justification on academic grounds. Should a university discontinue all of these as well, it might be asked, and if not, why ROTC?

The answer is twofold. First of all, remember that neutrality as it concerns us here is a property of the university as an institution, and governs only programs, policies, contracts, and so forth, representing an institutional commitment. This excludes from its scope the multitude of other events and activities like beer blasts and political rallies which merely occur within the university, usually on the initiative of individual students or student organizations, and are not in any real sense sponsored by the university as an institution. It is not only in keeping with, but indeed required by, the purposes of an open university that it allow as much freedom in these areas as is compatible with the preservation of academic values.

But second, there is a clear distinction between ROTC and even such institutionally sponsored programs and activities as nursing, football, and glee clubs. For in none of these other cases is the university party to a contractual arrangement whereby a student even before entering college makes a ten-year commitment to an outside agency;[17] becomes subject to immediate call to active duty if adjudged to have "willfully evaded" the terms of his contract; becomes subject to immediate separation from the program, with termination of financial support, any time it is deemed in the interest of the agency in question. . . . And in none of these other cases is the curriculum controlled (by law) in whole or in part by a noneducational outside agency which staffs a university department with its own paid representatives whose primary allegiance is to it (the university being only able to accept or reject nominees it puts forward) and in which federal law requires that the university appoint the agency's chief representative as chairman of a department at the rank of full professor.[18] If and when nursing, football, and glee clubs mark such a violation of the spirit of an open and autonomous community, or become as deeply committed on one side of the major issues of the day as the military, then by all means let us ask seriously whether they should continue to enjoy university sanction. But at present there is no significant analogy between them and ROTC other than that they all have their primary justification at least partly on nonacademic grounds.

A more difficult objection is that termination of ROTC would represent a de facto taking of sides with antiwar forces. This is the sort of objection advanced by those who hold the necessitarian view. Certainly a university *could* drop ROTC as a means of antiwar protest. But equally clearly, it need not do so and can take obvious steps to guard against being interpreted as doing so (such as by announcing that it is acting in the interests of neutrality). It is true that once an institution adopts a program which compromises neutrality, then to discontinue the program will gladden the hearts of those who oppose it. It is this which gives superficial plausibility to defenses of the status quo by appeal to neutrality and to the argument that a university cannot be neutral. But one must distinguish between dropping ROTC in order to take an antiwar stand and doing so in the interests of neutrality, since one and the same action could be taken on either ground. In the former case it would violate neutrality, in the latter not. When the foreseeable actual or symbolic benefit to one side in a controversy derives from an action necessary to undo an arrangement which compromises neutrality, such benefit cannot plausibly be said to be violative of neutrality. Otherwise, to side with those who favor neutrality would itself be to violate neutrality, which would mean that a principle of neutrality could never be implemented so long as there were some who favored it. And this would render the principle useless. Thus, if my analysis is correct, the objection that to discontinue ROTC would necessarily be to ally the university with antiwar forces cannot be sustained.

None of this is to deny that modern universities inevitably have complex ties with society. Nor is it to deny that it would be impossible and perhaps even destructive of the university to try to break all of these ties even if it were desirable to do so. These are the unchallengeable premises in the liberal position. But insofar as a principle of neutrality prescribes what a university *ought* to do, it applies only to what it *can* do. And while a university neither can nor should dissociate itself completely from society at large, there are some things it can readily do (like terminating certain contracts) and others toward which it can work in the long run (like altering investment policies when this is dictated in the interests of neutrality).[19] There are as well, as we have seen, many things violative of neutrality which it can refrain from doing.

. . . When faculty do address the broader issues, they often argue not so much from the benefit to the armed forces as from ROTC's supposed "moderating influence" upon the military: ensuring civilian control and a continuous infusion of civilian values into the military establishment.[20]

This is a seductive argument. Critics of the military rally to it as readily as supporters. It calls up images of a vigilant citizenry watching over a potentially dangerous military establishment (a necessary evil as long as there are threats to freedom in the world) and of the university as custodian of that citizenry's highest ideals, guaranteeing, as it were, that young men will emerge humane and responsible warriors, responsive to civilian leadership, if only they pass first through its portals.

Insofar, first of all, as the motive behind the argument is fear of a professional military elite insulated in background and education from the rest of society, ROTC probably does little to mitigate such a danger. The dangers of professionalism come not so much from enlisted men (as opponents of a volunteer army would have us believe) or junior officers as from the top-echelon officers' corps. And at that level, we already have a professional army with or without ROTC. It is worth remembering, in any event, that in Nazi Germany the strongest military opposition to Hitler came not from the younger officers and enlisted men but from the professional military elite, and yet it was the former who more nearly embodied the prevailing sociopolitical values of the civilian population.[21] The point is that the appeal to civilian values is next to meaningless unless those values are specified. If one means only certain values widely held by the civilian population, they may or may not be worth preserving. If one means values which are both widely held and properly so, then one must show, and not merely assume, that programs like ROTC will foster rather than undermine them.

ROTC, in any event, has had little impact of the alleged responsible and humanizing sort, at least as measured by the actions of the United States in Indochina. ROTC students have scarcely been identified with antiwar activity, much less in the forefront of it, which suggests either that ROTC does not attract young men much susceptible to the kind of influence in question or that it fails to instill in them the proper values—at least in sufficient strength to hold sway against military values like obedience—or both. Either way, the salutary influence of ROTC upon the military by one of the most obvious of criteria has been negligible.

This is hardly surprising. What is surprising is that it should seriously be thought that if you screen out a group of teen-age youths through the lure of an expense-paid college education, exact from them a military commitment at an age when they are still maturing, and place them throughout the duration of their higher education—when, ideally, at least, they should have the greatest freedom to grow intellectually and morally, and to do so with a minimum of pressure to conform and to obey external authorities—in a program of military training under the scrutiny of a commanding officer whose job is to screen them still further if necessary, the whole process will in the long run civilianize the military rather than militarize the citizenry. . . .

If one were seriously interested in exerting deliberate pressure upon the military through the universities—and if this were an appropriate use of the universities, which I contend it is not—this could better be accomplished by keeping the universities autonomous and expecting the military to transform itself in such a way as to attract college graduates in competition with other professions. As it is, it is no more the university's job to temper the military virtues than it is to foster them.

VI

The upshot is that neither the liberal student view nor the conservative faculty-administration view is adequate. Faculty and administrators have often had the better grasp of the principles[22] involved in their recognition that the university should strive to be neutral. Where they have gone wrong is in supposing that the current status quo is neutral. Students, on the other hand, have often had the more perceptive analysis of the actual facts and have seen that the universities long ago forsook neutrality, in fact if not by design and intention. Where they have gone wrong is in believing that the remedy lies in merely getting the university to serve other causes than it has served in the past. Recognition of what is sound in both of these positions leads to a more complex analysis than either one of them represents. And—as in the case of ROTC—it leads to conclusions which support many of the substantive changes students have urged over the years, but does so on precisely the grounds on which faculty and administrators have resisted those changes.

For all of this, there is considerable truth in B. H. Liddell Hart's claim that "if you wish for peace, understand war," and the one place above all others where such understanding should be attainable is the university. But its pursuit should be under the guidance not of those who are charged with the responsibility to wage war, but of scholars whose independence and objectivity is the same as that expected in any other academic discipline. For this reason, universities might seriously consider establishing programs of military studies. But they should be programs which deal with *all* aspects of the military, including the social, political, and moral dimensions. And they should be programs which are university initiated and controlled, staffed by scholars recruited in normal ways, and governed at all levels by properly established academic criteria. All of this is within the province of an academic institution's proper concerns. And insofar as public service is measured first and foremost by a university's contribution to a better understanding of the critical issues of the day, it may be among the more important services a university can render to society.

Notes

1. For a good historical study, see Frederick Rudolph's *The American College and University: A History* (New York: Vintage Books, 1962). See also Clark Kerr, *The Uses of the University* (New York: Harper & Row, 1966), chaps. 1 and 3, for a brief statement of this development and projection of where the universities are headed.

2. Such an assumption may not be self-evident, but it is sufficiently evident to stand until refuted, and is close to being a necessary article of faith for any philosophy of education.

3. A good attempt to clarify the notion with which I find much to agree is Robert L. Simon's "The Concept of a Politically Neutral University," in *Philosophy and Political Action,* ed. V. Held, K. Nielsen, and C. Parsons (New York: Oxford University Press, 1972), pp. 217–33. [Part I of this volume contains a statement of Simon's current views of neutrality.—Ed.]

4. The campus radicals perceived perhaps more clearly than anyone else that the status quo in American universities is not neutral. But instead of turning this to their advantage, they typically directed their fire against the concept of neutrality itself, claiming that it was a liberal camouflage of the real issues. Thus, they ended up defending the very principle they imputed to their opponents, i.e., that the university should serve political and ideological

causes. This open espousal of what they alleged their opponents to be holding covertly only widened the gap between themselves and other students and faculty, which in turn enabled administrations to play one side off against the other and (with a little luck, the whole thing could backfire) to emerge the beneficiary. This same phenomenon, attesting to the shallowness of so much of what passes for radicalism, is a recurrent one. Accurately perceiving the abuse of notions like "reason," "tolerance," and "nonviolence" by liberals and their allies, militants rise to the bait and reject the genuine as well as the counterfeits of these, thereby guaranteeing the failure of their appeals for support far more certainly than their opponents could ever do.

5. Henry David Aiken puts it that "a value-free academy, which is precisely what a university depoliticized in depth would try to be, is a contradiction in terms. At the least, the search for truth itself involves a commitment to the value of knowledge in every form, whether factual or normative. And an institution systematically committed to the search for and communication of truth in all its forms cannot in the nature of the case remain apolitical" (*Predicament of the University* [Bloomington: Indiana University Press, 1971], p. 97). In a similar vein, Robert Paul Wolff says: "As a prescription for institutional behavior, the doctrine of value neutrality suffers from the worst disability which can afflict a norm: what it prescribes is not wrong; it is impossible. A large university in contemporary America simply cannot adopt a value-neutral stance, either externally or internally, no matter how hard it tries" (*The Ideal of the University* [Boston: Beacon Press, 1969], p. 70). Whether the alleged impossibility here is of a logical sort, as implied by Aiken, or of a sort dictated by the circumstances in contemporary American society is not altogether clear.

6. I am not including religious issues here, though they may, and sometimes do, give rise to the same kinds of problems. Although I would defend the same conclusions with regard to those issues as I shall defend later with regard to the above, it would require a fuller discussion than I can engage in here.

7. Not only that, but one could push the argument further and point out that since the existence of state and federally supported universities depends upon funding, they for that reason have a stake in state and national elections and should therefore be active in supporting political candidates for office. To pursue this line of reasoning is quickly to involve the university as an institution in almost every major political issue, foreign or domestic.

8. Aiken (pp. 97–98) points this out when he says that "not every local political issue, of course, is a matter of immediate academic concern; nor am I contending that the university is obliged to take a stand on every matter debated in the state legislatures or the Congress. But this does not imply either that members of the university, in their capacity as scholars, or that the university itself as a collegial body, must remain aloof when, as in Nazi Germany, actions and policies of the state undermine the very possibility of

liberal learning or when, as in some of our own Southern states, prevailing social practices and prejudices radically limit the freedom of the academy in deciding policies of admission, appointment, or instruction." These remarks suggest not so much that the university *cannot* be neutral as that there are some circumstances in which it *ought* not to be neutral, which is the liberal rather than the necessitarian position. As will become clear later, I am in strong agreement with what Aiken says here, only I see it as having a different bearing upon the overall question of neutrality.

9. Aiken, in the first passage quoted above, seems to take neutrality in this exceedingly broad sense to signify neutrality with respect to any values whatsoever. Wolff sometimes sounds as though he takes it in a similar sense: ". . . every university expresses a number of positive value commitments through the character of its faculty, of its library, even through the buildings it chooses to build. Astronomy departments ignore astrology, psychiatry departments ignore dianetics, philosophy departments ignore dialectical materialism. Universities build laboratories for experimental research, thereby committing themselves to the importance of the scientific enterprise; libraries devote scarce resources to the accumulation of rare and ancient manuscripts; whole faculties are organized to teach and study social welfare, veterinary science, law, or business. Each of these institutional decisions embodies an evaluation which can easily become the focus of a political dispute." It is difficult to believe that anyone has ever seriously proposed that a university can or should be free of any value commitments whatsoever. If this is what the necessitarian means by neutrality, then his conception is not covered by the foregoing principles; but by the same token, conceding his position then does not entail an answer one way or the other to the normative question of neutrality as we have formulated it.

10. Of course, if one characterizes both the doing and the not doing of such things as the performance of "political acts," then one can logically ensure that universities cannot be neutral. But one does so at the cost of depriving his claim of any real significance. For when neutrality is made logically impossible to achieve, we give rise to the need for a new term to do the same service as it within the category of so-called political acts, enabling us to distinguish between acts we *can* do or refrain from doing and those we cannot. Wolff seems inclined to take this line in *The Ideal of the University* (pp. 70 ff.). While I do not find this plausible as an argument for the necessitarian position, it has the makings of a strong argument for the liberal position by calling attention to the fact that universities do have a certain amount of power (though less, I think, than is often suggested, and even less prestige) and implying that they should therefore apply it directly by taking stands on political issues. A full reply to this would require taking up in detail the question of what a university ought to be. I would suggest only that, if universities were the sorts of institutions they should be, they would not *qua* institutions have any particular political power to wield, and that it is only in

proportion, as they have forsaken their proper role that they currently possess such power. Rather, therefore, than accept the current trend and what it forebodes for the future (in which, in Clark Kerr's words, the university becomes a "prime instrument of national purpose"), I think it far better that effort be expended to transform the universities into genuine communities of learning, committed exclusively to the values which that implies.

11. Other than those which are inextricably allied with the pursuit of educational aims.

12. I shall later maintain that there are circumstances in which a university is justified in taking social and political action but argue that these are circumstances in which a university has abandoned its primary mission.

13. Controversiality, for example, is a relative notion, varying according to time and circumstance. Thus, although university-military ties during World War II were noncontroversial, they became exceedingly controversial during the war in Vietnam. It does not follow from this, of course, that they were ever a good idea, only that at one time they were not violative of neutrality as I have defined it while they were at another. While, as I shall maintain in the next section, neutrality is desirable, not everything which is consistent with neutrality is desirable.

14. I stress here considerations relating to the character and inner constitution of the university, because I think these are sufficient to establish the importance of neutrality. On the other side of the coin are all of the considerations relating to external pressures upon the university if it undertakes political action. As Walter P. Metzger points out regarding the landmark 1915 AAUP statement by Arthur O. Lovejoy, E. R. A. Seligman, and John Dewey, et al., "the norm of institutional neutrality was not just an ethicist's abstraction: it was a denial of the proprietary claims of trustees, donors, and their spokesmen, . . . it was an effort to reduce the sphere in which philistine administrators could take action" (*Dimensions of Academic Freedom* [Urbana: University of Illinois Press, 1969], p. 14). Beyond the encroachments of "philistine administrators," of course, are those of the state. And these have more recently come to be recognized as a danger inherent in institutional nonneutrality. Even Wolff, who maintains that the notion of neutrality is a myth, recognizes this and seems to support the perpetuation of the myth, citing the "ever-present threat of pressure, censorship, and witch-hunting by conservative forces in society at large. . . . Let the university once declare that it is a political actor, and its faculty will be investigated, its charter revoked, and its tax-exempt status forthwith removed. . . . It is a bitter pill for the radicals to swallow, but the fact is that they benefit more than any other segment of the university community from the fiction of institutional neutrality" (p. 75).

15. This situation is characterized by Aiken when he describes the circumstances in which the "actions and policies of the state undermine the very possibility of liberal learning" (see n. 8 above). I agree with him that at such time the universities should take action. It is just that, while he clearly thinks

the existence of such circumstances is sufficient to justify political action by the universities, he does not, if I understand him correctly, think that it is necessary.

16. The *Report of the Special Committee on ROTC* to the Secretary of Defense, September 22, 1969, headed by George C. S. Benson, backs ROTC on the grounds that it is a "major procurement source of officers for the Army, Navy and Air Force," arguing further that in assessing the relationship for the military to the universities, "one overriding priority must be recognized, namely, the national security of the country." The committee maintains not only that it is proper for universities to host ROTC units, but that they have a responsibility to do so—presumably derivative from an alleged responsibility to contribute to national security. This in turn is presumed to derive from the financial benefits which universities receive from the federal government: direct tax support in the case of public institutions and tax-exempt status in the case of private ones. The whole argument presupposes that the university as an institution has political obligations of a sort which preclude its being neutral on controversial moral and political issues. Interestingly, some of the staunchest advocates of university neutrality are among the first to insist that the university has an obligation to assist in national defense. Thus, a trustee of one university resigned in protest when his university's president signed a letter (joining thirty-six other college and university presidents) to President Nixon protesting the Cambodian invasion. He did so on the grounds that the university had no right "to become embroiled in public issues of political, military or economic importance." At the same time he deplored the university senate's vote to discontinue ROTC, on the grounds that it showed that the university "does not wish to be closely associated with the defense of the United States." One cannot have it both ways. If the university has an obligation to assist in national defense, this precludes it from being neutral on the whole constellation of moral and political issues attaching thereto.

17. Speaking here, and in what follows, of the NROTC Regular Student Program (see *Contract for Regular Students [NROTC]*, NAVPERS 1110/24 [6–67] [Washington, D.C.: Bureau of Naval Personnel]). There are variations in the programs from one service to the next. The NROTC student becomes a member of the armed service during his training and is committed to a minimum active-duty service period of four years following commissioning, plus two years of reserve duty. He may voluntarily disenroll during his first year, and thereafter only at the risk of being called to active duty.

18. The ROTC Vitalization Act of 1964 specifies that no unit may be established unless "the senior commissioned officer of the armed forces concerned who is assigned to the program . . . is given the academic rank of professor," and unless the institution establishes "as part of its curriculum, a four-year course of military instruction, or a two-year course of advanced training . . . or both, *which the Secretary of the military department concerned prescribes and conducts*" (italics added).

19. A university's investment policies pose more complex problems than does ROTC. Harvard has been notable in addressing itself to this aspect of the problem through a Committee on University Relations with Corporate Enterprise. The committee supported university neutrality but acknowledged certain issues—including "respect for freedom of expression, regard . . . for individual political rights and constitutional processes, and hostility (whether in the University's role as center of learning, contractor, employer or investor) to anything smacking of racism"—on which there presumably should be no room for question about where the university stands. Harvard has adopted the view that its investment policy should strive for maximum return, while nonetheless recognizing a "right and duty to achieve purposes other than educational purposes" through its investment practices. This latter qualification might be regarded as coming within the scope of our principle of neutrality by virtue of the further recognition that it arises "solely out of our obligations to take the long view of our education mission and to act as a good citizen in the performance of it" (as reported in *Harvard Today,* Spring 1971).

20. This argument was used in support of the original Morrill Act as well as more recently by the *Report of the Special Committee on ROTC* to the Secretary of Defense, which states ominously that "if ROTC were to be removed from the nation's campuses there would be grave danger of isolating the services from the intellectual centers of the public which they serve and defend." Secretary of Defense Laird played upon this same theme before Congress when he professed to be mystified "by those who on the one hand oppose the so-called 'militarization' of our society and on the other hand seem determined to dry up the important source of civilian trained officers of our armed forces" (*New York Times,* May 31, 1970).

21. See Telford Taylor, *Sword and Swastika* (Chicago: Quadrangle Books, 1969), p. 244.

22. Educational, not moral. They have often been remarkably insensitive to the latter.

Neutrality Precludes Divestment: College Trustees Should Not Make Moral Pronouncements on Such Political Matters as Divestment and South Africa

Martin Trow

The question of divesting stock in companies doing business in South Africa confronts boards of trustees of colleges all across the country. As they consider their response, board members must understand that they are deliberating not the morality of apartheid but the politics of divestiture.

I firmly believe, along with most other Americans, that racism is a moral evil and that a system of government based on it is morally indefensible. However, I also maintain that what institutions should do with regard to the South African regime is a completely different matter. That, I submit, is a *political* question, about which reasonable people of equal moral standing can—and do—differ.

Many academics of unimpeachable integrity are opposed to total divestiture. They include, to name just a few, David Gardner of the University of California; Derek Bok and David Riesman of Harvard University; and Alan Pifer, president emeritus of the Carnegie Corporation. As both a college trustee and teacher, I do not support the policy of divestment—either as a way of influencing events in South Africa or as a way to express moral indignation at the regime there.

Among the arguments against divestiture are that it is unlikely to bring about the abolition of apartheid and that, to the contrary, it will probably worsen the situation of black South Africans. As an article in the *New York Times* pointed out, "So far, the departures [of American companies] have tended to benefit the barons of corporate power in South Africa rather than the black majority divestment was supposed to help."

It is not my purpose to argue that the *Times*'s assessment of the effects of divestment are necessarily correct or that the presence of American-owned companies in South Africa would promote the democratic evolution of its society. I am simply saying that a decision

From *The Chronicle of Higher Education* (Sept. 20, 1987): B1–2.

158

to divest is a political, not moral, judgment—and that boards of trustees should not take positions on political issues about which moral people can disagree. What President Bok said in an open letter to the Harvard community a few years ago is still true: "Universities have neither the mandate nor the competence to administer foreign policy, set our social and economic priorities, enforce standards of conduct in the society, or carry out other social functions apart from learning and discovery.

Of course, a board can decide to divest stock in companies in South Africa for reasons dictated by prudent financial management. Such reasons aside, however, a college can make a decision to divest only on the ground that it is the moral thing to do. But it is dangerous for board members to transform a political issue into a moral one, simply to take sides, because when they insist on the moral superiority of one side, it becomes difficult for them to subordinate that position—now defined as a matter of conscience—to their common interest in the welfare of their institution. And it is precisely that interest, without regard to the political (or religious or ethnic or racial) loyalties and attachments of the members, that should govern a board's decisions.

"Moralizing" political issues also tends to lead to a demand that every institution in society demonstrate its virtue by taking a position—the "morally correct" position, of course—on the issue at hand. In this view it is not enough that the government take a position or that political organizations and interest groups advocate positions on political questions; educational institutions and professional and academic associations must also stand up and be counted. Such a demand asserts the primacy of political over all other social and cultural values. It also effectively denies the right of men and women of diverse political views to come together in non-political institutions with limited purposes, such as a college, to pursue those purposes cooperatively despite their political differences.

Freedom from having to take a position on every public issue is what enables a college to serve as an arena for discussion, debate, analysis, and reflection. Students, faculty members, and trustees are at liberty to take stands on political issues as citizens. But within academe, the job of students and faculty members is to raise questions, search for evidence, and above all to learn; the job of trustees is to make it possible for them to do so, by assuring that their college remains a free marketplace of ideas.

Boards must also take into account practical as well as intellectual considerations. For example, a college that firmly asserts its political neutrality and demonstrates it by offering its platforms and other resources for thoughtful examination of politically controversial issues will be able to attract support from advocates of all points of view. If, on the other hand, it takes a position on such issues, it must reasonably expect to lose the support of people who are politically committed in another direction. Loss of such support cannot help but weaken the capacity of an institution, both materially and morally, to serve as a place where all points of view can be represented and debated in a climate marked by civility, reason, and appeals to evidence.

With respect to such controversial issues, which inevitably engage strong passions and commitments, colleges should be committed to the *pursuit* of truth; they should not claim to be its possessor. Seventy years ago, just as this country entered the First World War, Senator Hiram Johnson observed that "the first casualty when war comes is truth." What we are seeing now in South Africa is a bitter civil war, with not just two but many sides. All have their own needs and their own ways to shape world opinion. The only thing we can be sure of in trying to follow events there is that we are seeing them through distorting lenses, and only in part.

Like most people, I have discovered that over time, with deeper knowledge and a broader perspective, I have had to revise—often substantially—my initial view of almost every major event that has occurred during my adult lifetime. I have no doubt that when, in time, we have learned more about events in South Africa, we will come to see them not only more clearly but also differently. I do not mean we will hate apartheid any less, just that the *factual* rather than the moral issues in South Africa will appear different to us. We may indeed come to hold different views in light of different facts.

That being the case, the role of colleges as institutions devoted to the pursuit of truth rather than to just one version of it is all the more important. Boards of trustees have a responsibility to preserve the necessary neutral ground for reasoned discussion. It is not their function to make moral pronouncements on such political questions. Indeed, academic freedom rests squarely on the self-restraint of trustees in resisting the temptation to so. Students and faculty members would be well-advised not to encourage a board to take overtly political positions. They may like the one their board takes this time, but they surely will not like the next one, or the one after that.

South Africa:
University Neutrality and Divestment
Richard Werner

In this paper I focus my attention on three widely circulated arguments against divestment. The first embraces the naiveté of divestment. The second concerns the fiduciary responsibility to maximize profits of trustees and CEOs. The third involves the neutrality of the university.

The Success of Sanctions

Many argued that divestment was at best a symbolic act. Divestment could not negatively affect the economy of South Africa to such a degree as to cause the end of apartheid. For a variety of reasons it was argued the divestment could not be successful. While symbolic acts like divestment may be praiseworthy, they are hardly obligatory. Consequently, divestment was not morally required.

In what follows, I will argue that divestment was successful and, as such, was not a mere symbolic act.[1] I was unable to find many of the facts that I am about to mention in the mainstream press, hence my frequent use of nontraditional sources. Indeed, even the sources I cite did not string together the facts to argue for the success of sanctions as I do. One was forced to read between the lines to find the best explanation of the effects of divestment.

While the news media and government worked hard to convince us of the success of violent war in the Persian Gulf, they failed to emphasize the success of nonviolent sanctions against South Africa. The point is more salient when one considers that the violent Gulf War failed in most of its stated objectives[2] while sanctions provided a remarkable success for nonviolent direct action.

During his presidency, George Bush (along with the news media) portrayed sanctions in South Africa as less than successful. Yet the facts speak for themselves. On the day that Bush announced the end of sanctions, Foreign Minister Roelof Botha gave a speech in South Africa explaining that sanctions had crippled the South African economy.[3] Both President F. W. de Klerk and Prime Minister de Plussey made similar pronouncements about the negative economic effects of sanctions in their public pronouncements.[4] When sanctions began, the South African GNP was growing at a rate of 2% per year. By the end of sanctions, the GNP was growing at a rate of -1% per year.[5] When sanctions began, the whites of South Africa enjoyed one of the highest standards of living in the world; when they ended, unemployment in South Africa stood at 40%—the highest level in the industrial world.[6]

Consider the following from *The New York Times*:

> About $10 billion in badly needed capital has hemorrhaged out of South Africa since the mid-1980's. American assets in South Africa dwindled from $2.6 billion to $1.5 billion. . . . [There are] estimates that an additional $2 billion was lost annually in bilateral trade and investment. And 197 American companies disinvested, leaving 129 companies still in place.[7]

Most of the arguments offered to show that sanctions are useless are *a priori* economic arguments. That is, they are arguments based on economic theory rather than facts. Some argue that corporations that left South Africa did not affect the economy there, for other corporations took their place. This ignores the cost to the economy of such transitions and the realization by the incoming corporation that it can take advantage of the situation by paying lower wages, charging higher prices, and seeking greater concessions from the government.

Moreover, as corporations left, it became increasingly difficult for Pretoria to purchase oil on the world market because of the stigma and risk attached to corporations in South Africa. Consequently, South Africa could expect to pay $5 to $10 per barrel above the market price once sanctions were in full swing.[8] Further, as the stigma and cost of operating in South Africa grew, the Pretoria government found it increasingly difficult to procure either international loans or investments. They were forced to pay higher interest rates for loans, if they could get them at all, while investors withheld money, fearing either stigma or the unstable economy.[9] The stigma of involvement in South Africa and the unstable economy also prevented other corporations from moving to South Africa.

While *The New York Times* initially opposed divestment on the grounds that sanctions would not work, *The Times* finally admitted the success of sanctions, although grudgingly.

> Yet liberals and conservatives now agree that sanctions must have contributed to the release from imprisonment of Nelson Mandela, . . . and to

the gradual dismantling of South Africa's racial segregation laws under President F. W. de Klerk. Sanctions, however, were hardly the sole factor at play, and conservatives minimize their contribution. . . . [T]he sanctions also coincided with a sustained campaign of opposition to apartheid by the black majority [of South Africa]. . . . Still, the American penalties cost the South African economy 1 to 3 percentage points of growth per year.[10]

The proponents of divestment never considered their actions the sole factor needed to end apartheid.[11] They conceived of divestment as *in*direct nonviolent action to further the effect of the *direct* nonviolent actions of South African black people and their supporters. Divestment was intended as an act of solidarity of people around the world with the nonviolent struggles of South African black people for freedom and emancipation from apartheid. But the task and risks were primarily those of South African blacks and their supporters.

In light of even the relatively few statistics and explanations concerning sanctions offered here, it is no surprise that the highest ranking officials in the Pretoria government begged President Bush to remove sanctions and spoke publicly about the devastating effects of sanctions, while at the same time Bush and the news media maintained that sanctions were less than successful. While the African National Congress initially opposed the lifting of sanctions as premature,[12] in early 1993 Nelson Mandela asked for the removal of all sanctions against South Africa. The continued success of sanctions jeopardized the future success of a new South African government.

My point here is that there is not merely a *correlation* between divestment and the beginning of the end of apartheid, but that there is adequate evidence to support the claim that sanctions helped *cause* the Pretoria government to move towards racial equality. Given the facts, the best explanation of the situation in South Africa is that the success of sanctions helped cause the beginning of the end of apartheid. As *The New York Times* put it, even liberals and conservatives can agree on this.

Fiduciary Responsibility

It is argued that divestment required trustees and CEOs to violate their respective fiduciary responsibilities to maximize profits for universities and corporations. But the argument proceeds as though these are the only responsibilities at issue or that the fiduciary responsibilities are absolute. Since the latter is silly, let me consider the former.

Trustees and CEOs do not lose their normal responsibilities as persons by adopting their new role. Nor do their basic moral duties disappear because of new role-specific duties. Among one's basic moral duties is one of nonmaleficence. This duty requires, specifically, that one refrain from harm and, generally and on at least some occasions, that one act to prevent harm.[13]

Yet investment in corporations in South Africa contributed to the harm done to blacks via the multiple forms of systematic oppression blacks suffer under the apartheid system.[14] Through investment in South Africa, both trustees and CEOs helped maintain the harm of apartheid and, thereby, violated their basic moral duty of nonmaleficence. The fact that the success of sanctions led to the dismantling of apartheid is clear evidence that investment in South Africa functioned to maintain the system of apartheid.

Some might argue that at the time of the divestment campaign those who invested in South Africa intended to benefit the victims of apartheid. The investors believed that through their investment the free market would promote civil rights for all in South Africa. But such beliefs were fantasy at the time. In the twenty years prior to the divestment movement, investment in South Africa had strengthened rather than weakened the apartheid system. While some corporations made token gestures such as the establishment of black schools that taught the racial superiority of whites or provided cars and trucks to the South African military and police, in the main corporations simply took advantage of a situation that meant high profits, low costs, and, in some cases, involved flagrant civil rights abuses of black workers. There was little economic incentive for corporations to seek change and strong economic incentives to maintain the status quo. Indeed, this is precisely why corporations moved to South Africa. Perhaps one could argue that investors merely intended to profit from their investment with no intention to maintain apartheid. Consequently, investors are not responsible for the evils of apartheid. But this line of argument ignores the obvious—investment did help maintain the evil of apartheid. Only through a conscious effort to ignore the facts could one not foresee that investment supported the apartheid system. It was foreseeable to anyone who cared to look with open eyes that investment supported apartheid. Moreover, if I engage in an activity that is obviously dangerous to the civil rights of others by threatening their basic freedoms and well-being, I am responsible for harm done to the others because of my act. This fact is even more obvious when those harmed did not consent to be in the position in which they find themselves but are, instead, victims of oppression.

Generally we are responsible for the foreseeable consequences of our actions simply because it is difficult to understand how one does not intend the foreseeable consequences of one's actions. While there are exceptions to this rule of thumb, the exceptions seem unhelpful for those who invested in South Africa.[15]

One might argue that investment in South Africa helped rather than harmed the black people of South Africa. After all, divestment caused serious damage to the South African economy and the brunt of that burden was passed to the underclass composed primarily of the black people of South Africa. According to this line of argument, apartheid was preferable to freedom for black South Africans since it produced better economic well-being for blacks. Yet few of us would trade improved economic conditions for our basic civil rights. Nor are these reasons advanced as an argument for the restoration of communism in the former Soviet Union and Eastern Europe. Surely the line of argument misses the point that after basic human economic needs are fulfilled, basic human rights become more important than increased economic well-being. As Steven Biko, a South African civil rights leader murdered by police in 1977, put it,

> Foreign investments support the present economic system of injustice. We blacks are perfectly willing to suffer the consequences of corporate withdrawal. We are quite accustomed to suffering.

A role-specific duty like fiduciary responsibility cannot override one's basic moral duty of nonmaleficence. Not even one's fiduciary responsibility to one's children, which is weightier than a trustee's or CEO's responsibility to a university or corporation respectively, overrides one's duty of nonmaleficence in the fulfillment of that duty. For instance, one cannot cause the violation of the basic civil rights of persons, through promoting murder or mayhem to provide for one's children's education. How, then, are trustees and CEOs justified in causing, at least in part, such foreseeable consequences of their actions, whether intentionally or not, by investment in South Africa? Certainly not because of a role-specific fiduciary responsibility that could be removed simply by declining to volunteer or resigning one's job on the board. Unlike role-specific duties, basic moral duties are inalienable and extremely weighty.

Even lesser role-specific duties, like the trustees' duty to provide for the education of students, can override their fiduciary responsibility. For instance, trustees' should not turn universities into sports palaces or pleasure domes to increase enrollments and eventually the endowment, since to do so would ignore the university's primary function to educate. Within the trustee's duty to education is an obligation to provide for the moral education of students.[16] By investment in South Africa, and thereby contributing to the violation of the basic civil rights of the black people of South Africa, trustees set a poor moral example for their students. Hence, they failed in their responsibility to educate morally their students.

University Neutrality

It is argued that universities and corporations should be ethically and politically neutral. To be otherwise would jeopardize the primary function of the former to educate and of the latter to maximize profits. So, it is argued, universities and corporations ought not divest, for to do so would be to abandon neutrality.

Let's begin by taking neutrality seriously. If it is true that a university or corporation should remain neutral, how does it do so by investment in South Africa? Let me suggest that it does not. To remain invested in South Africa is to take the side of those who oppose divestment—that is hardly a neutral stand with respect to divestment. As we have seen, it is to support the system of apartheid in South Africa—that is hardly a neutral stand with respect to apartheid.

Think of a neutral nation during wartime. It does not remain neutral by promoting one side or the other. It remains neutral by refusing to take a stand or promote either side. Likewise, a university or corporation does not remain neutral by promoting one side or the other with respect to divestment or apartheid. It remains neutral by refusing to take a stand. But how does a university or corporation refuse to take a stand concerning divestment? After all, one either divests or one does not. So one either sides with divestment or one opposes it. It would seem as though there is no neutral ground here. As the old saying goes, it would appear that one is either part of the problem or one is part of the solution.

But let me offer a suggestion for neutrality. First, to become neutral, the university or corporation would *disinvest* in South Africa. To remain invested is to promote apartheid, similar to a nonneutral country promoting a side during wartime. Second, to remain neutral, the university or corporation would stay disinvested until the issue is resolved. To reinvest is to take a side similar to a neutral country taking a side during wartime.

But isn't this merely a disguised argument for divestment? No, because the act of *disinvestment* is different from the act of *divestment*. The intention of the former is neutrality, the intention of the latter is to act in solidarity with the proponents of divestment and help end apartheid. Disinvestment and divestment are different acts because they have different intentions and, it is reasonable to believe, different foreseeable consequences. The actors in divestment intended to act in solidarity with numerous others and effect negatively the economy of South Africa thereby contributing to the end of apartheid. The intention proved successful since the intended solidarity and the foreseeable consequences came to pass. The actors in disinvestment intended to remain neutral with respect to the politics of South Africa. They foresaw that divestment might or might not prove successful and formed no intention with respect to the outcome or with respect to the divestor's intentions of the creation of solidarity. The two acts have different intentions as well as different foreseeable consequences and are, thereby, different acts. The argument here parallels the argument that neutrality on the issue of ROTC during the Vietnam War required that universities *not* offer ROTC but remain neutral with respect to the morality of that war.[17]

But suppose the opponent of divestment were to argue the following. To invest in South Africa to support apartheid is different from investing in South Africa solely in order to maximize profits. So they are different acts. To invest in South Africa in order to maximize profits is to remain neutral with respect to divestment. Hence, one is neutral, vis-à-vis divestment.

First, as argued, the act described here is not a neutral act but an immoral one. It violates the basic moral duty of nonmaleficence. Neutrality is not a convenient excuse for immoral behavior. By attempting to maximize one's profits, one knows, as a foreseeable consequence of one's acts, that one will contribute to the harm of innocent people through the systematic oppression of apartheid. How can one *knowingly* attempt to profit from the systematic oppression of a people, a moral catastrophe, and not expect to be held responsible, at least in part, for the consequences of that oppression?[18]

Second, because of these types of problems many contemporary philosophers, myself included, conclude that neutrality or impartiality is an impossibility, a fiction. We do not take neutrality seriously. Humans cannot adopt a point of view that is impersonal and dispassionate, separate from particular contexts or personal beliefs. One cannot both hold one's own subjective perspective, which is the only perspective one can hold, and, at the same time hold the objective perspective of impartiality or neutrality, the view from nowhere. One's perspective cannot be from two different places at once.[19] There are no immaculate conceptions.

Even if one became neutral, one would not be justified in the belief that one was neutral. The perspective of neutrality would seem as partial and subjective as one's old perspective—and as impartial and objective. All the old doubts about one's neutrality would remain—as would all the old confidence. Moreover, the notion of "more or less objective" makes little sense. Objectivity, like pregnancy and other similar concepts, does not admit of degrees. If the notion of neutrality is itself unknowable, how can one know whether one is closer to or farther from it? How can one know which of two perspectives is more objective if one does not know what objectivity is? So one is not warranted in the assertion, "my position is the neutral position" or "my position is more neutral than yours" unless one expresses it as an act of faith. Quite simply, no one of us can adopt the God's-eye point of view required for neutrality. As Richard Rorty puts it,

> One can, if one likes, see Kundera . . . as trying to overcome a common enemy: the tradition of Western metaphysics, the tradition which hints at One True Description which exhibits the underlying pattern behind apparent diversity. . . . For Kundera the way to overcome the urge to domination is to realize that everybody has and always will have this urge, but to insist that nobody is more or less justified in having it than anyone else. Nobody stands for the Truth, or for Being, or for Thinking. Nobody stands for *anything* Other or Higher. We all just stand for ourselves, equal inhabitants of a paradise of individuals in which everybody has the right to be understood but nobody has the right to rule.[20]

Some attempt to save a semblance of impartiality by arguing that neutrality is softer than previously thought. According to soft neutrality, neutrality entails only that there are universal rules of discourse, rules that all rational beings necessarily adopt if they are to communicate successfully, if they are to practice open and undistorted communication.[21]

But knowledge of these rules requires one to adopt the strong sense of impartiality. Unless one claims to adopt the God's-eye point of view, how can one claim to know which rules *universally* and *necessarily* govern all discourse? How is *a priori* knowledge possible without the God's-eye point of view? If the strong sense of neutrality is a fiction, *a priori* claims concerning the universal and necessary rules that govern all discourse are indefensible.[22]

If there are rules that govern discourse, let them emerge as part of the conversation. Let the participants identify the rules they want to govern their conversation. Let the rules remain fluid so that the participants can question the rules during the conversation. Otherwise we run the risk that privileged groups will unintentionally misidentify and apply seemingly *a priori* rules of discourse that favor the privileged groups and distort discourse. If there are necessary and universal rules that favor no one, that are needed for open and undistorted communication, these rules will emerge through trial and error over time. Yet even these emergent rules will be accepted provisionally in the light of pragmatic considerations. New facts may come to light, and new facts may disconfirm old rules. As C. S. Peirce recommended, adopt no rule that blocks the path to inquiry.

So where do I stand when I write? Don't my words presuppose the God's-eye point of view from which I pretend to write? Please do not take my words in that vein (or vain). I offer my words as suggestions or proposals to be considered and either accepted or rejected as the result of open and undistorted conversation. I consider open and undistorted conversation as the only means available to gain warrant for our beliefs. If the ideal outcome of such an open and undistorted conversation is not truth, it will surely do as the best available alternative.

But couldn't the defender of soft neutrality make the same appeal? Not without abandoning the claim that the rules of inquiry are known *a priori*. If they are not known *a priori*, there is no reason to believe that they are universal and necessary. If they are not universal and necessary, there is no reason to consider them *the* rules of inquiry.

So where are we? Either strong neutrality is possible or it is not. If it is possible, at best, it counts in favor of disinvestment. If it is not possible, then strong neutrality provides no sound argument against divestment for it cannot be argued that the university should be neutral if it cannot be. Either soft neutrality is possible or it is not. It seems that soft neutrality is parasitic upon strong neutrality, so it rises or falls with it and is, thereby, otiose with respect to the university neutrality issue. Consequently, we can conclude that the strongest claim that can be made from neutrality is that it requires disinvestment.

Moreover, given that neutrality is itself an increasingly suspect item, we can conclude that neutrality should not count for or against divestment—neutrality seems to demand no less.

Conclusion

None of the arguments against divestment considered here are compelling. Since investment in South Africa violates our basic moral duty of nonmaleficence, I conclude that divestment (or, at the very least, disinvestment) was justified from the start.

Notes

1. It was also reasonable to believe that divestment would be successful at the time of the movement and that it ought to be supported. See my "South Africa and the Consequences of Divestment," In *The Eye of the Storm: Philosophers Reflect on Militarism and Regional Conflicts,* ed. Laurence Bove and Laura Duhan Kaplan (Amsterdam: Rodopi Press, 1994) for the argument.

2. For substantiation, see Noam Chomsky, "The Global Protection Racket: Reflections on the Gulf War" and "Pascal's Wager" in *Chronicles of Dissent,* ed. Noam Chomsky and David Barsamian (Monroe, Maine: Common Courage Press, 1992).

3. *ABC News Nightline,* July 10, 1991.

4. *Ibid.*

5. *Ibid.*

6. *Ibid.*

7. *The New York Times,* Sunday, July 14, 1991, Section 4D, p. 3.

8. *National Public Radio,* "All Things Considered," July 10, 1991.

9. *Ibid.*

10. *Op. cit.* My additions in brackets.

11. For other explanations of the success of sanctions, see *The Manchester Guardian,* July 11, 1991, "South African Sanctions: Return of Foreign Finance Could Turn Tide of Decline," page 11.

12. *The New York Times, op. cit.*

13. For substantiation, see Henry Shue, *Basic Rights* (Princeton: Princeton University Press, 1980), or the more conservative moral analysis of Bernard Gert, *Morality* (Oxford: Oxford University Press, 1989), or the more demanding moral analysis of Peter Singer, *Practical Ethics* (Cambridge, Cambridge University Press, 1979), Chapter 8. Any one of the three will support the notion of nonmaleficence developed here.

14. For explanation of the notion of "oppression," used here, see Iris

Marion Young, *Justice and the Politics of Difference* (Princeton: Princeton University Press, 1990).

15. For an intelligent discussion of when we are and when we are not responsible for the foreseeable consequences of actions that cause the violation of basic civil rights, see Jeffrie G. Murphy, "The Killing of the Innocent," *Monist*, Vol. 57 (1983).

16. A distribution requirement in ethics that many universities endorse is evidence.

17. For instance, see Robert Holmes, "ROTC and University Neutrality," *Ethics*, Vol. 83, No. 3 (1973), reprinted in this volume.

18. I understand the systematic oppression of a people for racist reasons as one kind of moral catastrophe. Hence, the Nazi Holocaust as well as U.S. apartheid qualify as moral catastrophes. South African apartheid falls somewhere between these two examples in terms of its morally catastrophic nature.

19. Thomas Nagel, *The View from Nowhere* (Oxford: Oxford University Press, 1986) represents a soft formulation of this view. Hilary Putnam, *Reason, Truth and History* (Cambridge: Cambridge University Press, 1981) represents a moderate formulation. Richard Rorty, *Philosophy and the Mirror of Nature* (Princeton: Princeton University Press, 1979) represents a strong formulation. Any one of the three will support the arguments offered here, with the possible exception of those against soft neutrality that are in line with the Rorty perspective.

20. Richard Rorty, *Essays on Heidegger and Others* (Cambridge: Cambridge University Press, 1991), p. 75.

21. Jurgen Habermas, *The Theory of Communicative Competence*. Vol. 1: *Reason and the Rationalization of Society* (Boston: Beacon Press, 1983) and Robert Simon's contribution in Part I of this volume.

22. For an in-depth critique of weak neutrality, see Seyla Benhabib, *Critique, Norm and Utopia* (New York: Columbia University Press, 1986), pp. 327–51, and Young, *op. cit.*, pp. 106–7.

A Puzzle Concerning Divestiture
Steven M. Cahn

Suppose I hold 100 shares of stock in a company that has embarked on a policy I consider immoral. I therefore wish to divest myself of those 100 shares. In order for me to sell them, someone must buy them. But the buyer would be purchasing 100 shares of 'tainted' stock. And I would have abetted the buyer in this immoral course of action. Granted, the prospective buyer might not believe the stock 'tainted', but that consideration would be irrelevant to me, since I am convinced that, knowingly or unknowingly, the buyer would be doing what is immoral. Surely I should not take any steps that would assist or encourage the buyer in such deplorable conduct. Nor should I try to release myself from a moral predicament by entangling someone else. How then is principled divestiture possible?

From *Analysis* 47, no. 3 (1987): 175–76.

A Reply to Cahn
Daniel H. Cohen

Steven M. Cahn (*Analysis* 47.3, June 1987, pp. 175–6) asks how a principled divestiture of stocks is morally possible. The problem, correctly noted, derives from two premises. First, ownership of stock in a company whose policies are morally objectionable is itself morally objectionable. Second, it cannot be morally obligatory to perform an act which requires someone else to commit an offence of identical gravity. Because stocks can only be sold when there is a buyer, selling any such stocks accomplishes no net reduction of morally objectionable economic behaviour in the world. Divestiture, the argument concludes, is something of an ostrich act. It redistributes guilt instead of eliminating it. There can be no obligation to sell these stocks. It might be added that there are other, better models for moral behaviour: even if it is supererogatory to take the sins of the world upon oneself, we can at least be expected to refrain from casting our sins onto the shoulders of others.

For all its validity, the argument is specious, a straw man argument. The purpose of calls for divestiture of stocks in certain companies is not to cleanse individuals' portfolios and souls. The purpose is to bring pressure to bear on the companies in question to alter the odious practices. The line of reasoning is that a general increase in the numbers selling a given stock will increase the supply of that stock readily available on the market and so have a downward effect on the price of the stock. This would be the kind of message readable by even the most completely economic of agents. Divestiture is morally possible because it is a means, not an end. Accordingly, divestiture is successful only if it succeeds in having an effect. The divestiture that Cahn seems to have in mind would be successful as soon as the agent in question no longer owns the stock. His assessment of this is right: there is only a dubious moral value to be found in that. Influencing the policies of an Immoral-Corp can be a righteous goal; a clean portfolio is merely a self-righteous one. Of course, the two goals call for the same strategy, but identical strategies do not necessarily indicate the same goal. The distinction is not a new one: divestiture merely to clean one's own hands may be compatible with duty but no more.

From *Analysis* 48, no. 2 (1988): 109–10.

Morally Acceptable Divestiture
Kerry S. Walters

Steven M. Cahn (*Analysis* 47.3, June 1987, pp. 175–6) worries over whether principled divestiture of tainted stock is possible. Suppose I own stock in a corporation that's embarked on a policy I consider immoral. I therefore wish to dissociate myself from the corporation. To free myself of complicity I must sell the stock, which entails that a third party purchase it. But this 'entangles' the third party in a situation I deem reprehensible. And to knowingly entangle a third party in such a situation is likewise reprehensible, Cahn suggests, even if I apprise him of my reasons for divestiture. How then is principled divestiture possible?

The following analogy sheds light on Cahn's puzzle. Suppose I'm employed by a firm that's embarked on a policy I consider immoral. I therefore wish to dissociate myself from the firm. This entails my resignation. Moreover, my employer assures me I will be replaced. But one of the conditions of my contract, which I freely accepted at the time of appointment and still see as morally binding, is as follows. If I give intent to resign, I may legitimately step aside only after the firm has found my replacement and I have cooperated in his on the job training for a stipulated length of time. As a condition of employment, my replacement presumably will be required to acquiesce to or at least not oppose the firm's objectionable policy. Consequently, my resignation 'entangles' him in an immoral situation, and this is reprehensible. How then is principled resignation possible?[1]

Surely no one wants to suggest I'm duty bound not to tender my resignation merely because a third party will take my place. The ideal course of action, of course, might be for me to remain in the firm's employment and as an insider lobby against the immoral policy. That way no third party would become an accessory through my resignation. But such an action is supererogatory. If remaining goes against the grain, I may legitimately leave with no violation of duty if I conscientiously apprise my replacement of my negative evaluation of the firm. If he still willingly hires on, I can hardly be said to have 'entangled' him. My resignation is a necessary condition for his replac-

From *Analysis* 48, no. 4 (1988): 216–18.

ing me, but not for his ethical appraisal of and a subsequent response to the firm's immoral policy.

Similarly with divestiture. My ideal recourse might be to retain my stock, donate the dividends to charity and actively lobby for the reformation of corporate policy. True, I will remain a reluctant accessory in what I take to be an immoral situation, but at least I will avoid 'entanglement' of a third party. But I am under no obligation to retain the stock. Doing so makes me an incredibly decent fellow. It shows I'm willing to sacrifice my peace of mind for the sake of others. But it is clearly supererogatory. If it too abuses my conscience or endurance, I may sell with no violation of duty, provided I conscientiously apprise the buyer of my reasons for divestiture. If he still willingly buys, either because he disagrees with my ethical reservations or agrees without giving a damn, I can hardly be said to have 'entangled' him. My selling is a necessary condition for his purchase, but not for his ethical response.

Is this analysis merely a smokescreen for ethical buck-passing? I don't think so. I'm not claiming divestiture leaves me with spotless hands. I am, after all, retreating rather than redressing. But neither does it totally condemn me. Granted, divesting is a less than ideal recourse. But in light of the predicament's difficulty, it is morally acceptable. By morally acceptable I mean that course of action which falls within the bounds of ethical propriety without being fully virtuous. Given the complexity of certain ethical quandaries, it may be unlikely if not impossible to achieve a completely satisfying resolution. But this doesn't mean no resolution is possible. A careful examination may reveal courses of action which are acceptable although not what, in the best case scenario, one would desire. In short, shooting for moral acceptability is making the best of a bad situation. It may leave one with slightly soiled hands, but it may also be the best one can do under the circumstances.

Is, then, principled divestiture possible? If by 'principled' one means fully virtuous and completely satisfying, probably not. Moreover I suspect no—or at least very few—actions are principled in this strong sense. But if one more realistically takes 'principled' to mean morally acceptable, then yes. Principled divestiture is possible.

Notes

1. My colleague Chan Coulter has correctly pointed out that this analogy isn't perfect. If a shareholder wishes to sell, there is a logical entailment that

he involve a buyer. If an employee wishes to resign, it is probable but not necessary that a replacement becomes involved. Still, I don't think the analogy fatally limps, since the employee wishing to resign here considers himself under an ethical obligation to wait out his replacement. That is, a morally necessary condition for his leaving is that his position be filled by a third party.

Morally Principled Divestiture?
David Gordon and James Sadowsky

Both Daniel H. Cohen ('A Reply to Cahn', *Analysis* 48.2, March 1988, pp. 109–10) and Kerry S. Walters ('Morally Acceptable Divestiture' *Analysis* 48.4, October 1988, pp. 216–18) have attempted to show, in our view unsuccessfully, that a problem that Steven Cahn proposed (*Analysis* 47.3, June 1987, pp. 175–6) for certain advocates of divestiture can be solved.

(1) It is immoral to own stock issued by companies that, for example, invest in South Africa.

(2) To 'entangle' someone in an immoral action is itself immoral.

(3) Selling stock entails someone's buying the stock.

(4) Selling one's stock in a company that invests in South Africa entangles someone in an immoral policy;

Therefore (5) selling stock in a company that invests in South Africa is immoral.

Cahn did not claim that (1) is true: his argument, rather, is a problem for those who hold (1). This point is ignored by Cohen, who contends that the purpose of divestiture is, for instance, to bring pressure to bear on the South African government to end apartheid. Selling one's stock has no moral value in itself: 'it is a means, not an end'. (Cohen, p. 110).

If Cohen intends to construct an alternative argument for divestiture which does not depend on (1), he has left Cahn's problem untouched. Cahn's argument does not address the issue of whether one should, all things considered, divest: it poses a problem only to those who accept (1). That Cohen can take a position on divestiture without assuming (1) is, for the purpose of refuting Cahn, without significance.

Cohen may, however, wish his comments to be taken as an argument against adopting (1): if so, they do not succeed. If he is right that divestiture is a means, rather than an end, this does not remove divestiture from moral evaluation. To say that something is a means to an end does not entail that it is to be evaluated solely for its effective-

From *Analysis* 49, no. 3 (1989): 153–55.

ness in bringing about the end. Someone who holds that one ought not to use bad means to achieve good ends can consistently hold both (1) and (2) while agreeing with Cohen on the goal of divestiture. He need not hold that the purpose of divestiture is *only* to rid *oneself* of one's immoral holdings. Further, Cohen gives no argument that someone who does take the latter view of divestiture is self-righteous. Why isn't he simply trying to avoid immorality?

Walters devotes his principal attention to an attack on (2). He draws an analogy between (2) and a case of someone who is bound by a promise not to resign from an immoral job until a replacement can be found. If a consequence of accepting (2) were that on analogous grounds one must hold that 'principled resignation' is not morally possible, this indeed would throw (2) into question. But Walters has not shown this. His case depends on the existence of a promise not to resign until a replacement can be found. Since it is usually not held that promises bind unconditionally, one might argue that someone in a sufficiently immoral job need not abide by his promise. To the extent that the job involves one in evil, the strength of the promise, other things being equal, weighs more than the evil of remaining in the job, then there are some situations in which one is required to continue in a morally bad job. This hardly seems very damaging to (2).

And without a promise, Walters's case involves no violation of (2) at all. The issue here is neither entailment of the replacement nor its probability, but causation. If you resign from the job, you do not bring about your replacement, even if you know your employer will hire someone else. He makes an independent decision. But in the case of selling the stock, it is your action that directly entangles the buyer.

Walters's own solution to the divestiture problem suffers from a similar failing to Cohen's. He contends that although not morally perfect, divestiture may be doing the best one can in a bad situation. But neither divestiture nor his supererogatory solution avoids Cahn's problem, since each violates (1). Walters, rather than responding to Cahn, has instead presented an alternative view of the morality of divestiture, in this context an irrelevant enterprise.

Is Cahn's problem capable of solution? One approach might start from the premise that if one cannot avoid acting badly, the usual prohibition on the use of bad means to achieve good ends does not apply. If one must either retain or sell the stock, will not the chooser of necessity have to put to one side the (presumably equal) immorality of each alternative and decide on consequentialist grounds? But this argument assumes that holding and selling are the only alternatives.

Perhaps they are not: one might be able, e.g., to renounce one's stock ownership without selling it.[1] If so, Cahn's problem remains unsolved; we have not shown there exists a way of morally selling the stock.

Notes

1. We owe this suggestion to Mr D. R. Steele.

A Note on Divestiture
Steven M. Cahn

If you hold stock in a company that embarks on a policy you consider immoral, are you required as a matter of principle to sell that stock? In 'A Puzzle Concerning Divestiture' (*Analysis* 47.3, June 1987, pp. 175–6), I prescnted an argument in support of the surprising conclusion that principled divestiture is not even possible. For selling "tainted" stock passes the guilt of ownership from seller to buyer. And you should not attempt to release yourself from a moral predicament by entangling someone else.

Note that this puzzle does not purport to prove that divestiture is invariably a mistake but only that it cannot ever be justified as a moral imperative. Yet three recent attempts to solve the problem, those by Daniel H. Cohen (*Analysis* 48.2, March 1988, pp. 175–6), Kerry S. Walters (*Analysis* 48.4, October 1988, pp. 216–18), and David Gordon and James Sadowsky (*Analysis*, this issue, pp. 153–55), all seek to demonstrate how divestiture might be defended on grounds other than that of moral principle, a point not in dispute.

Walters agrees that by divesting one becomes 'a reluctant accessory in . . . an immoral situation'. Yet he defends divestiture as a second-best but still acceptable alternative for those more concerned with their own peace of mind than that of others.

Principled divestiture, however, is divestiture based on principle. The action is supposed to flow from moral duty. So the issue is not, as Walters would have it, whether divestiture is permitted but whether it is required. And he admits that far from being morally requisite divestiture is not even 'fully virtuous', since it results in 'slightly soiled hands'. So he has highlighted the problem but not solved it. As Gordon and Sadowsky put it, Walters' reply is 'an irrelevant enterprise'.

Cohen takes a different tack from Walters, responding that I have misunderstood the purpose of divestiture. It is not intended 'to cleanse individuals' portfolios and souls', a 'self-righteous' goal, but to force the stock's price down and thereby bring external pressure on the company to change its policy.

Gordon and Sadowsky rightly deem this rejoinder 'without signifi-

From *Analysis* 49, no. 3 (1989): 156–57.

cance', since the question is not whether divestiture can be defended on strategic grounds. Surely it can be. Likewise, it can be opposed on strategic grounds, for by not divesting a stockholder maintains the leverage to bring internal pressure on the company to change its policy. Either strategy may succeed or fail, depending in any particular case on a variety of factors, including the percentage of total outstanding shares held, the attitudes of the board of directors, social and economic conditions, and so on.

The puzzle I presented focused not on such empirical considerations but on the axiom that, regardless of circumstances, the only ethically proper policy is to sell "tainted" stock. So when Gordon and Sadowsky conclude that under the given conditions 'one cannot avoid acting badly' and must, therefore, make a decision based solely on 'consequentialist grounds', they themselves commit the same fallacy they detected in the other replies, viz. irrelevance.

As for the suggestion they attribute to D. R. Steele that a possessor of "tainted" stock might choose to renounce ownership rather than sell, this financially fatal strategy would amount simply to redistribution of the value of the divestor's shares among all other stockholders. The assets of those who had not divested would thereby be increased as would presumably their moral culpability.

The question thus remains as I put it previously: how is principled divestiture possible?[1]

Notes

1. I am grateful for the advice of my colleague David Rosenthal.

The Divestiture Puzzle Dissolved
Roger A. Shiner

Steven M. Cahn ([1], pp. 175–6) has offered an argument purporting to show the divestiture of shares in a company thought to be immoral cannot be required by moral principle. Many people think that such divestiture is a moral duty, and so Cahn's argument presents a challenge to such people. Cahn's argument turns on (A) the undoubted fact that Seller can only successfully sell such shares if someone else, Buyer, actually buys them, and [n] claims (B) that, given this undoubted fact, Seller thereby 'entangles' ([1], p. 176; [2], p. 156) Buyer in the same moral predicament from which Seller seeks to be disentangled by the divestiture, and (C) that it can never be a requirement of moral principle to entangle another in a moral predicament.

That the divestiture puzzle is not philosophically trivial is shown by Cahn's response [2] to the attempts so far published to solve it (see [3], [4], [6]). Cahn rejects all these attempts on the grounds that each of them in different ways shows how divestiture may be justifiable on grounds other than those of moral principle, grounds of a roughly consequentialist sort. If in fact divestiture cannot be justified on non-consequentialist grounds, but only on consequentialist grounds, then we would seem to have a powerful reason for rejecting non-consequentialist approaches to moral theory. That would not be a trivial matter.

(A) and (C) above seem to be unexceptionable. I shall show that (B), however, is treacherous. The term 'entangle' is too vague: if one disambiguates it, one can then show that (B) is mistaken. If (B) is mistaken, then Cahn's puzzle has no foothold.

First, another ambiguity. If a 'principled' divestiture is one that can be universalized, then we are to suppose Seller's 'I ought to sell my shares in Armaments Manufacturer' universalized to 'Everyone ought to sell their shares in Armaments Manufacturer'. In that case, since a seller requires a buyer who will then own the shares, of course principled divestiture is impossible. But it is trivially impossible, and Cahn is laughing at us behind our back. If a 'principled' divestiture is one such that Seller has a coherent non-consequentialist case for maintaining that he or she as individuals should sell their shares in

From *Analysis* 50, no. 3 (1990): 205–10.

Armaments Manufacturer, then the request for the form of such a case is non-trivial. I assume the problem Cahn has set is non-trivial.

There are two ways of looking at Seller's 'moral predicament'. The first concentrates on the state of Seller's soul, as it were, and regards Seller's soul as contaminated by association with the immoral company in which Seller holds shares. The second concentrates on the harm done—say, the economic support given to a corrupt regime—by the investment Seller had originally made. The 'entangling' of Buyer which purportedly takes place when Seller sells Buyer the shares might refer to either of these considerations.

Let us take the first one first. The thought here is that by the act of selling Seller purifies Seller's soul at the cost of passing on the contamination to Buyer. A certain kind of paradigm of immorality is presupposed here, cases where initially innocent persons have their moral sensibilities gradually blunted to the point where they become willing partners in some nefarious enterprise, or else where they are forced to participate in such an enterprise by blackmail or other form of coercion. Such cases require some self-conscious intention to entangle on the part of the entangler and some ignorance or reluctance on the part of the entanglee if 'entangling' with the relevant negative connotations is to be properly applied. Although we can imagine a case where Buyer is coerced by Seller into purchasing the latter's shares, the ordinary case of selling shares on the open market is quite different. For one thing, the mechanics of the electronic stock exchange put increasingly in doubt that shares have the kind of identity-conditions which secure the claim that any given Buyer is buying the very particular shares that some given Seller is selling. If there is a very small market in the shares, this may be possible; but if tens of thousands of shares are being regularly traded, it will not be possible. In the second place, Seller simply authorizes Broker to sell the shares; while Broker may know who Buyer is (though Broker may not, but sell only to another broker), Seller will not know. There are paradigms of harm being done to 'unassignable individuals', in Jeremy Bentham's splendid phrase—pollution of a river or of the air. The pulp mill may culpably know that some people will be harmed by its discharges although it does not know which people. If one is prepared to regard Seller's selling shares when it may not be possible to identify who buys them, or when, even if it is possible, Seller will be ignorant of Buyer, as contamination of 'unassignable individuals' comparable to a pulp mill discharging into a river, then I cannot confound that interpretation. But 'entangling' is already beginning to look like a tendentious description, and the distance of these cases from the paradigms of entangling is considerable. Third, as said, 'entangling' presupposes innocence or reluctance on the part of the entanglee. It is extremely unlikely that the ordinary case of shares being purchased on an open market involves any such ignorance or reluctance.

In short, cases where Seller really does 'entangle' Buyer and pass on the contamination of the soul, these are exceptional cases. What actually happens in the normal cases of a sale of shares would not support the description 'entangling' at all.

The second way of interpreting 'entangling' focusses on the harm done by the possession of the objectionable shares. Seller purportedly 'entangles' Buyer by causing Buyer to do exactly the same harm as Seller was doing. Indeed, as Gordon and Sadowsky note ([4], p. 155), the issue here is causation. Cahn's puzzle, and their support of it in this respect, require that, if Seller is to be rightly described as 'entangling', the causal connection from Seller to the harming investment remains unbroken by the act of selling the shares to Buyer. But it seems to me that this is simply not so. The voluntary purchase of the shares by Buyer on the open market is an intervening act which breaks the chain of causation from Seller to any harm done by the investment. Seller does *not* 'cause' Buyer to buy the shares, so long as Buyer has acted voluntarily in buying them.

The term 'cause' is slippery in this context. In one sense, it is perfectly true that Seller 'caused' Buyer's purchase (presuming the problem above of the identity-conditions for shares is solved). This is the sense of 'but for' causation, 'cause in fact', or necessary condition. 'But for' Seller's act of placing those shares on the market, Buyer could not have bought exactly those shares. Notoriously, however, the expression 'A caused B' means more than 'But for A's occurring B would not occur'. This sense of 'cause' is in common to both statements about inanimate ('The hail caused damage to the crop') and animate ('A's shriek caused B to jump') entities. The connection is termed by Hart 'causal responsibility', to distinguish it from 'legal liability-responsibility', the matter (crudely speaking) of a person's psychological relation to an occurrence (cf. [5], pp. 214–22). That the law, as well as ordinary talk, embodies this distinction between causal connections is not in doubt. The claim 'Seller entangled Buyer' requires more for its truth than simple 'but-for' causation. It requires genuine causal responsibility. But Buyer's voluntary intervention in the market negates Seller's causal responsibility.

Consider these two cases. (1) Vendor builds (it is indifferent whether the building is negligent, reckless, or intentional) a rickety porch on to a house. Vendor then sells the house directly to Purchaser, saying nothing when Purchaser fails to notice the condition of the porch. Shortly after, the porch collapses, injuring Lettercarrier. (2) Vendor builds the rickety porch as before, but commissions Realtor to sell the house. Purchaser purchases the house; Purchaser is merely a name on the contract to Vendor. Purchaser realizes the porch is rickety, but does nothing to fix it. Shortly after, the porch collapses, injuring Lettercarrier. In case (1), there is some plausibility to the claim that Vendor has 'entangled' Purchaser in the situation which led to harm to Lettercarrier. There is very little plausibility to this claim in case (2). Given Purchaser's voluntary purchase of the house, and awareness of the state of the porch, there is no longer any causal responsibility on the part of Vendor for the harm to Lettercarrier—even though it is true that, but for Vendor building the rickety porch, the harm to Lettercarrier would not have occurred. The case of Buyer's purchase of Seller's shares on the open market is analogous to case (2), not case (1).

In short, if 'entangling' is taken to refer to a causal connection between Seller and the harm Buyer is doing by investing in Armaments Manufacturer, then there is no such connection. Talk of 'entangling' is not justified.

Let us make one final attempt to reinstate the puzzle. We say to Seller, who we assume to have made a sincere speech along the lines of the above discussion, 'You still have not seen the point. You claim you have an obligation to divest yourself of your shares in Armaments Manufacturer. That is because you believe it is wrong to possess these shares because of the harm that this company's activities cause. But inevitably, if you *sell* your shares, then someone else will *buy* them. That person will then be doing the wrong you believe yourself now to be doing. So your action of selling is one that occasions a situation in which someone does wrong. It can never be a requirement of moral principle to occasion a situation in which someone does wrong. So you must be mistaken in thinking you have an obligation to divest yourself of your shares in Armaments Manufacturer.'

Seller can make the following reply. ' "Occasion" is a far cry from "entangle". I would indeed do wrong if I "entangled" another person in a situation in which that person did wrong. Whoever will own my shares will indeed do wrong. But that is not my problem. As things are, in no way do I force, coerce, entice, or otherwise influence Buyer, whoever Buyer may be, to buy my shares. In no way do I force, coerce, entice, or otherwise influence Buyer to do the wrong that

Buyer will do by owning those shares. I "occasion" Buyer's obtaining the shares, if you like, if we suppose (improbably, in the face of the facts) that, but for my shares being on the market, Buyer would not invest in Armaments Manufacturer. It is Buyer's own free choice to purchase those shares and make that investment. Consider the case of Executioner, who comes to believe that capital punishment is wicked and so resigns. Executioner, as an astute reader of the political tea-leaves, knows full well the state will have no trouble hiring another executioner, and that executions will continue. But it is absurd to say that by that resignation Executioner is "entangling" the new appointee in the wrong of capital punishment. The very notion of "responsibility" which you employ to hold me responsible is one that implies Buyer's or the new executioner's free choice makes them, not I or Executioner, "responsible". Executioner and I treat the other as an end, not as a means, in acknowledging the freedom to choose. We do what in conscience has to be done. Executioner's conscience is now clear, and so is mine.' Seller might even have spoken of 'clean hands' as well.

We can now see that we are in familiar moral territory. Both Seller and Executioner are persons who place a high value on *integrity*. It is important to both Seller and Executioner that they lack certain kinds of connection to wrong things that go on in the world. It may even be more important to them that they are not connected with wrongs than that the wrongs do not occur. Cohen ([3], p. 110) says (self-righteously?) that a 'clean portfolio is merely a self-righteous [goal]'. But those who value integrity despise such cynicism. The cases of Seller and Executioner throw into sharp relief the conflict between integrity-based moralities and utility-based moralities. In the name of the latter, Shareholder will urge Seller not to sell, but to work from within to change investment and manufacturing policies. Reformer may urge Executioner to remain and use the authority of a public position to campaign for abolition. Of such issues are agonies and tragedies made, both real and fictional. But, as long as integrity is of moral value, then the believer in integrity can repudiate entirely successfully the charge of 'entangling' in divestiture cases of the kind at issue.

I have shown that morally principled divestiture is indeed possible— this will be divestiture which is not 'entangling', and I have shown how *that* is possible. The key principle is the principle of integrity. Cahn also ([2], p. 156) puts the task he sets as showing whether there is a 'duty' to divest, whether divestiture is required. To show how principled divestiture is possible is not the same task as that of showing that everyone has a duty to divest. That task would require for its completion a powerful argument of normative substance, and not the solution of a philosophical problem about the possibility of a coherent argument. Cahn's puzzle as first posed was the theoretical one, not the substantive one. I have shown how it is that someone who believes in the duty to divest may show that the duty may be done in a principled way. The divestiture puzzle as put forward is therefore dissolved.[1]

References

1. Steven M. Cahn, 'A Puzzle Concerning Divestiture', *Analysis* 47 (1987) 175–6.
2. Steven M. Cahn, 'A Note on Divestiture', *Analysis* 49 (1989) 156–7.
3. Daniel H. Cohen, 'A Reply to Cahn', *Analysis* 48 (1988) 109–10.
4. David Gordon and James Sadowsky, 'Morally Principled Divestiture?', *Analysis* 49 (1989) 153–5.
5. H. L. A. Hart, *Punishment and Responsibility* (Oxford: Clarendon Press, 1968).
6. Kerry S. Walters, 'Morally Acceptable Divestiture', *Analysis* 48 (1988) 216–18.

Notes

1. I would like to thank Don Dedrick and Janet Sisson for valuable comments and encouragement.

Principled Divestiture and Moral Integrity

Steven M. Cahn

Assuming you own stock in a company that embarks on a policy you consider immoral, how can you engage in principled divestiture, for doing so passes the guilt of ownership from seller to buyer, thus exchanging one wrong for another?

In attempting to dissolve this puzzle I posed (*Analysis* 47.3, June 1987, pp. 75–6), Roger A. Shiner (*Analysis* 50.3, June 1990, pp. 205–10) argues that since the seller does not cause the buyer to act, does not 'force, coerce, entice, or otherwise influence' the buyer, but merely 'occasions a situation in which someone does wrong', the seller maintains moral integrity. As Shiner says, 'Whoever will own my shares will indeed do wrong. But that is not my problem.'

Selling, however, does not merely occasion buying; one person's selling *is* another's buying. 'A sells X to B' and 'B buys X from A' are not two events but one. Seeking to disentangle them is futile.

So is the attempt to avoid moral responsibility for one's desires. Your wish to sell your stock is logically equivalent to your wishing someone to buy it. But by hypothesis you believe it wrong for anyone to buy it. So your wish to sell is the wish that someone else do wrong. And that desire is immoral.

The divestiture puzzle thus remains unsolved.[1]

Notes

1. I am grateful for the advice of my colleague David Rosenthal.

From *Analysis* 51, no. 2 (1991): 112.

The Storm Over the University
John Searle

1.

I cannot recall a time when American education was not in a "crisis."
We have lived through Sputnik (when we were "falling behind the
Russians"), through the era of "Johnny can't read," and through the
upheavals of the Sixties. Now a good many books are telling us that
the university is going to hell in several different directions at once. I
believe that, at least in part, the crisis rhetoric has a structural
explanation: since we do not have a national consensus on what
success in higher education would consist of, no matter what happens,
some sizable part of the population is going to regard the situation as a
disaster. As with taxation and relations between the sexes, higher
education is essentially and continuously contested territory. Given
the history of that crisis rhetoric, one's natural response to the current
cries of desperation might reasonably be one of boredom.

A few years ago the literature of educational crises was changed by
a previously little-known professor of philosophy at the University of
Chicago in a book implausibly entitled *The Closing of the American
Mind: How Higher Education has Failed Democracy and Impoverished the Souls of Today's Students*. To me, the amazing thing about
Allan Bloom's book was not just its prodigious commercial success—
more than half a year at the top of *The New York Times*'s best-seller
list—but the depth of the hostility and even hatred that it inspired
among a large number of professors. Most of Bloom's book is not
about higher education as such, but consists of an idiosyncratic,
often original, and even sometimes profound—as well as quirky and
cranky—analysis of contemporary American intellectual culture, with
an emphasis on the unacknowledged and largely unconscious influence
of certain German thinkers, especially Weber and Nietzsche.

Why did Bloom's book arouse such passion? I will suggest an
explanation later in this article, but it is worth noting that Bloom
demonstrated to publishers and potential authors one thesis beyond
doubt: it is possible to write an alarmist book about the state of higher

From *The New York Review of Books* (Dec. 6, 1990): 34–42.

education with a long-winded title and make a great deal of money. This consequence appears to provide at least part of the inspiration for a number of other books, equally alarmist and with almost equally heavy-duty titles, for example *The Moral Collapse of the University, Professionalism, Purity and Alienation,* by Bruce Wilshire; *Killing the Spirit, Higher Education in America,* by Page Smith; *Tenured Radicals: How Politics Has Corrupted Our Higher Education,* by Roger Kimball; and *The Moral and Spiritual Crisis in Education: A Curriculum for Justice and Compassion in Education,* by David E. Purpel.

One difficulty with the more alarmist of these books is that though they agree that the universities are in a desperate state, they do not agree on what is wrong or what to do about it. When there is no agreement not only on the cure but on the diagnosis itself, it is very hard to treat the patient. Another weakness of such books is their sometimes hysterical tone. There are, indeed, many problems in the universities, but for the most part, they tend to produce silliness rather than catastrophe. The spread of "poststructuralist" literary theory is perhaps the best known example of a silly but noncatastrophic phenomenon. Several of these books try to describe current threats to intellectual values. How serious are these threats? Right now we can't tell with any certainty because we can't yet know to what extent we are dealing with temporary fads and fashions or with long-term assaults on the integrity of the intellectual enterprise.

I think the best way to enter this discussion is by examining at least briefly the current debate about the status of what is called the "canon" of the best works in our civilization, and what part the canon should play in the education of undergraduates. I have selected two books from the current flood, because they take such strong and opposing stands on just this issue. On the side of tradition is Roger Kimball's *Tenured Radicals,* and opposed are most of the articles included in *The Politics of Liberal Education,* a collection of essays originally given at a conference sponsored by Duke and the University of North Carolina on the subject "Liberal Arts Education in the Late Twentieth Century: Emerging Conditions, Responsive Practices."

Consider what would have been taken to be a platitude a couple of decades ago, and is now regarded in many places as a wildly reactionary view. Here it is: there is a certain Western intellectual tradition that goes from, say, Socrates to Wittgenstein in philosophy, and from Homer to James Joyce in literature, and it is essential to the liberal education of young men and women in the United States that they should receive some exposure to at least some of the great works in this intellectual tradition; they should, in Matthew Arnold's over-quoted words, "know the best that is known and thought in the world." The arguments given for this view—on the rare occasions when it was felt that arguments were even needed—were that knowledge of the tradition was essential to the self-understanding of educated Americans since the country, in an important sense, is the product of that tradition; that many of these works are historically important because of their influence; and that most of them, for example several works by Plato and Shakespeare, are of very high intellectual and artistic quality, to the point of being of universal human interest.

Until recently such views were not controversial. What exactly is the debate about? The question is more complex than one might think because of the variety of different objections to the tradition and the lack of any succinct statement of these objections. For example, many African Americans and Hispanic Americans feel left out of the "canon," and want to be included. Just as a few years ago they were demanding the creation of ethnic studies departments, so now they are demanding some representation of their experiences and their point of view as part of the general education of all undergraduates. This looks like a standard political demand for "representation" of the sort we are familiar with in higher education. If the objection to the "canon" is that it consists almost entirely of works by white males, specifically white males of European (including North American) origin, then there would appear to be an easy and common-sense solution to the problem: simply open the doors to admit the work of talented writers who are not white, or not male, or not European. If, for example, the contribution of women in literature has been neglected, there are plenty of writers of similar stature to Jane Austen, George Eliot, and Virginia Woolf who can be added.

Some of the opponents of the tradition will accept this reform, but most of the authors of *The Politics of Liberal Education* would not, and you will have misunderstood the nature of the dispute if you think that it can be resolved so simply. The central objections to the tradition are deeper and more radical, and they go far beyond the mere demand for increased representation. What are these objections?

To approach this question, I have selected the proceedings of the North Carolina conference not because they contain any notable or original ideas—such conferences seldom do—but because they express a mode of literary and political sensibility that has become fairly widespread in some university departments in the humanities and is characterized approvingly by some of the participants at the conference as "the cultural left." I doubt that "the cultural left" is a well-defined notion because it includes so many altogether different points of view. It includes 1960s-style radicals, feminists, deconstructionists, Marxists, people active in "gay studies" and "ethnic studies," and people of left-wing political persuasion who happen to teach in universities. But on certain basic issues of education these groups tend to agree. In describing the North Carolina conference in his concluding statement Richard Rorty writes:

> Our conference has been in large part a rally of this cultural left. The audience responded readily and favorably to notions like "subversive readings," "hegemonic discourse," "the breaking down of traditional logocentric hierarchies," and so on. It chortled derisively at mentions of William Bennett, Allan Bloom, and E. D. Hirsch, Jr., and nodded respectfully at the names of Nietzsche, Derrida, Gramsci, or Foucault.

Whether or not Rorty is justified in using the label, the views expressed show a remarkable consensus in their opposition to the educational tradition and in their hostility to those who, like Bloom, have supported a version of the tradition. Here are some typical passages:

Mary Louise Pratt, a professor of comparative literature at Stanford, writes,

> Bloom, Bennett, Bellow, and the rest (known by now in some quarters as the Killer B's) are advocating [the creation of] a narrowly specific cultural capital that will be the normative *referent* for everyone, but will remain the *property* of a small and powerful caste that is linguistically and ethnically unified. It is this caste that is referred to by the "we" in Saul Bellow's astoundingly racist remark that "when the Zulus have a Tolstoy, *we* will read him." Few doubt that behind the Bennett-Bloom program is a desire to close not the American mind, but the American university, to all but a narrow and highly uniform elite with no commitment to either multiculturalism or educational democracy. Thus while the Killer B's (plus a C—Lynne Cheney, the Bennett mouthpiece now heading the National Endowment for the Humanities) depict themselves as returning to the orthodoxies of yesteryear, their project must not be reduced to nostalgia or conservatism. Neither of these explain the blanket contempt they express for the country's universities. They are fueled not by reverence for the past, but by an aggressive desire to lay hold of the present and future. The B's act as they do not because they are unaware of the cultural and demographic diversification underway in the country;

they are utterly aware. That is what they are trying to shape; that is why they are seeking, and using, national offices and founding national foundations.

Pratt laments "the West's relentless imperial expansion" and the "monumentalist cultural hierarchy that is historically as well as morally distortive" and goes on to characterize Bloom's book as "intellectually deplorable" and Bennett's *To Reclaim a Legacy* as "intellectually more deplorable." In the same vein, Henry A. Giroux, a professor of education at Miami University of Ohio, writes:

> In the most general sense, Bloom and Hirsch represent the latest cultural offensive by the new elitists to rewrite the past and construct the present from the perspective of the privileged and the powerful. They disdain the democratic implications of pluralism and argue for a form of cultural uniformity in which difference is consigned to the margins of history or to the museum of the disadvantaged.

And according to Henry Louis Gates, Jr., a professor of English at Duke:

> The teaching of literature [has become] the teaching of an aesthetic and political order, in which no women and people of color were ever able to discover the reflection or representation of their images, or hear the resonance of their cultural voices. The return of "the" canon, the high canon of Western masterpieces, represents the return of an order in which my people were the subjugated, the voiceless, the invisible, the unrepresented, and the unrepresentable. Who would return us to that medieval never-never land?

Anybody who has been to such a conference will recognize the atmosphere. It is only within such a setting that Bloom and Hirsch (one a professor of philosophy in Chicago, the other a professor of English in Virginia) can seem (to people who are themselves professors somewhere) to exemplify "the privileged and the powerful."

One of the conferees, Gerald Graff of Northwestern, writes:

> Speaking as a leftist, I too find it tempting to try to turn the curriculum into an instrument of social transformation.

He goes on to resist the temptation with the following (italics mine):

> But I doubt whether the curriculum *(as opposed to my particular course)* can or should become an extension of the politics of the left.

It turns out that he objects to politicizing the entire curriculum not because there must be something immoral about using the classroom to impose a specific ideology on students, but because of the unfortunate fact that universities also contain professors who are not "leftists" and who do not want their courses to become "an extension of the politics of the left"; and there seems to be no answer to the question, "What is to be done with those constituencies which do not happen to agree . . . that social transformation is the primary goal of education." What indeed?

I said earlier that it was difficult to find a succinct statement of the objections to the educational tradition made by the so-called cultural left, but this is largely because the objections are taken for granted. If you read enough material of the sort I have quoted, and, more importantly, if you attend enough of these conferences, it is easy to extract the central objection. It runs something like this: the history of "Western Civilization" is in large part a history of oppression. Internally, Western civilization oppressed women, various slave and serf populations, and ethnic and cultural minorities generally. In foreign affairs, the history of Western civilization is one of imperialism and colonialism. The so-called canon of Western civilization consists in the official publications of this system of oppression, and it is no accident that the authors in the "canon" are almost exclusively Western white males, because the civilization itself is ruled by a caste consisting almost entirely of Western white males. So you cannot reform education by admitting new members to the club, by opening up the canon; the whole idea of "the canon" has to be abolished. It has to be abolished in favor of something that is "multicultural" and "nonhierarchical."

The word "nonhierarchical" in the last sentence is important and I will come back to it. In the meantime I hope I have given enough of the arguments from those who oppose the traditional conceptions of liberal education to make it clear why the dispute cannot be resolved just by opening up the club to new members, and why it seems so intractable. Even if the canon is opened up, even if membership in the club is thrown open to all comers, even after you have admitted every first-rate woman writer from Sappho to Elizabeth Bishop, the various groups that feel that they have been excluded are still going to feel excluded, or marginalized. At present there are still going to be too many Western white males.

The actual arguments given often speak of improving education, but the central presuppositions of each side are seldom explicitly stated.

With few exceptions, those who defend the traditional conception of a liberal education with a core curriculum think that Western civilization in general, and the United States in particular, have on the whole been the source of valuable institutions that should be preserved and of traditions that should be transmitted, emphatically including the intellectual tradition of skeptical critical analysis. Those who think that the traditional canon should be abandoned believe that Western civilization in general, and the United States in particular, are in large part oppressive, imperialist, patriarchal, hegemonic, and in need of replacement, or at least of transformation. So the passionate objections that are made by the critics to Allan Bloom often have rather little to do with a theory of higher education as such. (This is unfortunate, because there is plenty to object to in Bloom's book on purely educational grounds—for example, its failure to give sufficient attention or value to the study of history and its blindess to the achievements of contemporary analytic philosophy.) Their objection to the educational tradition is intended to make a political point about the nature of American society.

There is a certain irony in this in that earlier student generations, my own for example, found the critical tradition that runs from Socrates through the *Federalist Papers,* through the writings of Mill and Marx, down to the twentieth century, to be liberating from the stuffy conventions of traditional American politics and pieties. Precisely by inculcating a critical attitude, the "canon" served to demythologize the conventional pieties of the American bourgeoisie and provided the student with a perspective from which to critically analyze American culture and institutions. Ironically, the same tradition is now regarded as oppressive. The texts once served an unmasking function; now we are told that it is the texts which must be unmasked.

More puzzling than the hatred of Bloom is the hostility shown to E. D. Hirsch, Jr. After all, Hirsch's central idea is that it would be desirable for American schoolchildren to be taught a common body of knowledge, a set of elementary facts and concepts that Hirsch calls "cultural literacy." (Among the texts and ideas he believes should be "explained in depth" are, for example, the Bill of Rights, *Don Quixote,* and ecology.) It is hard to imagine how anybody could object to such an innocuous proposal for improving education in the grade schools and high schools. However, even this is greeted with rage; indeed, only Bloom and Bennett arouse more anger than Hirsch in these polemics. In a savage attack, Barbara Herrnstein Smith quotes Hirsch as saying that his project of cultural literacy will result in breaking the cycle of illiteracy for deprived children; raising the living standards of families who have been illiterate; making our country more competitive in international markets; achieving greater social justice; enabling all citizens to participate in the political process; bringing us that much closer to the Ciceronian ideal of universal public discourse—in short, achieving the fundamental goals of the Founders at the birth of the republic.

To this project, she responds:

> Wild applause; fireworks; music—*America the Beautiful;* all together, now: *Calvin Coolidge, Gunga Din, Peter Pan, spontaneous combustion.* Hurrah for America and the national culture! Hurrah!

Why the hysterical tone of opposition? Herrnstein Smith reveals her own preoccupations when she says that Hirsch is "promoting a *deeply conservative view of American society and culture* through a rousing populist rhetoric" (my italics). But of course there is no reason at all why students who become familiar with the range of facts and ideas compiled by Hirsch should not arrive at "radical" or "liberal" or other positions.

But what about the question of intellectual excellence? The very ideal of excellence implied in the canon is itself perceived as a threat. It is considered "elitist" and "hierarchical" to suppose that "intellectual excellence" should take precedence over such considerations as fairness, representativeness, the expression of the experiences of previously underrepresented minorities, etc. Indeed, in the recent debate at Stanford about the course in Western civilization, one of the arguments against the traditional curriculum (quoted with approval by Pratt) went as follows:

> A course with such readings creates two sets of books, those privileged by being on the list and those not worthy of inclusion. Regardless of the good intentions of those who create such lists, the students have not viewed and will not view these separate categories as equal.

I find this an amazing argument. One obvious difficulty with it is that if it were valid, it would argue against any set of required readings whatever; indeed, any list you care to make about anything automatically creates two categories, those that are on the list and those that are not.

One curious feature of the entire debate about what is "hegemonic," "patriarchal," or "exclusionary" is that it is largely about the study of literature. No one seems to complain that the great ideas in physics, mathematics, chemistry, and biology, for example, also come in large part from dead white European males. Historians of science have been showing how talented women were discouraged throughout modern history from pursuing scientific careers. But I have not heard any complaints from physics departments that the ideas of Newton, Einstein, Rutherford, Bohr, Schrödinger, etc. were deficient because of the scientists' origins or gender. Even in history of philosophy courses—as opposed to general education courses—there is little or no objection to the fact that the great philosophers taught in these courses are mostly white Western males, from Socrates, Plato and Aristotle through Frege, Russell, and Wittgenstein.

No doubt literature articulates the variety of human experience in ways that are unlike those of the sciences, but that is not enough by itself to explain the selective attitude that causes the humanities to be treated so differently from the sciences. To understand this difference you have to understand a second fundamental, but usually unstated, feature of the debate: in addition to having political objections to the United States and Europe, many members of the cultural left think that the primary function of teaching the humanities is political; they do not really believe that the humanities are valuable in their own right except as a means of achieving "social transformation." They (apparently) accept that in subjects like physics and mathematics there may be objective and socially independent criteria of excellence (though they do not say much about the sciences at all), but where the humanities are concerned they think that the criteria that matter are essentially political.[1] The argument goes: since any policy in the humanities will inevitably have a political dimension, courses in the humanities might as well be explicitly and beneficially political, instead of being disguised vehicles of oppression. These points are often stated in a kind of code. (In the code, to be "monumentalist" is to treat some works as if they were monuments, and to be "hierarchical" is to think that some works are better than others; I think "critical" used to mean vaguely Marxist as in some versions of "critical legal studies" but now it appears just to mean politically radical, as "critical pedagogy.")

For example, after having told us that "the most important questions facing both the liberal arts and higher education in general are moral and political" and that the university "is a place that is deeply political" Henry Giroux tells us the following about how we should teach "the canon":

How we read or define a "canonical" work may not be as important as challenging the overall function and social uses the notion of the canon has served. Within this type of discourse, the canon can be analyzed as part of a wider set of relations that connect the academic disciplines, teaching, and power to considerations defined through broader, intersecting political and cultural concerns such as race, class, gender, ethnicity, and nationalism. What is in question here is not merely a defense of a particular canon, but the issue of struggle and empowerment. In other words, the liberal arts should be defended in the interest of creating critical rather than "good" citizens. The notion of the liberal arts has to be reconstituted around a knowledge-power relationship in which the question of curriculum is seen as a form of cultural and political production grounded in a radical conception of citizenship and public wisdom.

He concludes that this transformation of our attitudes toward the tradition will link the liberal arts to "the imperatives of a critical democracy."

Notwithstanding its opaque prose, Giroux's message should be clear: the aim of a liberal education is to create political radicals, and the main point of reading the "canon" is to demythologize it by showing how it is used as a tool by the existing system of oppression. The traditional argument that the humanities are the core of a liberal education because of the intrinsic intellectual and aesthetic merits and importance of the works of Plato, Shakespeare, or Dante is regarded with scorn. Giroux again:

The liberal arts cannot be defended either as a self-contained discourse legitimating the humanistic goal of broadly improving the so-called "life of the mind" or as a rigorous science that can lead students to indubitable truths.

So the frustrating feature of the recent debate is that the underlying issues seldom come out into the open. Unless you accept two assumptions, that the Western tradition is oppressive, and that the main purpose of teaching the humanities is political transformation, the explicit arguments given against the canon will seem weak: that the canon is unrepresentative, inherently elitist, and, in a disguised form, political. Indeed if these arguments were strong ones, you could apply them against physics, chemistry, or mathematics.

From the point of view of the tradition, the answers to each argument are fairly obvious. First, it is not the aim of education to provide a representation or sample of everything that has been thought and written, but to give students access to works of high quality. Second, for that very reason, education is by its very nature "elitist" and "hierarchical" because it is designed to enable and encourage the student to discriminate between what is good and what is bad, what is intelligent and what is stupid, what is true and what is false. Third, the "tradition" is by no means a unified phenomenon, and, properly taught, it should impart a critical attitude to the student, precisely because of the variety and intellectual independence of the works being taught, and the disagreements among them. Fourth, of course the humanities have a political dimension at least in the sense that they have political consequences; so does everything else. But it does not follow from the fact that there is a political dimension to the humanities—as there is to music, art, gastronomy, and sex, as well as mathematics, philosophy, and physics—that the only, or even the principal, criteria for assessing these efforts should be political ones.

2.

Of the books I have read on the current "crisis" in education, the one I found the most fun to read is Kimball's *Tenured Radicals*. Kimball's announced aim is "to expose these recent developments in the academic study of humanities for what they are: ideologically motivated assaults on the intellectual and moral substance of our culture." One may doubt that he is right to characterize the current problems in the vocabulary of "crisis" and "corruption," but from my own experience it seems to me that he is right to say that "the situation is far worse than they [his readers, mostly outside of universities] are ever likely to have imagined." Mr. Kimball has attended a number of what would appear to be rather tedious academic conferences, and read a large number of books and articles in which many strange claims are made. He describes these patiently and often hilariously. He was not at the conference in North Carolina, but it seems unlikely that anything that happened there would have surprised him, because he recounts what happened at several other, similar conferences.

Kimball's method is to quote and paraphrase some of the more extreme views he encountered. For example, reporting a speech by Professor Barbara Johnson, he writes:

> Blending a deconstructionist's obsession with language and a feminist's
> obsession with male dominance, she summed up Professor Riffaterre's

paper as a "masterful demonstration" of "the fact" that "gynophobia [i.e., the fear of women] is structured like a language" and, conversely, that "language is structured like gynophobia."

... Women themselves conspire in perpetuating this unhappy situation, she told us, for "the collective linguistic psyche exists in symbiotic relation to the fallen woman." We also learned, by a similarly elusive logic, that the "literary canon is a defense against its own femininity," a defense "against the woman within." What any of this could possibly mean was never revealed, but no one seemed to mind; it all sounded so exquisitely chic.

Such a method will seem unfair if readers get the impression that in quoting extreme passages, Kimball is quoting only unusual or eccentric views. To judge by my own experience he is not being unfair; the sorts of things that he finds objectionable are, in fact, quite common. In fact, as Kimball knows, the audience at such a session will recognize Johnson's theses, at least in the sense that they know what ideas and authors she is invoking. The phrase about "structured like a language" is borrowed from Lacan; the reference to defending against the "woman within" derives from psychoanalysis, etc.

Kimball summarizes some of his general conclusions as follows:

It is one of the clearest symptoms of the decadence besetting the academy that the ideals that once informed the humanities have been corrupted, willfully misunderstood, or simply ignored by the new sophistries that have triumphed on our campuses. We know something is gravely amiss when teachers of the humanities confess—or, as is more often the case, when they boast—that they are no longer able to distinguish between truth and falsity. We know something is wrong when scholars assure us—and their pupils—that there is no essential difference between the disinterested pursuit of knowledge and partisan proselytizing, or when academic literary critics abandon the effort to identify and elucidate works of lasting achievement as a reactionary enterprise unworthy of their calling. And indeed, the most troubling development of all is that such contentions are no longer the exceptional pronouncements of a radical elite, but have increasingly become the conventional wisdom in humanities departments of our major colleges and universities.

Kimball is himself a journalist, an editor of *The New Criterion,* and his book is intended as polemical journalism, not scholarship. Nonetheless, it seems to me, even judged as such it has certain weaknesses. First, Kimball offers no coherent alternative vision of what higher education in the humanities should consist in. He simply takes it for granted that there is a single, unified, coherent tradition, just as his opponents do, and he differs from them in supposing that all we need to do to rescue higher education is to return to the standards of that tradition. But the situation is not that simple. In my experience there never was, in fact, a fixed "canon"; there was rather a certain set of tentative judgments about what had importance and quality. Such judgments are always subject to revision, and in fact they were constantly being revised.

Furthermore both the composition of our student bodies and the relation of the United States to the rest of the world have undergone some enormous changes in the past generation. For example, in my own university more than 50 percent of the freshman class are non-whites. And we are all aware that countries like Japan, China, and those of Latin America play a much larger part in our relations to the rest of the world than they did in the 1950s. It is an interesting question what influence these facts should have on our conception of the education of undergraduates. Perhaps in the end we will say they should have no effect, but it is not obvious.

Worse yet, the debate over college curriculum mainly concerns only a tiny fraction of undergraduate education, usually a single required freshman course in the humanities, together with other courses in literature which the scholars who describe themselves as the "cultural left" may seek to control, and which may (or may not) therefore be vehicles for promoting ideologies of "social transformation." Most undergraduate education—as well as our lack of any coherent theory of what we are trying to achieve in undergraduate education—is largely untouched by this discussion. Neither side has much to say about what actually happens in most college classrooms.

However, the debate about the freshman "core" course remains at the center of attention; the debate tends to be shallow because it is presented as a conflict between the cultural left, on the one hand, and the somewhat oversimplified views held by Bloom and Kimball, on the other. Why should one accept these as the only choices?

A second difficulty with Kimball's analysis is the thinness of his diagnosis. He argues that the radicals of the Sixties have now become tenured professors, and are carrying on, within the university, the same ideology that they espoused as student radicals a quarter of a century ago. This analysis seems superficial. One difficulty with it is that many of the people he cites most prominently, such as Paul de Man and Jacques Derrida, were not active as student radicals in the

Sixties. Indeed, most of the heroes of the cultural left had little to do with the sit-ins and the demonstrations against the Vietnam War or with any of the causes that concerned radicals in the 1960s.

Furthermore, the diagnosis still leaves too many questions unanswered. Why do the radical critics attack mostly the humanities? After all, tenured faculty in the humanities comes from the same generation as the current faculty in the natural sciences, in philosophy, and in the social sciences, but—leaving out such newly created departments as "Ethnic Studies"—the "cultural left" is not heavily influential outside the departments of French, English, and comparative literature and a few history departments and law schools. More pressingly, why should literature have become the academic home of radical left-wing politics? It ought to astonish us that the current university centers of activist radical political views are not in sociology, political science, or economics but in English, French, and comparative literature. We can all learn much about the nature of politics, culture, and history from Shakespeare, Balzac, and Conrad; but the study of poetry, plays, and novels is hardly the ideal basis for understanding modern structures of power or the mechanisms of revolutionary change.

Kimball has nothing to tell us about these questions. I think the issues are complex, but several factors help to explain the migration of radical politics from the social sciences to the humanities. First, as empirical theories of society or blueprints for social change, Marxism and other such theories have been discredited by recent events. The collapse of the Soviet empire only marks officially something that most intellectuals have known quietly for a long time. The standard versions of radical leftist ideology in the form of theories of society and social change, such as Marxism, Leninism, Stalinism, Maoism, and Castroism, are all in disrepute. The most congenial home left for Marxism, now that it has been largely discredited as a theory of economics and politics, is in departments of literary criticism.

Secondly, for reasons I do not fully understand, many professors of literature no longer care about literature in the ways that seemed satisfactory to earlier generations. It seems pointless to many of them to teach literature as it was understood by such very different critics as Edmund Wilson, John Crowe Ransom, or I. A. Richards; so they teach it as a means of achieving left-wing political goals or as an occasion for exercises in deconstruction, etc. The absence of an accepted educational mission in many literary studies has created a vacuum waiting to be filled. Perhaps the original mistake was in supposing that there is a well-defined academic discipline of "literary

criticism"—as opposed to literary scholarship—capable of accommo-
dating Ph.D. programs, research projects, and careers for the ambi-
tious. When such a discipline fails to be "scientific" or rigorous, or
even well defined, the field is left wide open for various fashions, such
as deconstruction, or for the current political enthusiasms.

Still, there is a fair amount of truth to Kimball's diagnosis. It is not
simply that some of the people he quotes have a history of student
radicalism, for many others do as well, but rather that often the
sensibility they express is much in accord with some of the simplistic
rhetoric of twenty-five years ago. As Gates puts it:

> Ours was the generation that took over buildings in the late sixties and
> demanded the creation of black and women's studies programs, and
> now, like the return of the repressed, has come back to challenge the
> traditional curriculum.

Suppose that one is dissatisfied with the low intellectual level of
the "cultural left," but that one feels at the same time that much
undergraduate education should be improved. This question was faced
in an acute form in the debate at Stanford, concerning the reform of
the curriculum in Western culture. Both the debate and its results are
instructive. Stanford had a required one-year course in Western culture
that had to be taken by all incoming students. This course was given in
eight different "tracks," corresponding roughly to different departments and schools. Among the tracks, for example, were history,
literature and the arts, philosophy, and Western thought and technol-
ogy. But all shared a required reading list, containing the Bible,
Plato's *Republic,* Homer, several medieval and Renaissance readings,
including Augustine, Dante, Thomas More, Machiavelli, Luther, and
Galileo, and of the moderns, Voltaire, Marx, Freud, and Darwin. In
addition, a list of writers ranging from Thucydides to Nietzsche was
"strongly recommended."

Many of the objections made to this course were predictable, reflecting the views of the cultural left I have mentioned, as were the
defenses. What emerged appears to have been a kind of compromise
arrived at after many months of debate. Unfortunately, the controversy became so fogged by political polemics and by partial and
inaccurate reports in the press that the central issues, and what
actually occurred, were not made clear to the general public.

The title of the course was changed to "Culture, Ideas, Values,"
("CIV" for short, with "Western" left out). The readings required for

all tracks now include the Bible, "a Classical Greek philosopher, an early Christian thinker, a Renaissance dramatist, an Enlightenment thinker," and readings from Marx and Freud. At least one non-European work must be studied and at some point in each academic quarter "substantial attention" must be given to "the issues of *race, gender,* and *class.*"

What was the upshot of these reforms in educational practice? It is too early to tell what the long-term results will be, but at present, of the eight tracks, seven are quite similar to the originals. To the required readings have been added such texts as Confucius, and the Koran, but I would guess that about 80 percent of the readings are by writers who are the same as, or comparable to, those in the previous program, though the texts used are not exactly the same. If anything, these seven tracks look to me like a slight improvement on the original course in Western culture, because they retain enough of the core readings so that the educational purpose of the original is not lost, and at the same time they enrich course work with readings from outside the European tradition.

The new plan also offered members of the faculty the possibility of formulating a completely revised course and some teachers have done so, with the result that the eighth track is a course called "Europe and the Americas." In this course, the required elements of the European canon remain, but they are read along with works of Spanish-American, American-Indian, and African-American authors. This eighth track presents a genuinely radical change from the earlier program, and it arouses the most objections from Kimball and other commentators.

However, it seems to me one can make a fairly strong case for the new course on purely educational grounds. Of eight tracks, it is not necessarily a bad thing to have one optional track where European civilization is taught as simply one civilization among others, and it does not seem to me at all worrying that Aristotle and Tocqueville are taught along with Frantz Fanon. Of course, as with all courses it all depends on how the course is taught. Yet even if we assume that the organizers have political goals, as I suppose they do, one of the most liberating effects of "liberal education" is in coming to see one's own culture as one possible form of life and sensibility among others; and the reading lists for the new course suggest that such an outcome is likely. Also, it is important to keep reminding ourselves that students are not just passive receptacles. In my experience, students are good at arguing back at professors, and indeed that is in large part what professors are for: to argue with. So my general impression from observing events at Stanford is that reports of the demise of "culture," Western or otherwise, in the required freshman course at Stanford are grossly exaggerated. If I were a freshman at Stanford, I might well be tempted to take "Europe and the Americas."

3.

One of the most ominous charges made in Kimball's book is that the cultural left in the humanities today has lost its traditional commitment to the search for truth. Indeed, according to Kimball, many no longer believe in the enterprise of an objective and disinterested search for truth, because they do not believe that such a thing is even possible. The claim is not that it is difficult and perhaps impossible to attain complete disinterest and objectivity, but rather that the very enterprise of trying to attain such things is misconceived from the beginning, because there is no objective reality for our objectivist methodology to attain. In short, many academics who make up the cultural left, according to Kimball, reject the "correspondence theory of truth"; they reject the idea that true statements are ever made true by virtue of the fact that there is an independently existing set of objects and features of the world to which such statements correspond.

Kimball's favorite target is a pamphlet produced by the American Council of Learned Societies, called *Speaking for the Humanities*. It is the product of a committee of six professors, five professors of English, and one professor of French and comparative literature. The pamphlet was explicitly designed to answer such critics as Bloom and Bennett, and it is written in a bland, academic prose. Its central sections, starting with "Ideology and Objectivity," begin somewhat condescendingly with the following: "Perhaps the most difficult aspect of modern thought, even for many humanities professors and certainly for society at large, is its challenge to the positivist ideal of objectivity and disinterest." But we learn after several pages that in fact this "positivist ideal" has been decisively replaced by something they call "theory," and that there are an overwhelming number of— unidentified—authorities who agree about this:

> Over the past two decades, traditional assumptions about ways of study- ing the humanities have been contested, in large measure because a number of related disciplines—cultural anthropology, linguistics, psycho- analysis, the philosophy of language—were undergoing major changes

that inevitably forced humanists to ask basic questions about their methods and the very definition of their fields.

Furthermore,

The challenge to claims of intellectual authority alluded to in the introduction of this report issues from almost all areas of modern thought— *science, psychology, feminism, linguistics, semiotics,* and *anthropology* [my italics].

And again,

As the most powerful modern philosophies and theories have been demonstrating, claims of disinterest, objectivity, and universality are not to be trusted and themselves tend to reflect local historical conditions [my italics].

As someone who takes more than a passing interest in "the most powerful modern philosophies," I know none of which it could be said that it "demonstrates" that such claims are "not to be trusted." Unfortunately the authors do not tell us exactly what results in these disciplines they have in mind. They also confidently quote "relativity and quantum mechanics" as supporting their new conception of the humanities. One wishes they had told us in some detail how the study of, say, inertial frames in relativity theory or the collapse of the wave function in quantum mechanics support their peculiar conception of the study of literature.

On first reading Kimball, it may appear that he is too hard on this pamphlet, but a close reading of the pamphlet makes it clear that he is not nearly hard enough. I do not here have the space to convey the smugness of its tone, the feebleness of its argument, or the weakness of its constant appeals to authority. Typical passages claim support from, "the most distinguished philosophers of science of our time," or tell us that, "the consensus of most of the dominant theories is. . . ."

One recurring fallacy deserves special mention. There is throughout the pamphlet a persistent confusion between epistemology and ontology; between how we know and what it is that we know when we know. It is an obvious fact that our epistemological efforts are undertaken by historically situated people, subject to all the usual imperfections, not merely of prejudice but of intellect. All investigations are relative to investigators. But it does not follow, nor is it indeed true, that all the matters investigated are relative to investigators. Real human investigators have to discover, e.g., that water is made of hydrogen and oxygen, but the fact that water is made of hydrogen and oxygen is not relative to any investigators.

Kimball sees that something very important is at stake in the debate concerning *Speaking for the Humanities*. He quotes Tzvetan Todorov's review of the pamphlet in the *New Republic*,[2] pointing out that its claim that most of the "dominant theories" reject the idea of disinterest and objectivity is "awkwardly reminiscent" of O'Brien's speech to Winston Smith in Orwell's *1984*:

> You believe that reality is something objective, external, existing in its own right. . . . But I tell you, Winston, that reality is not external. Reality exists in the human mind and nowhere else.

Kimball is mostly concerned with the political implications of this denial of an independently existing reality, but I would like to stress its purely intellectual implications. If you think there is no reality that words could possibly correspond to, then obviously it will be a waste of time to engage in an "objective and disinterested search for truth," because there is no such thing as truth. There are just various forms of discourse engaged in by various groups of people. Philosophers have a name for the view that there exists a reality independent of our representations of it. It is called "realism" or sometimes "metaphysical realism" or "scientific realism." An immediate difficulty with denials of metaphysical realism is that they remove the rational constraints that are supposed to shape discourse, when that discourse aims at something beyond itself. To paraphrase Dostoevsky, without metaphysical realism, anything is permissible.

Many arguments have been made against metaphysical realism, all of them in my view inadequate. This is not the place to go through each argument, but one can at least cite some of the texts. As a matter of the sociology of contemporary studies in the humanities, the two most influential attacks on metaphysical realism are supposed to have come from Thomas Kuhn's *The Structure of Scientific Revolutions* and Richard Rorty's *Philosophy and the Mirror of Nature*. Kuhn is supposed to have shown that science does not consist in the detached search for the truth, but that scientists instead are an irrational community, who grasp hold of one "paradigm" until they find it dissatisfying; then they have another "scientific revolution" and rush to another paradigm.

I do not for a moment believe that this is the correct interpretation of Kuhn's book, although he could have been clearer about whether he was referring to the sociology of scientific communities or the epistemology of scientific discovery. But whatever Kuhn's intentions, the effect has been to demythologize science in the eyes of people in literary studies, many of whom think that the claim of science to represent any independently existing reality has been discredited. When the authors of *Speaking for the Humanities* refer to "the most distinguished philosophers of science of our time," they clearly have Kuhn in mind.

What Kuhn did for science, Rorty did for philosophy. Rorty is supposed to have shown that philosophical claims do not correspond to an independently existing reality either. Both Kuhn and Rorty are supposed, oddly enough, to be supported by the deconstructive works of Jacques Derrida, who is alleged to have shown that the very idea of truth can be deconstructed, that the opposition between truth and falsity, between fact and fiction is an illusory one, and that is a "logocentric" prejudice to suppose that there is an independent reality that exists beyond texts. In fact, according to the literary theorists influenced by Derrida, there is nothing beyond or outside texts. So O'Brien is supposed to have triumphed over Winston after all.

Are there convincing arguments for metaphysical realism? The demand for a proof of the existence of a reality that is independent of our representations of reality is a puzzling one, because it looks like making the demand itself already presupposes what is demanded to be proved. The situation is a bit like those challenges one used to hear in the 1960s, when students would ask for a proof of rationality, "What is your argument for rationality?" But any demand for an "argument" or "proof" already presupposes standards of rationality, the applicability of which is constitutive of something's being an argument or proof. You cannot in the same breath appeal to argument and proof and deny rationality.

A similar point applies, but even more radically, to metaphysical realism. The person who denies metaphysical realism presupposes the existence of a public language, a language in which he or she communicates with other people. But what are the conditions of possibility of communication in a public language? What do I have to assume when I ask a question or make a claim that is supposed to be understood by others? At least this much: if we are using words to tell about something in a way that we expect to be understood by others, then there must be at least the possibility of something those words can be used to talk about. Consider any claim, from particular statements such as "my dog has fleas," to theoretical claims such as "water is made of hydrogen and oxygen," to grand theories such as evolution or relativity, and you will see that they presuppose for their intelligibility that we are taking metaphysical realism for granted.

I am not claiming that one can prove metaphysical realism to be true from some standpoint that exists apart from our human linguistic practices. What I am arguing, rather, is that those practices themselves presuppose metaphysical realism. So one cannot within those practices intelligibly deny metaphysical realism, because the meaningfulness of our public utterances already presupposes an independently existing reality to which expressions in those utterances can refer. Metaphysical realism is thus not a thesis or a theory; it is rather the condition of having theses or theories or even of denying theses or theories. This is not an epistemic point about how we come to know truth as opposed to falsehood, rather it is a point about the conditions of possibility of communicating intelligibly. Falsehood stands as much in need of the real world as does truth.

4.

I said earlier that we lack a coherent theory of undergraduate education. Is such a theory in *The Voice of Liberal Learning,* by the English philosopher Michael Oakeshott? In his book we are in an altogether different intellectual atmosphere from the debate about the "canon." The book is a collection of elegantly written essays, usually lectures delivered for a particular occasion or other. Both the elegance of the prose and the occasional nature of the articles sometimes get in the way of the presentation of a coherent, overall philosophy of education. Also Oakeshott uses certain words in special ways. He apparently thinks it is important that he does not say much about "education," "tradition," or "subjects," but talks instead of "learning," "inheritance," "voices," and "conversation." However, it is possible to extract from these essays something of Oakeshott's conception of the relationships between human beings and culture, and the consequences these have for what he likes to call "learning." Oakeshott is usually characterized as a "conservative," but if that is true, it is more in the sense in which Hume and Burke are conservatives, rather than in the sense of contemporary American or British politics.

Human beings, Oakeshott argues, are what they understand themselves to be; and the world that human beings inhabit is not a world of things, but of meanings. The understandings of these meanings requires an understanding of that understanding itself. It is a consequence of the relation between human beings and understanding that their inherited culture is not an addition to human beings, but is essentially what makes human beings human. "A man is his culture," and "What he is, he has had to learn to become."

A culture for Oakeshott is not a set of beliefs or perceptions or attitudes—and certainly not a body of knowledge or a "canon"—but a variety of distinct "languages" of understanding, including self-understanding. It is important for Oakeshott that culture does not consist in a set of "Great Books," but rather, as one learns and reads, in conversations that one continues to have with one's inheritance. In a "culture" there are a number of different "voices," and in "learning" one acquires access to these voices. There is a language of politics, of economics, of art, literature, philosophy; and learning consists in acquiring the ability to join these conversations. Liberal learning, especially at the university level, is therefore an introduction to this conversation, or rather to these series of conversations.

In learning, the teacher initiates the pupil into the inheritance of human achievements, but this inheritance consists of a variety of abilities. Each of these abilities combines "information" and "judgment." There are thus two components to knowledge, information and judgment, but judgment does not consist in a set of statements. It cannot be summarized in a set of explicit propositions, and it can only be acquired in conjunction with "information." Information can be "instructed," but judgment can only be imparted.

> "Judgement," then, is that which, when united with information, generates knowledge or 'ability' to do, to make, or to understand and explain. It is being able to think—not to think in no manner in particular, but to think with an appreciation of the considerations which belong to different modes of thought.

It is at this point that Oakeshott departs dramatically from the debate about the canon that we considered earlier. In that debate, both sides tend to think of education as matter of acquiring a certain body of knowledge, together with the appropriate attitudes. This is emphatically not Oakeshott's view. He thinks that what he calls "judgment" is more a kind of intellectual know-how than it is a set of beliefs or attitudes.

Universities should not be thought of as "artifacts" with a "purpose," but rather as a "manner" of human activity. The university is a place in which the various conversations go on, and it imparts the manners of the conversations. Such places of education have three essential characteristics: they are serious; they are places of study; and they are detached, apart from the rest of the society. It follows, according to Oakeshott, that concern with contemporary political and social issues is the very opposite of education.

Does all this amount to a coherent vision of education? The best way to approach this question is to see if we can extract from Oakeshott's overall vision a description of what he would regard as a well-educated person. The abstractness of Oakeshott's account leads to a certain vagueness in the conception of how we might carry it out in an actual program in a real university; however, we can at least discern the outlines of Oakeshott's person of learning. He or she is likely to be a person profoundly respectful of the "intellectual inheritance." He or she will have good intellectual "manners," and will have what Oakeshott calls "judgment." Such a person will also have a great deal of information, most of it about the past of human culture and achievements. In short, Oakeshott's educated person looks a lot like the ideal of a First Class Honours BA in Classics or History from my undergraduate days in the Fifties at Oxford. It is an attractive picture, but there are certain real weaknesses in it. First, Oakeshott does not have much to say about the critical purpose of education. His educated person does not look as if he would produce any intellectual revolutions, or even upset very many intellectual apple carts. What Oakeshott implies is not exactly conformity, but a kind of acceptance of the rules of the various discourses.

But perhaps the biggest single weakness of his conception of education is in the peripheral status it assigns to the natural sciences. The natural sciences do not fit his model, because, for the most part, the world of the natural sciences is not a world of meanings. It is a world of things; it is a world of entities, such as molecules or quarks, and forces, such as gravitational attraction or electromagnetic radiation. All of which are meaningless by Oakeshott's criterion. But, like it or not, the natural sciences are perhaps our greatest single intellectual achievement as human beings, and any education that neglects this fact is to that extent defective.

Because Oakeshott fails to allow for the ontology of the natural sciences as part of the world of our experience, he also cannot account for one of the great tensions in contemporary intellectual life, namely that between the modes of explanation that we have come to accept in the natural sciences, and the modes of explanation that are appropriate to mentalistic phenomena, such as those found in history, sociology, economics, and large parts of psychology. He correctly sees that it is bogus of the so-called "social sciences" to try to ape the explanatory apparatus of the natural sciences, but he fails to appreciate the power or even the nature of the model they are trying to ape.

The strength of his account is in perceiving that one of the great contributions of education lies not in what is explicitly said, but in the kind of sensibility that is imparted. What is said, by way of conveying information, is no more important than what is left unsaid. But the unsaid, as Oakeshott points out, can be imparted only by way of actually saying something.

Oakeshott overstates his pessimism about the possibilities of educating the new sorts of people who are entering the universities who would not have been admitted a century ago. In a chilling passage originally written in 1950, he says,

> In the past a rising class was aware of something valuable and enjoyed by others which it wished to share; but this not so today. The leaders of the rising class are consumed with a contempt for everything which does not spring from their own desires, they are convinced in advance that they have nothing to learn and everything to teach, and consequently their aim is loot—to appropriate to themselves the organization, the shell of the institution, and convert it to their own purposes. The problem of the universities today is how to avoid destruction at the hands of men who have no use for their characteristic virtues, men who are convinced only that "knowledge is power."

Kimball or Bloom might have written something very like this passage today. The characterization was true of some members of the new class of students who were entering the British universities after 1945, but it was not true of most of them. In the United States of 1990, it accurately characterizes a small number of academics who are attacking the traditional standards of rationality, intelligence, truth, and excellence in order to advance a political ideology. But for the most part, the new groups of people coming into the universities, many of them from poor families, are sadly unformed. It is not their aim to "loot"; they are often too bewildered to have well-formed aspirations. On Oakeshott's own account of culture, they are waiting for people like himself to impart to them enough "learning" so that they can form aspirations.

Our lack of a satisfactory theory of what a general liberal education for undergraduates should consist of would not be reprehensible if in fact our practice was so good that no theory was required. To do a good job of teaching, you do not necessarily need a theory. However, I think we are not doing a good job in general education. Faced with the well-known cafeteria of courses, and obliged to fill very few requirements, a student is more likely to be well educated as the result of chance, or of his or her determination, than as a consequence of planning by the university authorities. Why do we lack the confidence to require that each undergraduate acquire the rudiments of a good general education? After all, we were not always so lacking in self-confidence. When my grandfather graduated from Oberlin after the Civil War, he set out on his horse for what was then Indian territory, carrying Milton's *Paradise Lost* and the Bible in his saddle-bags. After the Second World War, when I began my education, it was no longer a matter of educating "Christian gentlemen," but we were quite confident of our theory of a liberal education. One was supposed to acquire a solid grounding in the humanities, the social sciences, and the natural sciences, usually in the first two years; and this grounding in turn provided a base for the selection of a "major." Furthermore, one was expected to be fairly proficient in English and in a foreign language.

In our current educational practice, we often do well at educating graduate students in Ph.D. programs. In fact, our better Ph.D. programs are the envy of the world and many students come from the best European and British universities to do graduate work in America. Professors feel that they know what they are doing when they prepare someone for a doctorate in history, philosophy, or physics. It is characteristic of American education that each stage is primarily designed to prepare the student for the next stage, so the best high schools prepare the student for college, and the best colleges prepare the student for graduate school. Since the professors think they know what they are doing in graduate education, it is not surprising that they also feel confident at designing undergraduate majors. The programs are designed to prepare the student for graduate work. In general education the failure of nerve derives from the fact that we do not know what we are preparing the student for.

Nonetheless, our lack of a well-defined objective is not a good enough reason to avoid stating some features of a general theory of education. In fact, it does not seem to me very difficult to describe some of the necessary conditions for being a well-educated person.

First the student should have enough knowledge of his or her cultural tradition to know how it got to be the way it is. This involves both political and social history, on the one hand, as well as the mastery of some of the great philosophical and literary texts of the culture on the other. It involves reading not only texts that are of great value, like those of Plato, but many less valuable that have been influential, such as the works of Marx. For the United States, the dominant tradition is, and for the foreseeable future, will remain the European tradition. The United States is, after all, a product of the European Enlightenment. However, you do not understand your own tradition if you do not see it in relation to others. Works from other cultural traditions need to be studied as well.

If these two streams, both the political-social and the philosophical-literary, are well organized and well taught, the claims of the various minorities should have their place. Intelligently taught social and political histories of Europe and the United States, for example, should recognize the history of all of the major components of European and American society, including those that have been treated unjustly. It is important, however, to get rid of the ridiculous notion that there is something embarrassing or lamentable about the fact that most of the prominent political and intellectual leaders of our culture over the past two thousand years or so have been white males. This is just a historical fact whose causes should be explored and understood. To deny it or attempt to suppress the works of such thinkers is not simply racism, it is unintelligent.

Second, you need to know enough of the natural sciences so that you are not a stranger in the world. This means, at a minimum, that you need to know enough about physics and chemistry to understand how the physical world is constructed. This would also include at least a smattering of knowledge of the general and special theories of relativity, and an understanding of why quantum mechanics is so philosophically challenging. Furthermore, at a minimum, you must have enough biology to understand the Darwinian revolution, and to understand recent developments in genetics and microbiology.

Third, you need to know enough about how society works so that you understand what a trade cycle is, or how interest rates will affect the value of the currency, for example. In short, you need to have some knowledge of the subject matter that used to be called political economy.

Fourth, you need to know at least one foreign language well enough so that you can read the best literature that that language has produced in the original, and so you carry on a reasonable conversation and have dreams in that language. There are several reasons why this is crucial, but the most important is perhaps this: you can never understand one language until you understand at least two.

Fifth, you need to know enough philosophy so that the methods of logical analysis are available to you to be used as a tool. One of the most depressing things about educated people today is that so few of them, even among professional intellectuals, are able to follow the steps of a simple logical argument.

Finally, and perhaps most importantly, you need to acquire the skills of writing and speaking that make for candor, rigor, and clarity. You cannot think clearly if you cannot speak and write clearly.

Just acquiring this amount of "education" will not, by itself, make you an educated person, even less will it give you what Oakeshott calls "judgment." But if the manner of instruction is adequate, the student should be able to acquire this much knowledge in a way that combines intellectual openness, critical scrutiny, and logical clarity. If so, learning will not stop when the student leaves the university. None of the books I have been reading about higher education makes even these elementary points.

Notes

1. Indeed, by "humanities" they do not mean everything that goes on under a Dean of Humanities but rather literature and cultural history.
2. July 3, 1989.

Multiculturalism/Political Correctness ("MC/PC"): Old Wine in No Bottles
David Paris

The debate on American campuses over "multiculturalism" and "political correctness" continues with little sign of compromise or settlement. Debates over curricular content and academic regulations continue despite talk about the need for dialogue and compromise, and opposing national organizations have sprung up to support or oppose MC/PC. Off campus, government agencies and the courts have joined the battle as well. A Supreme Court ruling on a municipal hate speech ordinance was, at least one justice suggested, influenced by attitudes toward the debate about cultural diversity.[1]

Critics of MC/PC have suggested that it politicizes the university. Curricula that openly support certain political views in the name of "diversity" and campus regulations restricting speech are, it is charged, inconsistent with the idea of the university as a neutral arena for rational inquiry and the free exchange of ideas. Proponents of the movement respond that academic institutions are already political. Claims of institutional neutrality and associated notions like objectivity or impartiality, it is argued, are at best misconceived and at worst merely a rationalization for existing power relationships within and beyond the academy. Thus the debate about MC/PC bears directly on questions of philosophical neutrality—of whether "neutral" (objective, impartial) inquiry is even possible or desirable—as well as parallel questions of political neutrality in (or of) academic institutions.

The goal of this essay is to clarify and examine what's at stake in the MC/PC debate by suggesting that it is a variation on a very old theme ("old wine"): the relationship between intellectual and political life. Specifically, this essay will describe in a broad way some of the possibilities for understanding this relationship in terms of philosophical and political neutrality. Developing these categories indicates that the multicultural project is often ambiguous, if not simply inconsistent, in its definition of this relationship ("no bottles"). There are some parallel, though less severe, problems in the more "traditional" account of this relationship.

Defining the Debate: The Politics of MC/PC

One hesitates to try to define "multiculturalism" or "political correctness." Any definition is likely to be taken as evidence that one is for (or against) one side or the other. Often what proponents call "multiculturalism" critics label "political correctness." Moreover, it is difficult to define this movement given the very different, if not simply contradictory, intellectual perspectives—from feminism to deconstruction, from Foucault to Lacan—associated with it. It is perhaps easier to find some unifying thread, if there is one at all, by noting the general political commitments of MC/PC and their specific manifestations on campus. Namely, this movement is committed to making significant changes in the academy that both focus on and benefit the cause of justice for the oppressed, specifically women, racial and ethnic minorities, and gays. It has been most typically and visibly expressed through two major campus issues: curricular debates about required courses and the "canon," and regulations concerning student speech and conduct. A multicultural curriculum is one that both contains texts by representatives of oppressed groups and deals with issues (racism, sexism, homophobia) critical to their experience. Regulations, as well as informal forms of encouragement and discouragement, concerning speech and behavior seek to promote a supportive ("politically correct") campus environment with regard to these groups.

These specific campus issues often lead to, and get hopelessly intertwined with, more general philosophical and political claims and debates. Arguments about required reading lists lead to the discussion of whether there is some objective or neutral measure of the value of a text, or whether all such judgments are the product—and serve the interest—of dominant groups. A debate over whether "hate" speech, somehow defined, is really action leads to arguments about whether free speech is a "neutral" value or the "prong of a strategy designed to delegitimize the complaints of victimized groups."[2] In all these areas, MC/PC contests many of the categories and understandings of more "traditional" views within disciplines and in the academy generally. Educational institutions are characterized as both structures of and instruments for oppression in society; for example, some claim there is a "mutual conspiracy between race doctrine and educational doctrine in America." The claims of the university to be a neutral arena for objective, rational inquiry, it is argued, ignore the fact that what is taken to be "neutral," "objective," and "rational" are merely

contingent, historically and culturally defined, and socially constructed—typically to the benefit of the powerful and to the detriment of
the oppressed. Thus the critique moves beyond specific challenges to
the university to a general critique of the dominant "Western" ("white
male," "sexist," "hegemonic," and so on) culture and philosophical
understandings. Finally, it encourages political activism, especially in
reorganizing the university, as necessarily following from its critique.[3]

Again, critics of this movement argue that it is an attempt to
politicize the academy in order to advance left-wing causes. The push
for "political correctness" often involves repressive regulations or at
the very least creates a hostile climate for dissenters who do not share
the political views of the proponents of multiculturalism. Still other
critics are more concerned with the philosophical premises underlying
the multicultural movement, claiming it is based on a kind of relativism
and even nihilism that is philosophically unacceptable. Whether the
critics focus on the narrower question of the proper administration of
college campuses or the broader philosophical and ideological questions about the nature of knowledge and the role of the academy in
society, they suggest that MC/PC is a dangerous intellectual movement. They claim it is contrary to the institutional neutrality essential
for academic life, its philosophy is destructive of rational inquiry and
discourse, and its politics are potentially or actually repressive.[4]

Supporters of MC/PC often claim to be offering a critique of the
academy from a sociological and historical (as well as a political)
perspective. Perhaps their claims, as well as those of their critics,
might be better understood by taking a sociological and historical
perspective on the relationship of intellectuals to political life, specifically in terms of the several ways "neutrality" might be understood.
Setting out categories concerning intellectuals' possible relationships
to the polity may not resolve the ongoing debate, but can tell us
something about how we might view it, especially with regard to
claims of neutrality.

Philosophers and Kings

The more radical proponents of multiculturalism often portray themselves as breaking with the intellectual tradition of "the West." This is
occasionally expressed in the rejection of "Eurocentrism" and of
canonical study of the "DWEMs," the Dead White European Males.
These critics also suggest that they are at odds with many, if not most,

contemporary political institutions that are, in their view, unjust, sexist, racist, and so on. So-called "traditionalists" agree that this is what multiculturalism stands for, and that is why they find it, and the pursuit of "politically correct" policies and regulations, objectionable. Both sides therefore agree that this movement involves a definitive break with the Western intellectual tradition and a critique of existing social and political institutions.

There is a certain irony in this agreement. Perhaps the chief figure in the disputed canon was also an intellectual who rejected the traditional wisdom of his society and was seriously at odds with it—so much so that he was executed (a penalty somewhat more extreme than the denial of tenure). Although Socrates is often seen as the paradigmatic figure in the traditionalists' canon, he was, like many in the multicultural movement, an intellectual who challenged the cultural and political traditions and assumptions of his society. Briefly exploring why Socrates was at odds with his society and how he understood and acted in response to that conflict suggests some categories for describing the possible relationships between intellectual and political life in terms of neutrality.

Socrates' intellectual challenge to common assumptions derived from sources of authority outside of his society. Whether that authority was the personal mandate of Apollo, the method of dialectical reason, or the theory of forms, or some uneasy combination thereof, it differed from and went beyond the culture and tradition of his society. Much of the force of the charge of impiety against him was precisely that he was seen to be posing basic (religious, metaphysical, epistemological) challenges to the dominant order. His intellectual stance put him outside the shared understandings of his culture and offered a perspective that he claimed was "independently authoritative." Indeed, Socrates made it quite clear on numerous occasions that he was skeptical of popular opinion, sought truth independent of it, claimed to rely on reason and dialogue rather than the authority of the poets, and frankly told the Athenian tribunal that he would obey God rather than his fellow citizens.[5]

That an intellectual might be at odds with his or her society, on whatever basis, does not have any necessary implications for political activity. That is, intellectuals may choose political responses ranging from entering the political fray to avoiding it altogether or finding some intermediate position that involves indirect political influence. Moreover, this choice may or may not directly follow from one's intellectual beliefs. Socrates did not undertake direct political activity to further his views. Apart from the normal discharge of his duties as a citizen, he stayed out of the political battles that racked the city. Indeed, his failure to act in times of crisis, as well as the antidemocratic tone of some Socratic dialogues, provokes I. F. Stone to denounce him as an elitist. However, it is also possible to see Socrates as a political "quietist" who consciously avoided political involvement for fear of being corrupted by it.[6] His dissent from the traditions and assumptions of his society did not lead him actively to enter specific political struggles, but instead to engage his fellow citizens in philosophical dialogues about the nature of virtue, knowledge, and so on.

This brief glimpse of Socrates suggests some categories for describing the possible relationships of intellectuals to political life in terms of neutrality. First, there is the question of the nature of the principles to which an intellectual might appeal as a source of his or her authority. We may distinguish, roughly, between appeals to principles that involve "external" as opposed to "internal" neutrality.[7] Neutrality in the broader, "external" sense involves appeals to principles beyond specific contexts or practices. It means placing oneself "outside" a practice or issue, suggesting noninvolvement, disinterest, or indifference. For example, a nation is neutral in war if it does not participate in the conflict. Similarly, an individual may be neutral between or among different items for consumption. Neutrality in this sense, however, need not be wholly passive or indifferent. It is often associated with the idea of objective observation or rational evaluation from a neutral point of view. For example, the idealized scientist is supposedly neutral between or among competing theories. He or she strives to create situations in which all individuals with access to the same data will agree on the truth of some theories or claims. Similarly, a philosopher, such as Socrates, might offer a principle (logical, moral) that would transcend the beliefs expressed in any particular situation or culture and be agreed to by all rational individuals. Whatever the philosophical or practical limits on such aspirations, it is clear that the concept of neutrality is often related to the ideal of objectivity, to appeals to a reality independent of specific historical and cultural contexts.[8]

"Internal" neutrality, on the other hand, involves understanding the application of rules and procedures within some specific or "local" cultural practice or set of practices. For example, a referee or judge is neutral insofar as he or she deals with and decides cases without reference to the persons involved but on the basis of some more or less recognized and settled principle(s). Neutrality in this sense implies the context of a practice or set of practices within which principles are applied and neutral (impartial) judgments rendered. The important point here is that this context typically provides all that is needed by way of justification. The referee need only appeal to the rules to justify his or her judgments, not justify the rules themselves; similarly, a judge need only cite the relevant law, not justify the law itself. The given context defines the appropriate rules and procedures (e.g., of a game, of judicial procedure) that can then be neutrally applied. Moreover, these "neutral" judgments are not neutral in terms of outcomes. Indeed, it is precisely their point to render judgments that often yield different outcomes (of a contest or case) for individuals, outcomes that typically benefit some individuals or groups over others.

To be sure, this distinction is hardly new or unusual. As Aristotle put it, "the question of the morally fine and the just—for this is what political science attempts to answer—admits of so much divergence and variation of opinion that it is widely believed that morality is *convention* and not part of the *nature of things*." Intellectuals' authority can involve appeals to external principles ("the nature of things") or internal ones ("convention"). Similarly, some of the force of the multiculturalists' arguments comes from at least making this distinction, if only to try to reduce the former to the latter. For example, Richard Rorty, hardly a traditionalist, also notes the difference between the arguments and self-understandings of "objectivity" and "solidarity," even though he claims they ultimately amount to the same thing. Similarly, "communitarian" critics of liberal political theory often claim that liberal notions of political rights and views on the individual often take as transcendent or rational truth what is historically constructed and contingent. Finally, there is a perennial debate within the social sciences about the relationship between the self-understanding of social agents, especially those in a different culture, and the accounts of an "external" observer. These debates, and many others in contemporary political theory, revolve around the nature and legitimacy of this distinction.[9]

Clearly, Socrates claims to be invoking externally neutral principles in defining his intellectual authority. It is also important to note that for intellectuals to locate their authority in this way need not put them at odds with prevailing beliefs. For example, the intellectual authority of the monastic orders was also based on appeals to a transcendent reality. But, unlike the case of Socrates, they shared the prevailing views. In both cases, however, there was no doubt that the intellectual principles involved were not merely conventional, contingent, or otherwise socially constructed. This is, moreover, not a feature solely of pre- or nonliberal societies. Liberal democratic theorists have also sought an "objective" foundation for their beliefs.[10]

Whatever the nature of the principles to which an intellectual subscribes, there is a separate question of whether he or she will remain neutral (distant from) or become engaged in the political battles of the society. Perhaps the more typical political posture of intellectuals is disengagement, whether the "quietism" of Socrates or the cloistered life of the monastery or even the relatively sheltered life of the contemporary academic in the university, "politicized" or not. But this need not be the case. An intellectual might decide to become actively involved in politics, especially on the basis of his or her principles. Lenin, for example, was someone who was both an intellectual and directly engaged in political action. Indeed, the Leninist party represents the attempt to institutionalize the unification of knowledge and power. Moreover, the source of authority for its intellectual claims are externally neutral, derivative from allegedly objective principles of historical development that stand outside of the particularities of tradition and culture. However, in this case the Leninist intellectual is not politically "neutral" or disengaged but actively involved in politics.

A simple table illustrates the two dimensions discussed thus far, the source of intellectuals' claims to authority and their actual political activity (Figure 1). The examples to this point have come only from the right hand side of the table, in which intellectual authority is derived from some external source. Another way to establish intellectual authority is to argue persuasively for certain interpretations of a culture's principles, to be able to give constructive, persuasive accounts of what society does or should regard as its principles. Socra-

Source of Authority

	Internal	External
Engaged	Constitutional Jurist	Lenin
Distant	Rawls	Socrates

Level of Political Activity

Figure 1: Intellectual Positions by Authority and Engagement

tes' archenemies and foils in some of the dialogues, the Sophists, claimed that they could speak effectively within their political setting and teach others to do so. They could persuasively use, or perhaps revise, society's conventions in establishing their authority. Indeed, as Machiavelli suggested, leaders might, as the occasion warranted, use rhetorical appeals to the founding of a regime or to some shared source of authority like a common religion (even as that religion claimed "external" warrant).[11] In either case there is the suggestion, similar to the multicultural critique, that the political realm is in some sense autonomous, contingent, and self-justifying.

A more contemporary, but far less cynical, example of such an appeal is John Rawls' recent claim that his principles of justice should be understood as "political, not metaphysical." Because "philosophy as the search for truth about an independent metaphysical and moral order cannot . . . provide a workable and shared basis for a political conception of justice in a democratic society," Rawls' proposes his principles as a "political charter" for liberal democracies that can limit serious conflict over philosophical issues.[12] Confining our attention to shared political principles (internal neutrality) as opposed to seeking "truth about an independent . . . order" (external neutrality) will better serve to form the basis for a "shared, workable order" among groups (in liberal democratic societies) that hold different and even incommensurable positions on philosophy, morality, and politics. In Rawls' case, intellectual authority is derived from appeals to shared perspectives ("convention") within a culture rather than ("metaphysical") appeals to the "nature of things."

As with appeals to externally neutral principles, the claim to this kind of intellectual authority need not lead to political engagement. That Rawls characterizes his principles as "political" does not imply that he is engaged in electoral or other direct political activity to have them authoritatively endorsed. On the other hand, there are examples of intellectuals, such as the Sophists or more contemporary counselors, writers, or other "public intellectuals," that are more directly engaged in the political arena without claiming "external" authority. Perhaps the purest model of this "engaged intellectual" is the jurist, especially in constitutional matters. While there might be considerable dispute about how judges ought to interpret the Constitution, there can be little doubt that they function within the broad parameters of our legal culture. Even the most expansive jurists cannot simply reject our tradition and laws in the name of some higher external authority but must elaborate their views of what our laws mean and require. Moreover, there can also be little doubt that judges are engaged political actors in the sense that they make authoritative allocations of values, ultimately backed by the force of the state.[13]

In order to get a better sense of how, if at all, the multiculturalist intellectual fits into these categories, it is necessary to add a third dimension to the categories of external/internal neutrality and political distance/engagement. To this point, little or nothing has been said about whether an intellectual's views are in conflict with or supportive of predominant cultural understandings and political practices. That an intellectual might appeal to an external or internal source of authority, or be more or less engaged in political activity, does not have any necessary implications for his or her support of existing political and social arrangements. As shown in Figure 2, there are other possibilities for intellectuals' relationship to politics that depend upon their view of existing understandings and arrangements. Thus though Socrates and the monastics share similar kinds of claims to (external) intellectual authority and both are disengaged from conventional political activity, they differ in whether their substantive views are congruent with those of their societies. Similarly, the engaged counterpart to the Leninist

Source of Authority

		Internal	External
Support of Dominant Culture			
Engaged	Critical	Social Critic	Lenin
	Supportive	Constitutional Jurist	"Best and Brightest"
Distant	Critical	Multiculturalist (?)	Socrates
	Supportive	Rawls	Monastics

Level of Political Activity (row label at left, spanning Engaged/Distant)

Figure 2: Intellectual Positions by Authority, Engagement, Substance of Views

might be the "best and brightest," those intellectuals actively involved in bringing "scientific" knowledge to the service of political power, whether it be through the development of weaponry or the "gaming" of guerilla warfare strategies.

At first glance it would seem that the multicultural intellectual is the critical counterpart of Rawls. Both eschew metaphysical claims and are not directly engaged in political activity, other than the various debates within the academy. Unlike Rawls, however, multicultural intellectuals have little interest in appealing to internally neutral, shared cultural principles, or seeking some common ground with the larger society. Rather, the aim is to criticize the larger culture from within the haven of the university and to give a voice to cultural alternatives. More generally, the more radical proponents of multiculturalism, especially in their "postmodernist" incarnation, often reject the notion that we can fix some principles, internal or external, as shared and governing of claims to knowledge and politics. Rather these are constantly negotiated and contested as our understandings evolve. Ultimately the "suspicion of all metanarratives," even those that might be internally neutral, suggests an intellectual style involving, to borrow a phrase, "a ruthless criticism of everything existing."[14] Historically one might find inspiration for this intellectual posture in someone like Rousseau or in the young Hegelians, cultural critics who seek to unmask society's claims to "objective" understandings that will transform society indirectly through intellectual criticism rather than direct political activity.

For lack of a better term, we seem to have found a "home" for the multicultural intellectual. Since many multicultural intellectuals reject any conception of (externally) neutral, objective inquiry, their authority derives from a critique of the larger culture, especially as represented by the university. The university is a good site for this kind of cultural criticism because it embodies, among other things, the pretense to neutrality and objectivity found in Western culture. Thus, they don't see themselves as "politicizing the university," but as challenging a political ideology (of neutrality, objectivity) that has been taken for granted and that has led to or supported the oppression of certain groups. Although they are not directly engaged in political struggle in the governing institutions of society, they still see the university as "political" in a meaningful sense because of its implicit ideology, an ideology they wish to subject to criticism and ultimately replace.

Whose Neutrality/Which Community?

It might be objected that the above distinctions are biased against multiculturalism. There is, it might be argued, a bias implicit in any distinction between external and internal neutrality or between political distance and engagement or, for that matter, between accounts that are supportive or critical of a dominant culture. To even use the language or "discourse" of neutrality, it might be argued, is to take the "traditionalist" view of what is "objective" to the detriment of other views. Distinctions between engagement and distance from political conflict are similarly suspect, attempting to mask the inherent political biases in the academy. Likewise, to suggest that the multicultural critique is contrary to dominant, existing ("neutral"?) understandings is to set it off as somehow different, abnormal, "other."

It might also be objected that these categories do the multicultural critique a disservice by exaggerating its challenge to "orthodox" epistemological and political views. Far from celebrating subjectivity or relativism, it might be argued, the multicultural critique offers insights into what is ignored by more mainstream perspectives and a more accurate account of social relations. It calls upon traditional scholars to live by their professed standards, to be truly objective and analyze the persistent patterns of discrimination and oppression in liberal democratic society. Indeed, it more persuasively expresses compelling ideals of democratic equality and justice. It calls upon scholars to take on the political task of being principled advocates for a society that better fulfills these ideals. Thus even if one accepts the above categories for "locating" intellectuals, multiculturalists are not so easily placed in some epistemologically or politically peripheral position relative to the dominant culture.

If we examine these objections more closely in terms of the categories in Figure 2, we can see some epistemological and political dilemmas that illustrate why the multicultural critique involves "old wine in no bottles." First, there is an epistemological dilemma concerning the source of intellectual authority for this critique. On the one hand, many multiculturalists are at least skeptical, and more often sharply critical, of prevailing disciplinary ways of thinking and standards for argument—appeals to external neutrality. In more extreme cases this leads to questions about fundamental notions of rationality and evidence more generally, and even scientific approaches and claims have been called into question. On the other hand, an important (theoretical) aspect of multiculturalism is what Paul Berman calls "68 Philosophy," that, simplistically put, "pictures culture and language as the giant hidden structure that permeates life." There is an underlying pattern to society of cultural conflict and dominance that is masked by the language of "rationalism, humanism, universality, and literary merit to persuade other people of their inferiority. But by shining the light of race/class/gender upon it, [it] can be revealed for the power play it is."[15] Though a simplification, this does illustrate the multicultural appeal to some general ("objective"?) analysis of social life, something that penetrates social convention and reveals the underlying nature of things (race/class/gender).

And herein lies a dilemma. The appeals to intellectual authority made by multiculturalists often deny the possibility of finding some rational, neutral ground for testing claims while offering a putatively objective, knowable account of the forces that shape society. It often emphasizes that what is taken to be objective is socially constructed, even to the point of denying that there is anything other than competing perspectives and denying the possibility or desirability of neutrality or objectivity. But at the same time, it is similar to more "traditional" approaches to politics and culture insofar as it offers "race/gender/ classism" as a (presumably "objective") description of social phenomena, one whose implications are presumably accessible to challenges of logic and evidence.

There is a parallel political dilemma. Multiculturalists often argue that politics is omnipresent and cultural institutions like universities are inevitably political; the question is what kind of political interests they will serve. Purportedly "neutral" standards, such as those governing academic inquiry and organization, are part of the traditionalist discourse that, again, hides the "power play" of the dominant culture. Their "neutrality" should be evaluated on the basis of how "neutral" the political outcomes of any rule or practice are, especially for historically oppressed groups. Indeed, the distinctions embodied in Figure 2 might be reduced to the single box in the upper-left-hand corner in which there is no "neutral" (privileged) epistemological or political positions but only cultural conflict and negotiation.

This notion is either politically self-defeating, if not simply incoherent, about this notion, even on its own terms, or it implicitly appeals to generally shared liberal democratic values. First, if "it is all political," then there is no neutral cultural and political ground for discussing and adjudicating competing claims, like the one proposed by Rawls, for example. Internal neutrality only applies within the major alternative cultures (alternatives to "white male" culture), having no "neutral" adjudication, only contested outcomes. If so, there is little reason, other than political preference or interest, to accept the multicultural critique or, for that matter, more traditional understandings. Moreover, this makes it difficult to define, let alone evaluate, the claims of competing cultural groups. The division of society into various tribes with their own cultures, and standards for judging issues or distributions, is potentially limitless. At the same time, the condemnation of some allegedly cohesive "white male culture" is also curiously reductive for an intellectual perspective that celebrates difference.[16] This kind of political reductionism provides little or no rational basis—the possibility of neutral values or standards for discourse (within a liberal democratic society)—for making the case for the critique or even defining the relevant groups whose fortunes are at stake.

The other horn of this dilemma stems from the fact that much of the force of the MC critique derives from its pointing out the historical injustices practiced by liberal democratic societies, in terms of their own values. The critique appeals to what were, and perhaps are, taken to be neutral, objective accounts of both the brute facts of historical discrimination and the (more or less) persuasive arguments about continuing sources of bias in both scholarly and political life. More important, it appeals to widely shared standards of respect for individuals, principles of right, and notions of equal treatment. Far from rejecting a common liberal democratic tradition in favor of celebrating cultural differences, the case for cultural respect and equal treatment often involves appeals to the basic concepts underlying liberal democracy.[17] Thus there is a political equivocation that parallels the epistemological ambivalence noted above. The multicultural critique simultaneously rejects the idea of a common culture even as it appeals to widely shared political notions.

These dualisms in the multicultural perspective are what make it "old wine in no bottles." As a critique of existing society, it partakes of a long tradition, going back to Socrates, of intellectuals' standing in opposition to the existing order (old wine)—but the ambiguities mentioned above deny it a clear platform for making its critique (no bottles). It is potentially powerful as it calls scholars to recognize some of the social biases embedded in traditional methodologies and ways of thinking—but it undercuts itself insofar as it reduces all knowledge claims to (biased) cultural construction. Similarly, in political terms, much of the force of multicultural critique derives from liberal democratic notions of rights, justice, and equal treatment—calling upon liberal democracies to live up to the values they espouse. But this is all too often mixed in with radical claims that liberal democratic values are inevitably sexist (racist, homophobic, and so on) and can be dispensed with when they do not serve the cause of certain groups. This often leads to actions that, though local to the academy, seem contrary to widely shared understandings and practices in liberal society—for example, concerning free speech—that make multicultural analyses and proposals less acceptable, even to those who would be politically sympathetic otherwise.

A cynical reading of this situation is that multiculturalism is selective in its skepticism, historicism, and cultural determinism, as well as in its appeal to shared political ideals. That is, whatever "traditionalists" say is relative to their (racist, sexist, hegemonic . . .) cultural frame of reference and therefore cannot claim to be the truth. Criticism of them and of society's fundamental flaws by multiculturalists, however, is not subject to similar critical scrutiny or skeptical doubt since it is an accurate and revealing portrayal of the fundamental social forces of race/class/gender embedded in language. Similarly, resistance to multiculturalists' proposals on the basis of interpretations of liberal democratic values are readily dismissed as (self-interested) rationalization or, worse, culturally determined blindness to the right values. Outcomes for the disadvantaged, rather than "neutral" principles, should determine the evaluation of policies within the academy and beyond. Thus, philosophical skepticism and political reductionism serve to clear the field so as to produce appropriate results, and anyone who notes the contradictions and ambiguities in the movement is open to a double whammy of being philosophically or theoretically unsophisticated ("logocentric") and politically incorrect (sexist, racist, etc.).

A more sympathetic reading of the multicultural critique would suggest that any intellectuals or groups of intellectuals will mix the categories of philosophical neutrality and political engagement. They will adopt positions or perspectives that will be admixtures of beliefs about what can be defended on some "objective" basis and views on what are (ought to be) shared values. They will likewise decide what level of political involvement or support of existing understandings is desirable and under what circumstances. Thus it should also be pointed out that more "traditional" intellectuals also often equivocate about the basis for their intellectual authority and, at their worst, indulge in parallel forms of reductionism. They are too confident about the objectivity of their own paradigms while overlooking the social context of knowledge construction. They often dismiss their opponents as "political" while overlooking their own political biases. Similarly, they fail to recognize that their political position often is not neutral—it is a function of institutional ideals and practices that have developed in liberal democratic societies and should be seen and defended as such. That is, traditional intellectuals also equivocate, perhaps inevitably, about where one "draws the line" or negotiates the tension between "political" and "metaphysical" accounts, between "distance" and "engagement."

But the key difference between multiculturalist and more traditional views is that the latter are less likely to be epistemologically and politically reductionist. That is, they are less likely to try to "relativize" categories and propositions in terms of some (typically racial or sexual) discursive community or to reduce political evaluation to evaluation of outcomes. A more traditional philosophical and scientific approach does not place justification within cultural structures or relativize belief to some ill-defined discursive community or culture, Eurocentric or otherwise. Rather it, ideally, tries to broaden the discussion by seeking to raise questions about cultural beliefs and practices from "neutral" vantage points. It is likewise less likely to view every issue as "political" and more likely to subject its political understandings to critical scrutiny in terms of general principles rather than the results for certain groups. To be sure, these epistemological and political aims are often lost or badly practiced, and what are taken to be neutral, objective vantage points are biased or simply inaccurate. Nonetheless, it is precisely the possibility of challenging such biases by appeal to (neutral) evidence and principles available to all in a liberal democratic society that makes possible a more sophisticated dialogue about the kinds of issues raised by the multicultural critique. As John Searle points out, our epistemological and political failings should not force us into a metaphysics that reduces reality to the cultural preferences of an observer or a community.[18]

To put the matter another way, it is not trivial to point out that the assumptions of academic or other discursive (or political) communities often reflect cultural bias rather than objectivity or neutrality. But it is too easy to make that observation do more argumentative work than it can bear or, worse, make it serve as a substitute for dialogue and argument. If there is no authority for intellectual life and no neutral position, internal or external, and if every arena is political and there is an ongoing cultural conflict in which we are all engaged whether we acknowledge it or not, then there is the profound risk of reducing intellectual life to political power. There is little chance of dialogue if we begin with the presupposition that intellectual inquiry and political discussion involve little more than the assertion of cultural domination. Perhaps the most sympathetic reading of the denial of neutrality and the elevation of politics in the multicultural movement is that it is a function of rhetorical excess rather than a real break with ordinary modes of argument. By reminding of us of some of the underlying assumptions and misuses of common understandings of what is philo-sophically and politically neutral, the multicultural approach can assist us in reexamining, and if necessary changing, these assumptions.

Finally, in light of the above it is tempting to suggest that there is some available, sensible, easily attainable compromise. Universities can be more sensitive to the legitimate issues raised by new forms of scholarship and by their increasingly diverse student populations. Supporters of the cause(s) of multiculturalism can reject extreme rhetoric and organizational coercion as the vehicles for promoting their aims. Traditionalists' apocalyptic rhetoric can likewise be toned down in favor of appropriate responses to these changes. Indeed, the tradi-tional resolution of intellectual differences through study and open dialogue will serve multiculturalists and traditionalists alike.

Without gainsaying such a compromise there is something about it that misses an important point. The multicultural critique promises to reveal the nature and purposes of social and political institutions through critical examination of their historical and social functions. This includes a healthy suspicion and skepticism of expressed ratio-nales for social arrangements as well as a critique of culture generally. But in this assault within the academy it seems to take for granted what traditionalists do as well, namely that universities are important because they shape the minds of young adults. Therefore the canon wars are, for both traditionalists and their multicultural critics, a struggle for the souls of the young.

But are these assumptions true? Put most bluntly, does college matter? One might well imagine a critique of the university that did not focus on the canon or political correctness but rather discussed the role colleges and universities play in sorting students and passing out credentials. Similarly, one might ask what students actually take away from their college educations or what impact educational institutions have upon a variety of communities. One might wonder what a pro-gram of testing akin to the SAT or NAP at the end of college would show about changes in students' knowledge or skills. Indeed, such a program would not even capture the upwards of forty percent of students that drop out of postsecondary schools, a rate higher than the much-maligned secondary schools. In short, neither the multiculturalist nor the traditionalist stops to look directly and critically at the impact of college, let alone their debates, on their students or the larger community.[19]

These may seem rather cynical points. On the contrary they are an expression of regret that an opportunity seems to be missed, and may be slipping away, for asking some hard questions about how the academy actually relates to its students and to the larger community. For all the talk about politics, perhaps the most unfortunate outcome in the multicultural debate is the absence of real discussion about these political relationships. The questions of intellectuals' relationships to the larger society are still with us, as they have been since Socrates. They deserve to be more honestly engaged.

Notes

1. For recent surveys of the debate, see Paul Berman, ed., *Debating P.C.* (New York: Dell, 1992); Patricia Aufderheide, ed., *Beyond PC: Toward a Politics of Understanding* (St. Paul: Graywolf Press, 1992). See also "High Court Voids Law Singling Out Crimes of Hatred," *New York Times,* June 23, 1992, p. A1, 17, from Justice Brennan's opinion, "I fear that the Court has been distracted from its proper mission by the temptation to decide the issue over 'politically correct speech' and 'cultural diversity'," p. A17.

2. Stanley Fish, "There's No Such Thing as Free Speech and It's a Good Thing, Too," in Berman, *Debating P.C.,* p. 242.

3. See Ted Gordon and Wahneema Lubiano, "Statement of the Black Faculty Caucus," in Berman, *Debating P.C.,* pp. 250: "Simple exposure [to other cultures] is absolutely meaningless without a reconsideration and restructuring of the ways in which knowledge is organized, disseminated, and used to support inequitable power structures."

4. Occasionally critics have offered more sociological and generational accounts that claim that "tenured radicals," activists in the 1960s and academics now, are responsible for this politicization. See Roger Kimball, *Tenured Radicals* (New York: Harper and Row, 1990). For other critiques see Dinesh D'Souza, *Illiberal Education* (New York: Free Press, 1991); David Bromwich, *Politics by Other Means* (New Haven: Yale University Press, 1992). For a more sympathetic view of the multicultural movement see Gerald Graff, *Beyond the Culture Wars* (New York, Norton, 1992); Henry Louis Gates, Jr., *Loose Canons: Notes on the Culture Wars* (New York: Oxford University Press, 1992).

5. On "independently" and "dependently authoritative" claims to knowl-

edge, see Charles Lindblom and David Cohen, *Usable Knowledge* (New Haven: Yale University Press, 1979). Obviously, there are many different ways to interpret Socrates' views, but the key point here is their claim to some warrant independent of cultural context and common opinion.

6. See I. F. Stone, *The Trial of Socrates* (Boston: Little, Brown, 1987); Gregory Vlastos, *Socrates, Ironist and Moral Philosopher* (Ithaca: Cornell University Press, 1991). For commentary about Socrates "quietism," see M. F. Burnyeat, "Cracking the Socrates Case," *New York Review of Books,* March 31, 1988, pp. 12–18; Martha Nussbaum, "The Chill of Virtue," *The New Republic,* September 16, 1991, pp. 34–40.

7. For a more complete discussion of the distinction between internal and external neutrality, see David C. Paris, "The 'Theoretical Mystique': Neutrality, Plurality, and the Defense of Liberalism," *American Journal of Political Science,* 31, 4 (1987), pp. 909–39.

8. As William Galston puts it, "we cannot help noticing the ways in which moral and social thought breaks through the bound of specific community practices, not in response to some external and exorcisable metaphysical need, but rather in accordance with its own inner and inescapable activity. Social philosophy that begins by seriously attending to the contradictions of everyday social practice necessarily ends by moving some considerable distance from its point of departure." *Liberal Purposes* (New York: Cambridge University Press, 1991), p. 24.

9. See Richard Rorty, *Contingency, Irony, and Solidarity* (Cambridge: Cambridge University Press, 1989); on the debate between communitarians and liberals, see Patrick Neal and David Paris, "Liberalism and Communitarianism: A Guide for the Perplexed," *Canadian Journal of Political Science,* XXIII, 3 (1990), pp. 419–440; on "interpretive" approaches in the social sciences, see James Reynolds and David Paris, *The Logic of Policy Inquiry* (New York: Longman, 1983), Ch. 6.

10. In the words of one commentator, "it has been the objective of many liberal writers to demonstrate that their political conclusions logically follow from either incontestable metaphysical claims or indisputable factual evidence." D. J. Manning, *Liberalism* (New York: St. Martin's Press, 1976), p. 119.

11. "It is therefore the duty of princes and heads of republics to uphold the foundations of the religion of their countries, for then it is easy to keep their people religious, and consequently well conducted and united. And therefore everything that tends to favor religion (even though it were believed to be false) should be received and availed of to strengthen it; and this should be done the more, the wiser the rulers are, and the better they understand the natural course of things." The masses see religion as having "external" warrant while the leaders see it as being "internally" neutral. Nicolo Machiavelli, excerpt from *Discourses on the First Ten Books of Titus Livius* in Jere Porter, ed., *Classics in Political Philosophy* (New York: Prentice Hall, 1989), p. 223.

12. John Rawls, "Justice as Fairness: Political, Not Metaphysical," *Philosophy and Public Affairs*, 14 (Summer, 1985), p. 230.

13. It is important to note that this does not necessarily mean that intellectuals agree with their society's principles. They may seek a redefinition or radical change in those principles, even as they recognize that those principles are conventional or contingent. For example, those engaged in "critical legal studies," like those in the multicultural movement, argue that jurists should attend to the consequences of the law for the disadvantaged rather than be bound by precedent and prior doctrine. The latter are seen as supporting oppressive and discriminatory arrangements. See Allan Hutchinson, ed., *Critical Legal Studies* (Savage, MD: Rowman and Littlefield, 1989).

14. The "suspicion . . ." phrase is Jean-Francois Lyotard's, *The Postmodern Condition: A Report on Knowledge* (Minneapolis: University of Minnesota Press, 1984), p. xxiv. The most radical version of "postmodern" thinking might reduce these categories to a single one represented by the upper-left-hand corner of Figure 2.

15. Berman, *Debating P.C.*, p. 14.

16. In criticizing "filiopietism and ethnic boosterism," Diane Ravitch points out the simplifying assumptions of the multicultural movement in public education, "In the particularist analysis, the nation has five cultures: African American, Asian American, European American, Latino/Hispanic, and Native American. The huge cultural, historical, religious, and linguistic differences within these categories are ignored, as is the considerable intermarriage among these groups, as are the linkages (like gender, class, sexual orientation, and religion) that cut across these five groups. No serious scholar would claim that all Europeans and white Americans . . . all Asians . . . all people of African descent are of the same culture. Any categorization this broad is essentially useless." "Multiculturalism," in Robert Long, ed., *The State of U.S. Education* (New York: Wilson, 1991), p. 97.

17. These are also values, as Simon's examination of neutrality suggests, that are shared with more "traditional" defenders of the idea of institutional neutrality, for example, respect for students and faculty as autonomous persons. More generally, as Benjamin Barber puts it, "Think for a moment about the ideas and principles underlying anticanonical curricular innovation and critical multiculturalism: a conviction that individuals and groups have a right to self-determination; a belief in human equality coupled with a belief in human autonomy; the tenet which holds that domination in social relations, however grounded, is always illegitimate; and the principle that reason and the knowledge issuing from reason are themselves socially embedded in personal biography and social history, and thus in power relations. Every one of these ideas is predominantly the product of Western civilization." *An Aristocracy of Everyone: The Politics of Education and the Future of America* (New York: Ballantine Books, 1992), p. 147.

18. See John Searle, "The Storm Over the University," *New York Review*

of Books, December 6, 1990, reprinted in this volume, on the need to distinguish the difficulties related to the "epistemic point about how we come to know truth as opposed to falsehood" from "metaphysical realism" as "the condition of having theses or theories or even of denying theses or theories. . . . Falsehood stands as much in need of the real world as does truth" (p. 209 of this volume).

19. For a similar point about the issue of hate speech, see Henry Louis Gates, Jr., "Let Them Talk," *The New Republic,* September 20, 27, 1993, "the grip of this vocabulary has tended to foreclose the more sophisticated models of political economy that we so desperately need. I cannot otherwise explain why some of our brightest legal minds believe that substantive liberties can be vouchsafed and substantive inequities redressed by punishing rude remarks" (p. 48). The same comment could easily be rephrased in terms of education generally and directed at those who believe postsecondary education could be improved by getting rid of "political correctness."

Politics and the College Curriculum
Laura M. Purdy

> For us to attempt to reform the education of our brothers at public
> schools and universities would be to invite a shower of dead cats,
> rotten eggs and broken gates from which only street scavengers and
> locksmiths would benefit, while the gentlemen in authority, history
> assures us, would survey the tumult from their study windows with-
> out taking the cigars from their lips or ceasing to sip, slowly, as its
> bouquet deserves, their admirable claret.
>
> Virginia Woolf, Three Guineas

> American education has been profoundly compromised in the past
> two decades. Standards have been eroded, curriculum has been
> debased, and research trivialized or distorted by ideology.
>
> Statement of Editorial Purpose, Academic Questions

Introduction

There is a war on over the curriculum in higher education and the
scholarship that supports it. It is an important war because curricular
decisions define in large part what educated people will know and
think, and that in turn makes a significant difference in how we all live.

Many people (I shall call them "traditionalists") think the curriculum is basically fine the way it is. According to them, it is now in part
a neutral representation of truth (or reality) and is, for the rest,
composed of works chosen for their excellence according to objective
principles. Its content constitutes the canon. Although the curriculum
could no doubt be improved in various ways, changes ought to be
made in accordance with these principles of neutrality and excellence.
I take these claims to be typical of writers such as Allan Bloom, as well
as of the academics represented by the National Association of Scholars.[1]

The critics (I shall call them "revolutionaries") believe that the
picture of the world presented by much of the traditional curriculum,
by failing to take into account such categories of analysis as gender,
race, and class, is seriously biased. They also maintain that the
allegedly objective principles according to which works are judged
worthy of inclusion in the curriculum are by no means neutral with
respect to these categories, so that many factors apart from excellence
play a part in constructing the canon.

236

Revolutionaries come in two basic varieties. "Radicals" want more time for "outsiders' " works, to remedy what they view as rampant exclusions in the curriculum—exclusions that, among other things, marginalize white women and all persons of color. They seem to see the content of the curriculum in terms of a political battle: It is a reflection of who has power. It is therefore neither neutral nor excellent, no matter who controls it.

Some revolutionaries ("liberals") see the matter quite differently. They argue that changes are necessary "to provide a more truthful account of our history and cultural heritage."[2] Thus these changes are not just a matter of politics. They also hold that in at least one important sense of the word "neutral," incorporating the perspectives of gender, race, and class make the material studied more neutral, that is, less reflective of a single (and partial) point of view. They also believe that many works are now excluded because selection principles are blind to certain kinds of excellence.

Traditionalists see these revolutionary arguments as being, at best, demands for equal time, and at worst, demands for including obviously inferior works in the curriculum in order to satisfy purely political goals. Thus a statement published by the National Association of Scholars asserts that "a sound curriculum cannot be built by replacing . . . [accepted intellectual and aesthetic] standards with the principle of proportional representation of authors, classified ethnically, biologically, or geographically." And, although the association endorses the study of other nations and ethnic subcultures, it must "proceed in a manner that is intellectually honest and [must] not serve as a pretext for inserting polemics into the curriculum." The association also "views with alarm" the "growing politicization" of the humanities and social sciences as they are being "subordinated" to "ethnic studies, the study of non-Western cultures, and the study of the special problems of women and minorities in our society."[3] Such responses suggest that traditionalists conflate the liberal with the radical position.[4]

Are these condemnations the scholarly equivalent of dead cats and rotten eggs—or are revolutionaries truly destroying our valuable cultural heritage? Or is the truth somewhere in between?

Such is the general outline of the war over the curriculum, one that is raging ever more fiercely as different constituencies struggle to determine what should be taught. My aim in this paper is to see what, if anything, can be said on behalf of feminist philosophy, one kind of revolutionary thought, in response to traditionalist objections to it.

Why feminist philosophy? The reason for limiting my investigation to this relatively narrow field is that the debate is now so broad that few, if any, academics are competent to deal with it in its entirety. Not only do different disciplines pose somewhat different problems, but traditionalists tend to lump together many strands of criticism, such as deconstructionism, feminism, multiculturalism, and gay and lesbian studies.[5] Deconstructionism seems to me to be in any case different enough to require its own analysis. And, although there are important connections among the last four, I doubt that many scholars have the expertise to deal well with them as a group.[6] However, the conclusions reached with respect to feminism often will nevertheless be relevant for the larger context.

In particular, our examination will explore whether revolutionary contributions necessarily weaken the curriculum and the extent to which revolutionary scholarship is compatible with rigorous critical inquiry, the central element of Simon's conception of institutional neutrality.

Historical Observations

Ignorance of history leaves us with unrealistic conceptions of both past and present. It is therefore helpful to have some reminders about the history of higher education and about women's place in human society.

It is tempting to imagine a calm and rational Golden Age of higher education. For instance, John Silber writes:

> In the past, the belief that there were transcendent principles by which
> we could guide our lives helped give society a goal and an understanding
> of the human condition. There was a shared vision, a set of standards
> which could measure conduct and a motivation to strive for excellence.[7]

Attractive though this image is, we should be asking what principles Silber is referring to, and by whom they were formulated and "shared."

Furthermore, knowing a bit of history undermines the vision he presses upon us. Few scholars are taught that the first colleges were religious institutions geared toward educating a small elite; women were barred from them.[8] Florence Howe writes: "by the mid-nineteenth century, such education produced Christian *man*, not so much for a particular vocation, but for what Lawrence Veysey calls 'manliness,' a combination of culture and piety, a posture substituting for American aristocracy'' (222). The rise of science and a broader conception of democracy changed this narrow religious focus into a more widely useful enterprise.[9] Many new disciplines were created, and specialization flourished. The curriculum was constantly changing and developing. Howe emphasizes:

> It is important . . . to keep remembering how new the "traditional" disciplines are. Some of those grouped under the rubric "humanities" . . . are even newer than the sciences and social sciences. In one sense, modern English departments and the literary curriculum, especially in American literature are hardly fifty years old. In general also, the basic characteristic of the curriculum these past hundred years has been its instability. . . ." (226).

The process of change was hardly a model of rationality at work. For instance, William Rudolph describes one notable decision at Yale:

> . . . for years it had been possible to teach Greek without teaching Homer, and then along came James Luce Kingsley, who told President Timothy Dwight of Yale that he would like permission to use Homer as well as the New Testament in teaching Greek. The problem presented by Professor Kingsley was almost insurmountable, so challenging was it to the idea that Yale had of itself. Greek was recited on Mondays, and Dwight would not allow Yale to be put in a position of requiring Yale students to study an infidel author on Sundays; Homer was made optional, but at the price of having raised doubts about the capacity of Yale to retain its Christian character . . . (56).

Somewhat later, Yale faced another dilemma: students wanted to learn not only classical languages, but modern ones. Yale brought in teachers—

> French in 1825—and, then later, Anglo-Saxon in 1839 and German in 1841. These noncredit options, simply courses available for those who thought that they mattered, were clearly unsatisfactory from the view of the students, but alarming from the view of the authorities. The arrival of Anglo-Saxon as an option prompted Yale's president, Jeremiah Day, to sigh: "It might soon be necessary to appoint an instructor in whittling" (66).

Such narrow-mindedness was not unique. Those who conceive of history as a centrally important and rigorous discipline may be surprised by its late appearance in the curriculum. It was not until 1881 that Cornell University set up the first history department. Five years later, Princeton's president defended the meager offerings provided by its one professor of history: "I think the numerous narrative histories of epochs is just a let-off to easy-going students from the studies which require thought" (125–26).

Furthermore, the curriculum, far from being the flower of human thought was "sometimes a creature of convenience." For example, in the early 1900s all upper division courses were made elective at the University of Illinois because there wasn't enough laboratory space to accommodate all the students in time for graduation (Rudolph, 20). Rudolph suggests, furthermore, that "while what from the point of view of the faculty looked like a systematic curriculum was often, as experienced by the students, something of a shambles" (53).

It also seems that the intellectual environment now mourned by traditionalists is very recent, a product of the flood of applications made possible by the G.I. Bill. For the first time, many colleges and universities could select for students "who represented 'the academic culture'—the curriculum, the intellectual life—setting the tone of undergraduate society, instead of that traditional turned-off or indifferent majority who found their purpose in the extracurriculum" (11–12).

Not only then has higher education changed over time to accommodate social values, but such change has been thought desirable. A cursory look at the history of American higher education shows it adapting—not promptly, and for the most part not very willingly—but nonetheless, in the end, adapting to those changes.[10]

How is all this information relevant to the question at hand? I think it requires us to see college curricula as constantly evolving constellations of courses and programs that are responsive to a variety of influences.[11] Some are internal, including no doubt the same kind of personal ambitions and idiosyncracies that now play a considerable role in academic decision making, and some are external, created by the larger currents within society as a whole. And although the general direction of curricular changes can be judged positively, there is certainly little here to suggest that the curriculum has ever been the coherent and rigorous expression of a wise educational ideal.

Let us now turn to the woman question.[12] Most influential Western thinkers, from Socrates to Nietzsche, have thought women were different from men in ways that go beyond mere biological difference. At best, they have viewed women as complementary to men, playing a perhaps important but basically subsidiary role in society.[13] At worst, and unfortunately most typically, they have asserted women's inferiority, equating us with unthinking nature and unchecked emotion, unable to reason well or think morally. What little argument buttressed those claims has rested on unfounded assumptions, bad logic, and transparently self-serving moral claims.[14]

The central problem here is, in my opinion, that society has been unwilling to see women as agents, as people with legitimate interests of our own. Hence there has been considerable resistance to the notion that what is good for us could sometimes take precedence over what is good for others. One manifestation of that resistance is the reluctance to take seriously our own conceptions of our interests.[15]

Because of our alleged intellectual and moral inferiority, it has been difficult for women to become educated. In the United States, higher education has been available to women for little more than a hundred years. In fact, it was not until the 1960s that women were admitted to the most prestigious men's institutions.[16]

Given this history, it is not surprising that there are few influential women in academe. It is well known that most women are to be found in the least prestigious institutions, in the lowest ranks, and spend the bulk of their time teaching, not writing or setting academic policy. Because of the power structure of academe, this means that our voices have relatively little weight in discussions about curriculum, and, to the extent that prejudice against women still exists, those voices command even less attention than would otherwise be the case.

Now, higher education is important. Not only does good education help develop mind and character, but it is crucial for social mobility. Yet our system of higher education was shaped largely by men with allegiances to a tradition that has, for the most part, found women intellectually and morally wanting.[17] Given this history, it is surely appropriate for the burden of proof to rest on the shoulders of those who maintain that it nonetheless responds equally well to the interests of women and men, contrary to the NAS assertion that it is "ludicrous" to think that the "liberal arts oppress minorities and women."

The importance of this question is still further underlined by the following consideration. Technical institutes could prepare people for highly skilled jobs, so why do we need colleges and universities at all? The answer, it seems to me, is that they are expected to provide society with wise citizens and leaders, and it is the liberal arts—the humanities in particular—that are to do that.

No wonder, then, that there is such bitterness about the proper content of the humanities when there is so much disagreement about

what they should achieve. Wisdom, after all, is not the mere instrumental ability to get to B from A, but much more importantly, knowing
which Bs are worth having. Likewise, conceptions of the good society
involve a host of judgments about the good life and about what justice
requires. None of these claims consist solely of facts that could be
established by means of the relevant observations, but rather involve
value judgments about what activities and states of affairs are good,
worthwhile, and fair. No such judgments are therefore neutral in the
sense that the claim "the worm creeping up on my foot is brown" can
be neutral. The extent to which value judgments can be neutral (or
objective) in some other way is perhaps the central question underlying
the curriculum debate.

How, more precisely, do the humanities create wise citizens and
leaders? Some traditionalists hold that they tell us what wisdom is.[18] A
second major strand of traditionalism defends the humanities not
because they have the answers about life, but because they grapple
with the right questions.[19]

Revolutionaries are somewhat less forthcoming about the general
aims of liberal education. *Speaking for the Humanities*, a revolutionary
pamphlet put out in 1989 by the American Council of Learned Societies, suggests that the humanities should be conceived of "as fields of
exploration and critique rather than materials for transmission. . . ."
(8).[20] Other scholars emphasize their importance for teaching democracy, or for making people's lives better.[21] Still others emphasize the
role of the humanities in helping students see new possibilities and
making judgments about good lives.[22]

Oddly then, there is surprisingly widespread agreement about the
importance of rational examination of the basic question of how we
ought to live, as individuals and as a society. So what is the problem?
Despite substantial basic agreement about the aim of education, traditionalists object to revolutionary work on a number of grounds, most
prominently, relativism and "politicizing" scholarship. But what do
these claims mean? And, are they justified?

Relativism

Traditionalists appear to be convinced that revolutionaries are relativists. By this, they mean that revolutionaries either doubt the existence
of any objective world about which we can make judgments that are
true or false, or else that although such a world does exist, we cannot

know enough about it to make these kinds of judgments. Furthermore, traditionalists also attribute to relativists the view that it is impossible to make objective value judgments, either because no acts or states of affairs are better than any others or because we couldn't ever know enough to do so. Therefore, revolutionaries are believed to have given up the search for truth, abdicated from judgments about the quality of literary and artistic work, and to have concluded that power, not reason, is the only possible basis for "moral" action.

What is the evidence for revolutionary relativism? John Searle, in his review of several recent books on higher education, repeats Kimball's view that

> . . . the cultural left in the humanities today has lost its traditional commitment to the search for truth. Indeed, according to Kimball, many no longer believe in the enterprise of an objective and disinterested search for truth, because they do not believe that such a thing is even possible. The claim is not that it is difficult and perhaps impossible to attain disinterest and objectivity, but rather that the very enterprise of tying to attain such things is misconceived from the beginning, because there is no objective reality for our objectivist methodology to attain (39).[23]

Is this accusation true? Granted, radical revolutionaries have given up on truth and reason.[24] There is also a good deal of wild talk. Liberal revolutionaries who aren't philosophers quite often say things that seem to imply relativism. In my experience, however, when pressed, they back off and reformulate their claims more carefully. Yet in the survey of the literature I did for this paper, there was not a single assertion of relativism.[25]

At the eye of this storm is the ACLS pamphlet *Speaking for the Humanities* (*SH*).[26] Although it has been attacked on several fronts, the charge of relativism is central to the case against its alleged position.[27]

Let us consider in some detail one such charge. In a recent defense of traditionalism, Dinesh D'Souza writes, "the American Council on [sic] Learned Societies . . . maintains that democracy cannot be justified as a system of government inherently superior to totalitarianism; it is simply an 'ideological commitment' that the West has chosen" (159).[28]

When I went back to the passage in question, here is what I found.[29] First, it asserts that democracy has little to fear from the recognition that all thought arises from particular perspectives, for "a system of thought that is alert to the way interests generate thought and ideological assumptions govern the most self-evident truth has a better chance to understand and analyze arguments effectively than a system that does not question assumptions." Second, it asserts that "to locate ideology is not necessarily to condemn." Failing to recognize democracy as an ideology would mean that we (inaccurately) see it as a given truth, one that is not subject to argumentation or choice. Third, it asserts that "we should not equate truth with our own political ideology." Again, we must recognize the living nature of ideology, which means that there is always a need to confront and reconcile different conceptions of democracy. It points out that people often claim that their views are objective and disinterested as a way to hide the necessarily ideological element in it. Finally, and perhaps most significantly, *SH* maintains that "one need not make an absolute commitment to the view that no thought can be 'uncontaminated' by interests in order to see how intellectually fruitful that view can be." That helps us notice weak arguments and covert ideology.

In a sense, *SH* does play into the hands of those who are looking for relativism because of its somewhat imprecise use of language, especially the way it uses "ideology." The latter seems increasingly to be used, especially by nonphilosophers, to describe any systematic theory that includes moral or political values. Yet this use obscures the crucially important distinction between an outlook based on mere taste and impervious to critical analysis, and one that is the product of empirical testing and reasoned reflection. The first use is suggestive of relativism, the second is not.

However, a careful reading of the passage in question should dispel the temptation to think that *SH* is asserting relativism—quite the contrary. It says that all ideas are produced by humans, and humans have points of view and interests. However, in paragraph 1, it also says that this fact threatens democracy *only if* reason does not help us make political choices. The comment that democracy has less to fear from this epistemological reality than any other political philosophy implies that *SH* thinks it the best justified one. In paragraph 2, *SH* says that "we may wish to argue that a commitment to democracy is not ideological but a recognition of universal truth, disinterestedly achieved, and unavailable to other more partisan cultures." Read out of context, this might be interpreted as a denial that democracy is the best-justified political theory, but it is more plausible to see it as an epistemological assertion about the nature of political judgments. In other words, political and empirical judgments are different kinds of beast, and no political judgment can be as solid as the best verified empirical one.

The same is true of the first statement of paragraph 3 ("We should not equate truth with our own political ideology."). The fact/value distinction may be less clear than it used to seem, but it still does useful work here: Moral and political judgments are *value judgments*, not assertions of fact. But it doesn't follow from their not being facts (therefore not statements of which it is appropriate to predicate truth) that they cannot be more or less defensible. The rest of paragraph 3 simply points out the obvious truth that people often claim to be objective and disinterested when in fact they are not.

Last, and most important, paragraph 4 is a clear denial of relativism. There the authors emphasize the importance of careful scrutiny for *all* claims, as they come from particular humans. But such scrutiny— eradicating irrational elements and looking for disguised ideological assumptions—is not an activity that relativists engage in, because the only reason for doing so would be to get closer to the truth. Relativists, however, don't believe in truth.

In short, it would be surprising if the authors of *SH* were to prefer D'Souza's interpretation of their position on democracy[30] to the one below:

> We need to acknowledge that we are teaching children a political philoso-
> phy, democracy, that values some states of affairs and disvalues others—
> one of a number of possible different political theories. By acknowledging
> this, we immediately raise the question of justification, for if we are
> choosing such a political philosophy, children will want to know why this
> is the one we ought to live by, rather than some other. It is possible to
> give good reasons for choosing democracy over other possible ap-
> proaches, and we should be teaching children these reasons. However,
> we need to be clear about the fact that there are certain disadvantages to
> democracy, too, and it would be dishonest to ignore or deny them.

My rewriting of *SH*'s claims about democracy makes it clear that it is a *choice*, but a reasonable one. We think that presenting democracy to children as the only possible political view, or as "objectively true," would be both inaccurate and indoctrinatory. But we do not therefore deny it to be the best-justified theory. Surely telling children the truth, despite its complications, is the only justifiable course of action. Perhaps traditionalists fear that in doing so some children will decide that democracy is not the best theory. That might well happen, but that result is still preferable to the lip service devoid of understanding or commitment that arises from indoctrination rather than education about democracy.

What, overall, are we to make of this discussion of *SH*? That D'Souza, who is not a philosopher, should conclude that Levine and his coauthors are relativists on the basis of a passage such as the one analyzed here is somewhat surprising, but perhaps no more sloppy than one might expect from a popular book. However, it is a good deal more puzzling to find John Searle making the same judgment.

In his review piece "The Storm Over the University," Searle repeats Kimball's view of the revolutionary conception of truth: "they reject the idea that true statements are ever made true by virtue of the fact that there is an independently existing set of objects and feature of the world to which such statements correspond." (39) Both Kimball's and Searle's understanding of the claims in *SH* may have been influenced by Tzvetan Todorov's review of it, "Crimes Against the Humanities," which illustrates what he thinks *SH* is saying by the following quotation from *1984*:

> You believe that reality is something objective, external, existing in its own righ. . . . . But I tell you, Winston, that reality is not external. Reality exists in the human mind and nowhere else (Searle, 39).

Searle himself takes this quotation to represent the revolutionary position and goes on to argue for the existence of an objective reality. His argument for metaphysical realism is right on the mark—but irrelevant, since there is no evidence in *SH* of the confusion between epistemological uncertainty and ontological nihilism at which it aims. That is, *SH* is warning against assumptions of infallibility, not denying that there is a truth to be found through reasoned argument and discussion.

What, precisely, is at issue here? Three different kinds of criticisms can be raised with respect to objectivity:

1. The claim that a particular assertion fails to meet agreed-upon criteria of objectivity.
2. The claim that a particular conception of objectivity is inadequate.[31]
3. The claim that there is no such thing as objectivity.

Searle (and other traditionalists) appear to believe that revolutionaries are arguing for (3). I believe, however, that despite some language suggestive of (3), liberal revolutionaries are arguing only for (1) and sometimes for (2).

Why is there such serious confusion? It appears to arise from the position in *SH* that "all thought develops from particular standpoints, perspectives, interests" (10). In other words, human thought may be influenced by the views of those who produced them. This position is being interpreted as a claim that it is therefore impossible to attain objectivity: Even widely accepted "truths" are inevitably tainted by irrelevant interests, and conflicting points of view are irreducibly contradictory.

But this interpretation of the position that thought arises from persons is not the only one, and given what we have already seen of *SH*, certainly not the most plausible one. It can instead be taken as a reminder of the importance of scrutinizing the origins of ideas to see where bias is most likely to creep in; disagreements can be taken as evidence that further investigation and argument is needed, not that argument and inquiry are necessarily ineffective.

What *SH* emphasizes is the difficulty of achieving an objective view; never is it asserted that there is nothing to be known or that reason is impotent in helping us find truth or make judgments. *SH* explicitly addresses this issue, recognizing that people will find its position threatening, for they may take it to mean that "it gives license to anything since there would appear to be on this account no objective grounds of argument, only various versions of personal or political interest" (9). But, it says, this inference is mistaken: "At its best, contemporary humanistic thinking does not peddle ideology, but rather attempts to sensitize us to the presence of ideology in our work, and to its capacity to delude us into promoting as universal values that in fact belong to one nation, one social class, one sect" (11).

What is being said here is that claims of objectivity have often been in fact mere partial accounts that have presented only part of the story. *SH* asserts that contemporary theory presses us about the "boundaries and limits of knowledge, about where we stand when we claim to speak with authority," but does not deny the possibility of definite knowledge claims (13).[32]

In sum, *SH* points out that political judgments are not facts, and that ideas come from human beings. Both of these claims are plausible and widely accepted. They are nonetheless widely interpreted as assertions of relativism, despite a reasonably successful effort on the part of its authors to distinguish their position from relativism. How is it possible to escape the conclusion that either the critics of *SH* are unacceptably sloppy or that they deliberately sought to mislead readers about its position?[33] Skeptics should go look for themselves.

Now, it may well be true that some of the excerpts traditionalists quote would, if followed up, yield expressions of relativism by *radical* revolutionaries. But even if they did, traditionalists would be no closer to making their case, which has to be that revolutionary challenges to the curriculum are *necessarily* relativistic and therefore not worth taking seriously. In other words, in order to avoid dealing with the specific details of revolutionary claims, traditionalists often rely instead on rather general epistemological claims that they believe pull the rug out from under every revolutionary case. Thus, by attributing relativism to revolutionaries, traditionalists suggest that the assertion that gender makes an empirical or moral difference is incoherent. Once the charge of relativism is shown to be untenable, however (by showing that many revolutionaries neither consider themselves to be relativists nor are relativists in fact), the discussion must focus on the plausibility of specific claims. It should be clear by now that a significant segment of the revolutionary camp denies relativism. Nor is it reasonable to construe revolutionary claims relativistically—quite the contrary, for the most part they assume both an objective empirical world that is best understood by using gender as a category of analysis and a moral world that can be made better by doing so. Hence, for example, feminists object to the common practice of doing biological research on exclusively male samples. In these cases, the possibility that gender makes a difference is ignored, even though it may be, as in the study of the effects of aspirin ingestion on heart attacks, a matter of life or death.

Thus it seems that traditionalist refusal to take revolutionary work seriously on the basis of its relativism is unwarranted. Let us now turn to the second fundamental traditionalist objection to revolutionary work—that it "politicizes" academe.

"Politicization"

"Politicized" work is work that inappropriately injects political considerations into the scholarly world. But such a claim requires analysis both of "inappropriate" and "political."

"Inappropriate" could mean injecting political considerations where they appear to have no place whatsoever, or raising the wrong issues in value discourse. One possible target of the first claim might be feminist work in epistemology and the philosophy of science. This work is predicated on the assumption that most of our existing theory was created by men, mostly middle- and upper-class white men, and that, although the fields are apparently nonpolitical in nature, they might still incorporate certain political biases common to this group. The traditionalist interpretation of this assumption as the claim that biology somehow determines thought is insensitive to the point that individuals with different experience may well see the world differently and that theory can only benefit from the contribution of diverse perspectives.

Now, I am myself unconvinced of some of the more far-reaching claims by the work I have read so far.[34] However, the idea here that our most fundamental conceptions about knowing are at present marked in unnecessary and perhaps harmful ways by their genesis is interesting, and, if true, would constitute a clear advance in theory. That none of this feminist work has so far been unambiguously successful ought neither to be surprising, given its short history, nor grounds for the contempt now being heaped upon it. How many radical new intellectual perspectives got it right immediately? We cannot, in any case, say *a priori* where politics will turn out to be relevant.

The view that it is possible to raise the "wrong" questions in value discourse will be examined later. Let us now turn to questions about the meaning of "political."

One of the interesting features of the curriculum debate is the glaring absence of definitions of this key word. So we need to start here by looking at the way the word gets used. One clear implication of the claim that a given piece of work is "political" seems to be the view that politics are incompatible with good scholarship.[35] That could mean either that political conviction is incompatible with scholarly integrity or that it is incompatible with appropriate scholarly openness.[36]

That political conviction is incompatible with scholarly integrity is rarely articulated in a straightforward way by traditionalists, but it forms an unmistakable undercurrent in their work. In some cases, it may be an appeal to the clearly false claim that all revolutionaries are relativists, since integrity is irrelevant for scholarship that makes no truth claims. The new charge would have to be that revolutionaries' political convictions override all other values, including honesty. So they are believed to ignore inconvenient evidence, take material out of context, twist their opponents' arguments, gloss over contradictions in their own positions, and indulge in a variety of fallacies such as straw person, hasty generalization, and red herring.

The simplest version of this position is that revolutionaries, unlike traditionalists, have political convictions, and political convictions are necessarily connected with lack of integrity. The obvious objection to this position is that everybody has political convictions, and so it cannot be that having them is tied to lack of integrity unless one is willing to concede that nobody has it. Political convictions are, after all, simply our most basic judgments about justice. As such, all thinking citizens—including traditionalists—have them, even if unarticulated and inconsistent.

Perhaps having traditionalist convictions protects your integrity either because defending the status quo is less compelling a passion than pressing for change or there is something especially noxious about revolutionary beliefs. But repelling attacks on a beloved status quo isn't necessarily less urgent a concern than pushing for change. Nor has it yet been shown that there is anything especially noxious about revolutionary visions of justice.

The difficulty in evaluating this matter is obvious: The impact of political beliefs on scholarship is hard to measure, partly because no one is free of political leanings and partly because of the enormous scope of the inquiry. I believe, however, that there are some basic rules of good scholarship and they can help us tell good work from bad.[37] Nobody using those rules could conclude that revolutionaries have a monopoly on bad scholarship. In fact, I found a great deal of such work on the part of traditionalists at junctures where one would, on the contrary, expect them to be scrupulously careful, namely in their case against revolutionaries.[38]

Unfortunately, it looks as though inadequate scholarship often characterizes traditionalist criticism of feminism. Common but faulty patterns of argument include equating feminism with its most speculative claims and rejecting it on that basis, leaving untouched its basic claims about justice.[39] Another is the "chamber of horrors" account. There we find catalogs of obviously ridiculous positions interspersed with quite reasonable claims that the author wants us to consider beyond the pale—without argument.[40] A variation of this technique lists a series of outrageous incidents, but given the general level of accuracy I have been discovering in this literature, I have become skeptical that many of them occurred as described.[41] No doubt a few did, but it is fallacious to condemn a theory on the basis of wild claims propounded by some of its adherents. Last, there is a good deal of emotionally loaded language in traditionalist work, hardly the sign of dispassionate scholarship that relies solely on reason.[42] It seems, at the very least, that traditionalism is no guarantee of good scholarship.

Let us now go on to consider whether feminism undermines good scholarship by interfering with scholarly openness. Before looking in detail at this question, we need to get clear about what it means to be a feminist. Although I cannot speak for every feminist, it is generally agreed that women's interests are not treated with the same respect as those of men and that justice requires that this state of affairs be remedied.[43]

Narrowing the question now to philosophy, and in particular to ethics and political philosophy, what does feminism mean? Alison Jaggar suggests that feminist philosophers are committed to eliminating male bias in ethics.[44] Many readers are no doubt skeptical that there is any significant male bias in ethics, and hence regard this project with jaundiced eye. Before dismissing it, however, recall that the discipline of ethics has been until lately the creation of men.[45] It is therefore quite possible that despite their attempts to be rational and objective, ethics now bears the marks of distinctively male interests—in both senses of the term. Surely it is better to be alert to this possibility so as to detect bias if it exists than to be so convinced of its absence that it wouldn't be noticed even if it were there.

Jaggar maintains that this project assumes the wrongness of women's subordination and the equal seriousness of women's and men's moral experience. These assumptions in turn require us to use gender as a category of analysis, as it is always possible that women and men are not similarly situated. When they are not, it is important to investigate whether the differences are either a result of or a source of hitherto unnoticed unfairness. They also require us to keep in mind the broad consequences of actions and to extend moral reasoning to the domestic realm (97–99).[46]

What, in practical terms, are the consequences of these guidelines? First, because of our conviction that women are as important as men, we notice when women's interests are discounted or ignored, or where issues that are especially important to our lives are not considered worthy of investigation at all.[47] Second, these concerns lead us often to adopt a number of specific strategies. One is an interest in understanding the reasons why people behave as they do. Another is making sure we look at a given situation from the point of view of all the affected parties, and over the long run. Still a third is attempting to come up with solutions to moral conflicts that involve structural rather than purely individual change and to find remedies that spread costs as equally as possible. In short, we try to be quick to understand and sympathize, and slow to condemn.[48]

Apart from these approaches, feminist work is mostly conducted in the usual ways. We try to get a full picture of the problematic situation, consider alternative explanations of how it got that way, and try to envision different possible solutions. We sift through arguments and objections, evaluating claims according to reason, employing principles, logic and evidence. The diversity of feminist viewpoints means that we spend substantial amounts of time criticizing each other in the attempt to come up with solid answers. For example, I often disagree with radical feminist critics of new reproductive practices. In that work I give grounds for rejecting some of their basic premises, argue for the relevance of facts they ignore, and point out bad consequences of their proposed solutions. My arguments—and theirs—can be judged by the usual criteria for scholarship.

Is there anything unscholarly about these interests, strategies, or approaches? On the contrary, I contend that they are an improvement over the less thorough and humane work now quite common in applied ethics.[49] Traditionalists may criticize our overall goal of eliminating male bias in ethics, but it remains to be shown that this goal is any more "political" than the conviction that ethics is fine the way it is.[50] Thus it would be unwarranted to reject feminist ethics on the grounds that they are "politicized" or biased.

We have, in the course of this discussion, crept into the realm of value judgments where the centrally important disagreements lie. It is here that accusations that feminists think that the wrong questions are important,[51] or that we look at the right questions in the wrong way, find their mark.[52]

Now some people seem to believe that moral discussion itself is out of place in academe. However, other influential traditionalists concede its importance; for them, remember, the function of the humanities is to give us a forum for discussing the good life. But "the good life" tends to be categorized as a moral question, even though its political ramifications cannot be ignored by any adequate treatment. But for now we can put off discussion of the difference, for Bloom himself admits that the low quality of *political* thinking in our society is the fault of the university. In the 1960s, according to him, "the university had abandoned all claim to study or inform about value—undermining the sense of value of what it taught, while turning over the *decision* about values to the folk, the *Zeitgeist*, the relevant" (313). Now whether Bloom's claim is historically accurate or not, we can certainly agree that *if* political discourse is rejected as inappropriate for academe, where will people learn to distinguish good argument from bad? In that case, both students and professors are likely to adopt unexamined principles based on perceived self-interest or popular opinion. So he is right that for the university to reject moral and political discourse as an appropriate preoccupation is asking for ignorant, ill-thought-out political rhetoric and action, not only in academe but elsewhere as well. Furthermore, his conception of political discourse as *reasoned* discourse is certainly right—discourse where conceptual analysis, logic, and empirical evidence play a significant role.

Bloom mourns the "apolitical character" of the humanities, "the habitual deformation or suppression of the political content in the classic literature, which should be part of a political education" (353). In particular, he mourns the fact that "no one even tries to read [the Great Books] as they were once read—for the sake of finding out whether they are true" (373). His view, quite rightly I think, is that the reason for reading Greek ethics is to find out what a "good man" is—not just to find out what the Greeks thought he was like (373). Alas, he says, the "professors who now teach them do not care to defend them, are not interested in their truth" (374).

Apparently, however, feminists do not count ("no one even tries to read them as they were once read—for the sake of finding out whether they are true."). For it is we who avidly read Aristotle (and Plato and Kant and Nietzsche . . .), to see how well supported is the case for our inferiority. It is true that we have less interest than Bloom in the question of what makes a "good man." We are far more interested in what it takes to be a good person—a question Aristotle fails to consider. Humans, for him, are divided into radically different kinds, each with their appropriate virtues. And like many of his successors, Aristotle thinks that women's inferiority justifies using us to further men's interests, not our own. Yet that conclusion, to the extent that Aristotle stoops to argue for it, is based on patently absurd claims.[53]

Why does our attention not win Bloom's approval, the Bloom who asserts that "the latest enemy of the vitality of classic texts is feminism"?[54] He says that feminists either attempt to "expunge the most offensive authors—for example, Rousseau—from the education of the young or to include feminist responses in college courses, pointing out the distorting prejudices, and using the books only as evidence of the misunderstanding of woman's nature and the history of injustice to it" (66). I doubt many feminist instructors believe in "expunging" sexist "great men"; for one thing, it is far too much fun—and far too instructive—to analyze what they have to say! Humor aside, what is wrong with "including feminist responses"?

Underlying Bloom's comments is the premise that we are making mountains out of molehills. The comments on women constitute only a small part of Aristotle's works, and his misogyny is an aberration that does not affect the whole in any important way. We are simply to ignore what he says about women, and pretend to be men. That is, after all, what many of us did in graduate school when we first confronted the issue.[55] But, as feminist writers have been pointing out for some time now, "add women (delete, in this case) and stir" won't work. For not only are we unlike men in some important ways, but to lose serving women leaves a gaping hole in the support system for men. How can men exercise their liberal virtues if no one is tending the babies and making dinner? Or are Aristotle's "natural slaves" to fill the gap? Ignoring such a central problem in Aristotle's ethics and politics, as traditionalists tend to do, suggests that it is neither serious nor important. Feminists contend that it is both.

No less important is Aristotle's influence on Western civilization's attitude toward women. To say that this attitude and its consequences are unimportant is to say that social inequality, in general, and the subordination of women, in particular, is unimportant. This is, of course, a political judgment—just like our objection to it—and both need to be backed up by argument.

Without a definition of "politics," we can make no further headway here. Once we rule out the objection that to be "political" (as opposed to justifiably "moral") is to deny that reason has a prominent place in judgments about value, what is left? Is there a distinction here between "the political" and "the moral" such that it is appropriate ("moral") to discuss certain carefully circumscribed questions about the good life, but inappropriate ("political") to consider the associated broader questions about the justice of every basic social institution?

There is some reason for thinking that some such notion is at work here, even if not explicitly supplied by traditionalists. For example, it seems clear that they are reluctant to extend moral analysis to the private realm, where until lately most middle- and upper-class Western women have been confined.[56] The issues represented by the feminist slogan "The personal is the political!" crystallize the disagreement here. Traditionalists are clearly uncomfortable with the conception of women as individuals having their own interests. To see women as such agents is to have to admit the possibility that their interests will sometimes be in conflict with those of men, and that the instrument we use for adjudicating between men's conflicting interests, justice, might also be appropriate for the ones that arise between women and men.

Thus, for example, Virginia Hyman objects to the feminist insight that there may be conflicts of interest between women and men. She says that feminists hold that "the relationship between men and women is essentially one of conflict" (13). She points out that feminists admit that "this view is 'perhaps its hardest premise to absorb into general social analysis' " (13). She goes on to say:

> Why this view meets with such resistance is never examined. The possibility that relationships between the sexes may be complementary and interdependent, to say nothing of sexual, is not considered. Granted their view that sexual and family relationships may be viewed as power struggles, such relationships may also be viewed as complex networks of dependency. How can anyone ignore the fact that women as well as men enter these relationships freely, and that they can be based on deep feelings of love, affection, and commitment? (13)

Perhaps there are radical feminists with the view Hyman attributes to feminism as a whole, but the position she refutes is a caricature of the most reasonable and widely-held feminist position about the relationship of the sexes. This position sees women entering into relationships with men more or less freely, depending on the economic and social factors that constrain their choices. That these relationships may be based on love and that they involve mutual dependence, including sexual dependence, is undeniable. However, feminists also see women as agents with their own interests, and hence conflicts of interest between women and men in marriage are both possible and quite common.[57] Hyman seems to be unable to think in any but all-or-nothing terms here, both with respect to the position she attributes to feminists and in her own view. Furthermore, anybody who has even a nodding acquaintance with recent work in feminist ethics knows that it most commonly sees connections with other humans, not conflict, as primary.[58]

Traditionalists' preferred image is that of women and men living harmoniously together so that there is no need for justice. Distaste for importing justice thinking into the domestic realm seems to me to be in fact close to the core of the accusation that revolutionaries are "politicizing" scholarly treatment of such matters.

On the one hand, this position might simply represent the rejection of a kind of philosophy that concerns itself with limited, particular questions rather than the most universal ones, a kind of philosophy that, according to Stephen Toulmin, was dominant until Descartes' time.[59] Yet it is no secret that most of the influential philosophers have themselves made distinctions between the different kinds of good lives suitable for different categories of people. Does that mean that Plato and Aristotle, Kant and Nietzsche, weren't doing philosophy? Perhaps there is room here for a legitimate difference of opinion about the appropriate scope of philosophical discourse, but why should that issue engender such emotion?

On the other hand, this question of the appropriate scope of philosophy isn't relevant to the central moral and political questions raised by feminism. First, it is easy to forget that gender is not something just women have, so studying gender isn't just studying women.[60] Second, despite their premise that women are as important as men, feminist moral philosophers are, like those famous philosophers who preceded them, fundamentally interested not in women but in women's proper place in the social web.[61] But unlike most of those philosophers, we are criticizing, not shoring up, the status quo.

Women, say feminists, are unjustly treated. By rejecting such claims as mere "political" campaigns on the part of "special interests," traditionalists can push away the demand that they come to grips with the evidence offered in defense of that claim. They can also get away without having to provide a case for their own view that women have no pressing complaints. Certainly, none of the objections offered so far on behalf of that position justify its failure to respect the feminist challenge. The discussion here *is* political, and the attempt to argue that some particular stand with respect to it is not political is untenable—as writers like Bloom who concede its political nature must recognize.[62] Therefore when we hear that feminist treatments of Aristotle or Kant, Rousseau or Nietzsche are "politicized"—but never that the writers themselves are "politicized"—it is hard to escape the conclusion that arguing for equal consideration for women is "political," whereas being satisfied without it is not.

Conclusion

At the beginning of this paper I said my aim is to see whether traditionalist criticisms of academic feminism have any merit. This is obviously a large subject, about which a good deal more needs to be said. However, it should be clear that the most prevalent and serious criticisms are groundless: Feminism is neither a kind of relativism nor does it pursue an inappropriately political program. By concentrating on such criticisms, traditionalists take a weak part of the revolutionary movement for the whole, and, having refuted that part believe that they have come to grips with the whole. This is a classic case of the straw-person fallacy. Consequently, the automatic rejection feminist work gets in some quarters is unjustified; in particular, efforts to gain a place for feminist concerns in the college curriculum deserve respect and support.

It should not be inferred from what I have said that I think that all work done in the name of feminism is sound or that every feminist criticism of professors, courses, or research is defensible. It is an unfortunate fact that any powerful social movement will include some who have only half understood it as well as those who are more interested in power than in justice. Nor should those who lose sight of truth in the pursuit of justice be forgotten.[63] However, to reject feminism on the basis of their doings is intellectually and morally irresponsible.

More generally, given the opposing conviction about deeply-held values that underlie the debate, it is especially important to insist on rigorous standards of evidence and rationality. Emotionally satisfying as it may be to join the outcry against the latest outrages (whether traditionalist or revolutionary), doing so on the basis of unsubstantiated accounts and prejudice deepens rifts instead of promoting healing dialogue. Feminists and nonfeminists alike therefore have a duty to constructively criticize teaching, scholarship, and criticism itself. They must also counter attempts to suppress honest discussion, whether by censorship, disruption, distortion, or name-calling. Properly understood, the best of revolutionary scholarship is no less compatible with rigorous standards of inquiry than the best of traditional scholarship. Rigorous argument, reasoned discourse, and critical inquiry are not the exclusive domains of traditionalism but are central to a variety of diverse nontraditional perspectives, including feminism. If a neutral university simply is one committed to critical inquiry, feminism and critical neutrality are not necessarily in conflict.

Notes

1. Allan Bloom, *The Closing of the American Mind* (New York: Simon & Schuster, 1987). The National Association of Scholars is an organization formed to counter the influence of revolutionaries. It emphasizes traditional approaches to scholarship and claims that only such approaches maintain the highest standards of excellence.

2. From the "Statement of Principles" of *Teachers for a Democratic Culture*, a group formed to counter the influence of conservatives. Patricia

Aufderheide, ed., *Beyond PC: Toward a Politics of Understanding* (St. Paul: Graywolf Press, 1992), p. 67.

3. "Is the Curriculum Biased?" A Statement by the National Association of Scholars, *APA Newsletters*, Vol. 898, No. 1 (Fall 1989): p. 102.

4. The "Statement of Principles" of Teachers for a Democratic Culture, an organization formed to counter the NAS, also makes this point. Traditionalists, it asserts, "make no distinction between extremists among their opposition and those who are raising legitimate questions about the relations of culture and society." [Patricia Aufderheide, ed., *Beyond PC: Toward a Politics of Understanding* (St. Paul: Greywolf Press, 1992), p. 68.]

5. See for example Roger Kimball, *Tenured Radicals* (New York: Harper & Row, 1990), Preface.

6. For this reason, and because this paper is already far too long and complicated, I will not be raising obviously relevant examples and points as I go along. It should not be inferred that I doubt either their importance in their own right or their intrinsic connection with feminism.

7. John Silber, "The Alienation of the Humanities," *Academic Questions*, Vol. 2, No. 3 (Summer 1989): p. 16.

8. Florence Howe, "Breaking the Disciplines," in Florence Howe, *Myths of Coeducation* (Bloomington: Indiana University Press, 1984), p. 222.

9. Frederick Rudolph, *Curriculum: A History of the American Undergraduate Course of Study Since 1636* (San Francisco: Jossey-Bass, 1977), pp. 14–15.

10. Rudolph writes: "Some young professor once said of the possibilities of curricular reconstruction in his institution: 'The progress of this institution will be directly proportional to the death rate of the faculty.' " Rudolph comments: "The professor was an optimist. College faculties by the late nineteenth and early twentieth centuries had developed an authority that made the course of study a jealously guarded compound of special interests. By then it seldom mattered who died . . ." (17–18).

11. Rudolph tells us that "by 1960, 2,452 different kinds of degrees had been conferred, 832 of which had been abandoned, casualties of changing academic fashion, curricular consolidation, or a revision of standards" (9).

12. It is easy to forget how recent is women's access to higher education, or indeed, to anything resembling equality under the law in the United States—or any other society. We have been voting citizens for less than a hundred years, and it is important to remember that this central right of citizenship was not won by sweet reason. A hard look at the statistics that measure the differences between women and men supports the conclusion that there is a serious imbalance of power, freedom, and welfare between them. It is plausible to believe that this state of affairs is both a result of negative attitudes about women and of the inadequate education stemming from those attitudes in the first place.

13. Two well-known exceptions here are Plato and Mill. Plato examined the possibility that women might be fitted to rule, in the *Republic*, and Mill argued forcefully for women's equality in *The Subjection of Women*.

14. See Aristotle, for instance.

15. This problem is somewhat more complicated than I describe here, given the powerful social pressures that tend to obscure women's views of what is in their interest.

16. A review of reasons used over the years to keep women out of higher education doesn't inspire confidence in the wisdom of tradition. Consider, for instance, the notorious Dr. Clarke, who held that brain activity drained energy from women's reproductive organs and led to a depressed birthrate among the "best" women. Even once the point was won, it is instructive to note how long it has taken for colleges and universities to reject the idea of a special women's curriculum intended to prepare us for domesticity. See Edward H. Clarke, *Sex in Education: A Fair Chance for the Girls* (Boston: James R. Osgood and Company, 1873).

17. To be sure, feminists now utilize egalitarian principles initially proposed by traditionally important writers. The problem is that those who, like Mill, saw women as persons to whom such principles apply, have been less influential than those who did not, or who, like Aristotle, held fundamentally hierarchical views.

18. A different and fairly common view is that the aim of the humanities is the development of our capacity for aesthetic judgment and enjoyment. For instance, Irving Howe says that

> . . . we should want our students to read Shakespeare and Tolstoy, Jane Austen and Kafka, Emily Dickenson and Leopold Senghor, not because they "support" one or another view of social revolution, feminism, or black self-esteem. They don't, in many instances; and we don't read them for the sake of enlisting them in a cause of our own. We should want students to read such writers so that they may learn to enjoy the activity of the mind, the pleasure of forms, the beauty of language—in short, the arts in their own right.

A related view seems at times to be espoused by Allan Bloom, who, according to Martha Nussbaum sees the university as a refuge for those who wish to practice "a philosophy that is not practical, alive, and broadly distributed, but contemplative and quasi-religious, removed from ethical and social concerns, and the preserve of a narrow elite."

These views are not in themselves political, but they have, by omission, important political consequences.

19. See for example, Thomas Pangle, "Entering the Great Debate," *Academic Questions*, Vol. 2, No. 2 (Spring 1989): p. 24; and Allan Bloom, *The Closing of the American Mind*, p. 251.

20. George Levine, Peter Brooks, Jonathan Culler, Marjorie Garber, E. Ann Kaplan, and Catharine R. Stimpson, *Speaking for the Humanities* (American Council of Learned Societies, ACLS Occasional Paper, No. 7, 1989). Hereafter, *SH*.

21. See Elizabeth Kamarck Minnich, "From Ivory Tower to Tower of

Babel?" *The Politics of Liberal Education, The South Atlantic Quarterly*, ed. Daryl J. Gless and Barbara Herrnstein Smith, Vol. 89, No. 1 (Winter 1990): pp. 181–94; and Richard Rorty, "Two Cheers for the Cultural Left," in Gless and Herrnstein Smith, pp. 232–33.

22. Consider Florence Howe, "Literacy and Literature," in Howe, *Myths*.

23. John Searle, "The Storm Over the University," *The New York Review of Books*, (December 6, 1990): pp. 34–42 reprinted in this volume.

24. Some radicals may simply be epistemological relativists; others, more fundamentally, may be ontological ones.

25. It did not include deconstructionist accounts, which I gather are relativistic.

26. Levine et al.

27. Among those who attack it are Kimball, Searle, and Tzvetan Todorov in his "Crimes Against the Humanities," *The New Republic*, (July 3, 1989): pp. 26–30; and Dinesh D'Souza, *Illiberal Education: The Politics of Race and Sex on Campus* (New York: The Free Press, 1991).

28. D'Souza, *Illiberal Education*, p. 159. D'Souza's unreliability is conceded even by some who are apparently favorably disposed toward him. For example, see C. Vann Woodward, "Freedom and the Universities," in Aufderheide. He writes: ". . . it would be wise to bear in mind that *Illiberal Education* is a polemical work written with strong conviction to condemn and persuade, and that it is largely a collection of negative examples. Its moderation in tone and style may put readers off guard for its occasional stretching of evidence and logic to score a point. When I first wrote on the book I accepted its purely factual statements as true; on the whole, for a subject so heatedly debated up to the last moment, the investigation seemed reasonably thorough, the rhetoric comparatively temperate, and the documentation fairly detailed, if sometimes very selective. Unfortunately, the book turned out to contain some serious and irresponsible factual errors" (29). Considering that the curriculum debate focuses in part on scholarly integrity and standards, this writer seems remarkably tolerant of D'Souza's errors.

29. *SH* is both a quasi-official revolutionary document and the focus of much traditionalist criticism. Therefore, it seems to me to be a fair and representative piece to consider in detail here. The passage in quote is a continuous passage, but to make it easier to read and refer to, I have separated and numbered the paragraphs.

30. I am using"democracy" in a broad and undefined way here since the context requires nothing more, and it would take us far out of our way to consider its many meanings.

31. I take it that is the import of the claim that the literary canon excludes works that belong in it, not necessarily because they represent the output of certain categories of humans, but that they are excellent in a way that the canon does not recognize.

32. The puzzling issue here is whence arose this tempest about relativism.

How can a philosopher like Searle be led so far astray by the occasional sloppy use of language in *SH*, especially since he is fully aware that the authors are not philosophers, and are therefore likely to be imprecise in ways philosophers wouldn't be? One might well disagree with a good deal that they say without thereby having any justification for concluding that they are relativists— certainly not, as Todorov claims, that they "gladly confess to the crime of which they are accused. They explain that there is no such thing as truth or objectivity. . . ." (28) Hence Todorov's reference to *1984* is irrelevant. Yet it is repeated by both Kimball and Searle.

33. Remember that these critics are important personages. Todorov and Searle are major scholarly figures, Searle, a philosopher; Kimball has written a popular and widely-cited book.

34. For example, although the work of Evelyn Fox Keller and Genevieve Lloyd contains much of interest, I do not think they have succeeded in making a compelling case for their respective theses. But a great deal more work on rationality, objectivity, and science has come out in the last few years, and it is increasingly powerful and sophisticated.

35. Virginia Hyman, "Conflict and Contradiction: Principles of Feminist Scholarship," *Academic Questions* Vol. 1, No. 1 (Winter 87–88), pp. 5-17; D'Souza, pp. 210–11.

36. See for example, Hyman, p. 9.

37. A goodly part of the contemporary feminist critique of scholarship has to do with scholars' refusal to apply their own public standards properly. Another part does address those standards, attempting—sometimes success-fully—to show that the rules wrongly exclude certain kinds of worthwhile insights and others are biased in gross or subtle ways that lead to skewed results. But those cases must themselves meet basic standards of logic, well-supported empirical claims, completeness, honesty and fairness. What those in turn require is sometimes open to dispute, but that does not mean that they are never useful.

38. For a particularly striking example of dishonest traditional scholarship, see Virginia Hyman, "Conflict and Contradiction: Principles of Feminist Scholarship," *Academic Questions*, Vol. 1, No. 1 (Winter 1987–88), pp. 5–17. This piece is a review of Ellen Carol DuBois, Gail Paradise Kelly, Elizabeth Lapovsky Kennedy, Carolyn Korsmeyer, and Lillian S. Robinson, *Feminist Scholarship: Kindling in the Groves of Academe* (Urbana and Chicago: University of Illinois Press, 1985). There is no space here to analyze the issues, but I urge skeptical readers to read both Hyman and the relevant passages in DuBois et al. Not only does Hyman seriously misrepresent DuBois et al., but she relies on even more dubious assumptions than the ones she criticizes in that work.

I am by no means unaware of the shoddy revolutionary scholarship. Among other things, different versions of this paper have been on the receiving end of some of the most sloppy and absurd criticisms I have ever seen from feminists!

39. See Berger, for example.

40. See, for example, Kimball, especially Chapter 1. On page 15, for example, he says that feminism seeks to "subordinate literature to ideology by instituting a fundamental change in the way literary works are read and taught." But it's not immediately clear why such fundamental change might not be *more* objective nor is argument given against the suggested change.

41. Discussions of some of the standard entries in the catalog of horrors are now appearing in the media. Consider for instance the oft-quoted "Hey, hey, ho, ho. Western culture's got to go" chant that was elicited by Jesse Jackson's visit to Stanford at the height of the debate about the Western Civilization course. Bob Beyers, who directed the Stanford University News Service from 1961 to 1990, writes in the *Chronicle of Higher Education* that these accounts leave out Jesse Jackson's response to the students: " 'The issue is not that we don't want Western culture. We're from the West.' But, he added, other cultures also should be studied." Beyers goes on to point out that "the chant was never repeated at Stanford." Yet that ending is never included in the story (June 19, 1991, B2).

Another infamous incident alleged to have occurred at SUNY-Binghamton is discussed at length in a *Mother Jones* article by David Beers; Beers provides substantial evidence that media reports of the affair bear little relation to what took place there. Similarly, Jon Wiener shows that D'Souza's account of the Thernstrom case at Harvard is thoroughly inaccurate. [David Beers, "PC? B.S." *Mother Jones*, Vol. 16, No. 5 (September–October, 1991): pp. 34–35, pp. 64–65; Jon Wiener, "What Happened at Harvard," *The Nation* (September 30, 1991): pp. 384–88.] Beers and Wiener are reprinted, along with other illuminating accounts, in Aufderheide.

It seems to me that these responses raise extremely serious questions about the accuracy of the most broadly circulated versions of these events and require thoughtful persons to (at the least) suspend belief in them. Furthermore, given the central role accounts of such cases are playing in the debate over curriculum and scholarship, careful observers surely need to reserve judgment about alleged nefarious influence of revolutionary ideas in academe.

42. For good examples of loaded language, see Brigitte Berger, a professor of sociology at Wellesley College. Her paper "Academic Feminism and the 'Left,' " *Academic Questions*, Vol. 1, No. 4 (Spring 1989), pp. 6–15, is a textbook example of what to avoid. See also Kimball, for instance p. 7.

Berger's paper reflects several of the other problems listed here. For example, she discusses the idea that in circumstances of oppression, the oppressed can have a clearer view of the situation than the oppressors. She comments: "by a sleight of hand, the alleged subjugated position of women in public and private life, the very foundation of feminism as a social movement, is thus transformed into an epistemological and moral advantage. The logical absurdity of all this is beyond description" (14). To assert that something is absurd is not, after all, to give us reasons for thinking so. This particular idea has a respectable history and is taken seriously by many nonfeminist scholars. Since it is not self-evidently ridiculous, Berger surely owes her readers some account of her position.

43. How these premises are formulated varies widely, as do views about such questions as the origins and nature of women's inequality, together with judgments about the steps necessary to rectify it. Such disagreement should not be surprising, given the short history of academic feminism and the difficulty of the issues with which it deals.

44. Alison Jaggar, "Feminist Ethics: Projects, Problems, Prospects," In *Feminist Ethics*, ed. Claudia Card (Lawrence: University Press of Kansas, 1991), p. 97.

45. This fact, as far as we know now, is clear, as those who want to use it to assert superior philosophical talent of men can hardly deny.

46. I have concentrated on the issues most relevant for applied ethics; Jaggar discusses other issues more pertinent to theoretical ethics.

47. See *Hypatia*, Vol. 4, No. 2 (Summer 1989), especially Purdy, Sherwin, Warren, and Bell. (Laura M. Purdy, "Feminists Healing Ethics," pp. 9–14; Susan Sherwin, "Feminist and Medical Ethics: Two Different Approaches to Contextual Ethics," pp. 57–72; Virginia Warren, "Feminist Directions in Medical Ethics," pp. 73–87; and Nora K. Bell, "What Setting Limits May Mean: A Feminist Critique of Callahan's *Setting Limits*," pp. 169–78.)

48. I do not deny that there is some feminist scholarship that does not follow this pattern. But as elsewhere, I would argue that to condemn all feminist work on the basis of the bad is a case of hasty generalization.

49. See for more details, Sherwin, "Feminist and Medical Ethics," and Warren, "Feminist Directions in Medical Ethics."

50. This conviction could amount either to the view that men's and women's interests are equally satisfied, or that if they aren't, that state of affairs is nonetheless justifiable. Defending either claim involves the same kind of moral and political argument as their denials, of course.

51. See for example, London, p. 7.

52. D'Souza, p. 208; Hyman, p. 7; Helprin, p. xix.

53. The injury here is all the more bitter because of Aristotle's reputation as a careful observer of biology.

54. P. 65. Bloom's first objection focuses on the study of literature. He complains that feminist attention to literature is limited to a litany of its sexism.

55. See, for instance, Sheila Ruth, "Methodocracy, Misogyny and Bad Faith: The Response of Philosophy," *Men's Studies Modified*, ed. Dale Spender (Oxford: Pergamon Press, 1981).

56. Feminist scholars have recently been pointing out that the so-called "private" world is nonetheless a creation of the "public" world. It is, after all, the latter that lays out the boundaries of the former as a world where the usual standards do not apply.

A traditionalist philosopher who does address this question in some detail is

Michael Levin. Levin objects to feminist environmentalism and attributes to biological differences the differences in women's and men's social situations. He concludes that they are fixed and therefore inevitable; hence they cannot be unjust.

57. Christina Hoff Sommers, who concedes that women do have interests, is reluctant to see conflict: She infers from her claim that "most young mothers" believe that their interests are being satisfied, that they really are. She goes on to assert that

> even this basic insight of the feminist theoretician—that gender roles are essentially inequitable, favoring the male as free subject and discriminating against the female as object and victim of male oppression—is still no more than an intriguing and contentious perspective on social reality shared by some elitist intellectual women. . . . (106)

Sommers does not support her claims with any discussion of the issues. [Christina Hoff Sommers, "Should the Academy Support Academic Feminism?" *Public Affairs Quarterly*, Vol. 2, No. 3 (July 1988), pp. 97–120.]

58. In this it contrasts with a good deal of traditional liberal theory that sees conflict between humans—male humans, anyway—as basic. Why it fails to extend this assumption to relationships between the sexes is an interesting question that deserves further inquiry. See Susan Moller Okin, *Justice, Gender, and the Family* (New York: Basic Books, 1989).

59. See Stephen Toulmin, "The Recovery of Practical Philosophy," *Arts & Sciences*, Northwestern University, Spring 1988.

60. Just as race is not just something that is predicated of people of color, class is not only what the poor have, and sexual orientation not just what homosexuals have. See Elizabeth V. Spelman, *Inessential Woman* (Boston: Beacon Press, 1988).

61. The neglect of women fed by the view that they are unimportant means, however, that we tend to focus on women more than men.

62. That is probably why, despite his scorn for feminism, he, unlike more naive writers, does not reject it for its political nature.

63. Thanks to Spencer Carr for this point.

Index

AAU. *See* American Association of
Universities
AAUP. *See* American Association of
University Professors
ABC News Nightline, 170n3–6
Abram, Morris, 110, 111, 127
absolute neutrality, model of, 19–22
academic ethic, 2–99; criticism of, 6;
in curricular revision, 80; vs
racism, 91
academic values, 9–11; core, 4
Ackerman, Bruce, 16n4
activism: faculty, 108; student, 112,
114–19, 130–31
administration, 124; view of
university neutrality, 151
affirmative action, 91–93, 95n9–10
African National Congress, 163
Afrocentrism, debate over, 67–68,
191
Agresto, John, 84n4
Aiken, Henry David, 71, 72, 84n7,
110–26, 153n5, 153n8–9, 155n15;
response to, 127–35
alcohol use, regulations on, 42–43
American Association of Universities
(AAU), tenure rules, 133
American Association of University

Professors (AAUP), 129, 130,
155n14; tenure rules, 133
American Council of Learned
Societies: reports, 70; *Speaking
for the Humanities*, 205–8,
242–47, 260n29, 261n32
American Philosophical Association,
119–20
American Workers Party, 129
antiracism, 91; core, 91; ideological,
91–92
apartheid, 171n18. *See also*
divestment
Aristotle, 111, 221, 259n14, 259n17,
263n53
Army Reserve Officer Training Corps
program, 147. *See also* ROTC
programs
Arnold, Matthew, 191
Aufderheide, Patricia, 232n1, 257n2,
258n3–4, 262n41
autonomy, 44
awards, criteria for awarding, 48–53,
65n5

Baldwin, Roger, 129
Barber, Benjamin, 234n17
Barsamian, David, 170n2

Contributors to Part II

Henry David Aiken
  Philosophy, Brandeis University (deceased)
Steven M. Cahn
  Philosophy, City University of New York, Graduate Center
Daniel H. Cohen
  Philosophy, Colby College
David Gorden
  Philosophy, Los Angeles
Robert Holmes
  Philosophy, University of Rochester
Sideny Hook
  Philosophy, The Hoover Institute (deceased)
David Paris
  Government, Hamilton College
Laura Purdy
  Philosophy, Wells College
James Sadowsky
  Philosophy, Fordham University
John Searle
  Philosophy, University of California, Berkeley
Roger Shiner
  Philosophy, University of Alberta
Martin Trow
  Public Policy, University of California, Berkeley
Kerry S. Walters
  Philosophy, Gettysburg College
Richard Werner
  Philosophy, Hamilton College
Robert Paul Wolff
  Philosophy, University of Massachusetts, Amherst